FALSE SUMMIT

McGill-Queen's University Press
Montreal & Kingston | London | Chicago

FALSE SUMMIT

GENDER IN MOUNTAINEERING NONFICTION

JULIE RAK

ISBN 978-0-2280-0626-8 (cloth)
ISBN 978-0-2280-0627-5 (paper)
ISBN 978-0-2280-0772-2 (ePDF)
ISBN 978-0-2280-0773-9 (ePUB)

Legal deposit second quarter 2021
Bibliothèque nationale du Québec

Printed in Canada on acid-free paper that is 100% ancient forest free
(100% post-consumer recycled), processed chlorine free

This book has been published with the help of a grant from the Canadian
Federation for the Humanities and Social Sciences, through the Awards
to Scholarly Publications Program, using funds provided by the Social
Sciences and Humanities Research Council of Canada.

We acknowledge the support of the Canada Council for the Arts.
Nous remercions le Conseil des arts du Canada de son soutien.

Library and Archives Canada Cataloguing in Publication

Title: False summit : gender in mountaineering nonfiction / Julie Rak.
Names: Rak, Julie, 1966– author.
Description: Includes bibliographical references and index.
Identifiers: Canadiana (print) 20200415948 | Canadiana (ebook)
    20200416014 | ISBN 9780228006268 (cloth) | ISBN 9780228006275
    (paper) | ISBN 9780228007722 (ePDF) | ISBN 9780228007739 (ePUB)
Subjects: LCSH: Mountains in literature. | LCSH: Mountaineering in
    literature. | LCSH: Sex role in literature. | LCSH: Mountaineering
    expeditions.
Classification: LCC PN56.M7 R35 2021 | DDC 809/.9336—dc23

Set in 11/14 Sina Nova with Alternate Gothic Compressed, Trade
Gothic LT Std, and Univers Next Pro Condensed
Book design & typesetting by Garet Markvoort, zijn digital

One of the reasons I read memoir is to know I am not alone.

Sharon Wood, *Rising: Becoming the First Canadian Woman to Summit Everest*

CONTENTS

FIGURES

ACKNOWLEDGMENTS

This book has taken me a decade to write. Along the way, there were many changes in my life and my work. I'm very grateful to everyone who helped me through those changes.

Thanks to the Social Science and Humanities Research Council (SSHRC) for providing me with the funding to conduct early research, and for agreeing to prolong funding when illness meant that I could not continue for some time. Thanks to the students in English 402 Mountaineering Writing, who helped me to think about this project in its early stages. Thanks to the anonymous reviewers for the manuscript, whose suggestions made the book a better work of scholarship.

Thanks to my colleagues who are part of the growing community of mountaineering studies, especially the members of the Canadian Mountain Studies Initiative (CMSI) at the University of Alberta who have been so supportive of this project: PearlAnn Reichwein, Zac Robinson, Liza Piper, David Hik, Jeff Kavanaugh, Stephen Slemon, and Colleen Skidmore.

Special thanks to these brilliant international colleagues: Katie Ives and the incredible publication Alpinist, Peter Hansen, Maurice Isserman, Harald Höbusch, Amrita Dhar, Helen Mort, Kerwin Klein, Ela Klimek, Catherine Hollis, and Caroline Schauman. Philippe Lejeune sent me books in French I could not find anywhere else. Li JieMei read material in Chinese for me. Thanks also to my University of Alberta colleagues who generously helped me with film and textual resources or who provided advice as I wrote: Dianne Chisholm, Bill Beard, Keavy Martin, Amy Kaler, Lianne McTavish, Liz Czach, Mark Simpson, Sarah Krotz, Judy Davidson, Corrinne Harol, Teresa Zackodnik, Jaime Baron, Jonathan Cohn, Christine Wiesenthal, Heather YoungLeslie, and Daphne Read. As always, thanks to my fantastic colleagues in life writing studies: Anna Poletti, Laurie McNeill, Kate Douglas, Margaretta Jolly, Craig Howes, Eva Karpinski, Ricia Chansky, Alfred Hornung, John Zuern, Cynthia Franklin, Lena Kurvet, Sidonie Smith, Julia Watson, Philippe Lejeune, Gillian Whitlock, Sara Brophy, and Candida Rifkind. Special thanks to Joan Waters for her care and support. Thanks to Mini Aodla Freeman, who taught me not to point at the mountains when I talk about them. Special thanks to Lou Kaskischke for his kindness and generosity. Special thanks to Yumiko Hiraki for her invaluable feedback and comments.

Thanks also to my friends and guides from the climbing world. Special thanks to guides Anna Keeling and Abby Watson, who taught me so much that I needed to know about how to be in the mountains.

I am grateful for interspecies care from Mr T and Loki as I worked on this book. I thank the environment I get to be in, the land of Treaty Six and the traditional Métis territory where I live and work, and everything in them – the earth, the water, the sky, the air, and especially the mountains. Most of all, I thank Danielle Fuller for sharing her life and work with me, and for being the best companion on so many adventures.

Previously published material in this book is reproduced here by permission:

Rak, Julie. "The Afterlife of a Disaster: Everest 1996 Memoirs as Gendered Testimony." In *Inscribed Identities*, edited by Joan Ramon, 172–90. London and New York: Routledge, 2019.

Rak, Julie. "Social Climbing on Annapurna: Gender in High-Altitude Mountaineering Narratives." *English Studies in Canada* 33, nos 1–2 (2008): 109–48.

FALSE SUMMIT

To me, [climbing] is one of the most wonderful
feelings a woman can have.

Jimena Lidia Huayllas, "The Cholita Climbers of Bolivia
Scale Mountain in Skirts"

INTRODUCTION

BECAUSE GENDER IS THERE

On 23 January 2019, five Aymara women aged forty-two to fifty – Indigenous women who had worked as cooks and porters for years in the
Bolivian climbing industry – did something extraordinary. In full traditional Aymara skirts and shawls, Lidia Huayllas Estrada, Dora Magueño
Machaca, Ana Lía Gonzáles Magueño, Cecilia Llusco Alaña, and Elena
Quispe Tincutas climbed Aconcagua, the highest summit on the South
American continent. Five years earlier they had formed a group of
eleven, with other Aymara women, dedicated to climbing the mountains
where they had worked in service, with the ultimate goal of climbing
Aconcagua (figure I.1). According to Huayllas Estrada, even when they
worked as cooks and porters, they always "felt the desire to go to the top
and see how it felt. So in December 2015, we did." In a video about the
Aconcagua climb, they refer to themselves as *cholita* climbers, reclaiming

Figure I.1 | Bolivia's "cholita" climbers descend a glacier at the Huayna Potosí mountain in the Cordillera Real range.

the derogatory term *chola* (meaning "mixed" Indigenous woman) as a way to resist discrimination against them, and to assert their pride in who they are. They climb in skirts and shawls, using modern equipment, as an expression of their cholita identity. And they are dedicated to resisting sexist ideas about climbing, even in their own community: "We've always had a culture of machismo here in Bolivia. They [men] would say, 'How can a woman climb up a mountain? That's wrong!' I [Huayllas Estrada] would encourage my girlfriends, I told them: 'Why can't we climb just like men do'" (Clarke 2019).

The successful ascent of Aconcagua by cholita climbers would not be seen as ground-breaking by any traditional mountaineering[1] body. The first recorded summit of Aconcagua was in 1893, and more than 2,000 successful summits are made every year by the normal route, which does not involve technical climbing. But in every other way, the achievement of the cholita climbers is noteworthy because of the invisible barriers to becoming a climber, which include narrow ideas of what achievement in climbing is. The challenge here was to become a diverse climber in an environment where that had been unthinkable. Each member of the team had to overcome the barriers preventing them not only from climbing, but from climbing *as themselves*, in a style that made sense to them, even if the climbing community ignored the magnitude of that achievement. For more than two centuries, ideas of what good climbing is have had the effect of policing who gets to be a climber, and in some cases excluding climbers from participating in mountaineering culture, except as servants or members of the interested public. How has this come to be, and why is it still happening?

The answer to these questions lies in the position mountaineering has held in the development of abstract ideas about gender and nature, particularly as they developed in Western Europe. Since the eighteenth century, the act of climbing the highest mountains has played a central role in the way that much of the world has imagined conquest, human achievement, and the place of wilderness in social life. People have been living in mountainous areas and climbing mountains much longer than that, but the idea of climbing a mountain for reasons other than human survival, religious obligation, military strategies, or as part of a journey is connected intimately with the development of what Peter Hansen has called "modern man," a European idea of humanity connected to individual growth, self-cultivation, and mastery – or sovereignty – over the environment as well as over one's self (2013, 17–20). But in that phrase "modern man" is something so obvious that it mostly escapes critique: more than two centuries after the practice began, mountaineering is still foundational to the maintenance of a narrow version of masculinity, and that masculinity is the preserve of a certain kind of man, writ large in the hundreds of accounts of classic mountaineering expeditions, from the nineteenth century to the latest IMAX film about Mount Everest. It is undeniable today that there are now female climbers, climbers of every gender who are not white, climbers who are neither from the Western world nor heavily influenced by European or North American culture, and climbers who do not participate in discourses of heroic masculinity. There are some encouraging signs of support and recognition of diversity within climbing communities.[2] And yet, much of the world of mountaineering has remained remarkably resistant to imagining any other kind of identity for its participants until very recently, even as everything else about climbing has changed.

False Summit: Mistakes and Other Stories

I think of the resistance to other ways of understanding climbing beyond the well-worn white male heroic adventure story as a kind of "false summit." What can this mean? False summit means two things in hiking and climbing. The first meaning has to do with a disappointing mistake: when a climber reaches what looks like the summit of a mountain, but it turns out that it is a lesser summit on the way to the "true" summit, or the actual highest point, the lower point is the false summit. A false summit can be intensely disappointing to reach because it represents the dashing of someone's hopes (Unruh 2020). But false summits presuppose "true" ones as well. In other words, the belief that mountaineering is about reaching the highest point (and not about the experience of getting there, the difficulty of the climb, or even the identity of the climber) *creates* the idea of a lesser climb, or one that does not count. When female climbers, disabled climbers, or climbers who are not white are treated as if they are not "true" mountaineers, I believe that, metaphorically, they have encountered a false summit. Such a "summit" becomes a block for marginalized climbers when authentic climbers tell them that they cannot achieve their goals because their achievements, their identities and even their bodies do not matter to climbing. In other words, they do not have what it takes to be an elite climber.

False Summit seeks to critique that assumption, because the falsity of the false summit is not actually about climbers who want to change things. It lies in the faith in authenticity itself, just as the "false" summit highlights assumptions about what matters in climbing, and that there is only one way to climb a mountain. False summits exist because of an exactness in climbing that should be called into question. Perhaps the persistence in thinking of climbing as an activity with only one dominant narrative of achievement indicates that it is time for other stories of achievement to matter as well. As Katie Ives points out, a lack of interest in the climbing community in Eberhard Jurgalski's discovery (2019) that many important summit records for 8,000-metre peaks are mistaken or false could indicate that there is a flaw in mountaineering's emphasis on summits. She writes, "There's another outcome [of the lack of interest in correcting false summits] that could arise: a growing awareness of the fallibility of dominant ways of envisioning climbing. The location of particular summits might not be the only matter we've been getting wrong" (Ives 2020). In other words, a false summit as a metaphor for *another idea of being a climber* can be understood as a critique of a dominant discourse in climbing. If getting to the top is all that matters, there will be a hierarchy within climbing. But what if that is not what matters, after all? Who would get to be a climber if other stories of climbing start to matter?

The other meaning of false summit Ives is discussing has to do with the false claim of summiting, which can happen because of the financial and reputational benefits attached to achieving a summit (Horrell 2010). The climbing world's focus on summits, rather than climbs, adheres to the origin of contemporary climbing in a western European binary logic attached to truth and falsehood, success and failure, fame or obscurity. The logic has its benefits, and so in effect the idea of the summit creates benefits that are worth lying about. Therefore, false summits are not just about misperception and disappointment, but are also about the position of truth, evidence, and veracity in climbing, and in reporting about it. False summit accounts therefore connect story-making with climbing, which in turn connects stories about climbing to the concerns of nonfiction itself, with its emphases on experience, truth claims, and memory as part of what makes such stories circulate.

Nonfiction and Mountain Climbing: Connections

To understand how and why resistance to changing the heroic narrative of climbing has happened and keeps happening, *False Summit* looks to the extensive body of nonfiction writing about mountaineering – particularly climbing memoirs, biographies, and accounts of expeditions to the Himalayas and the Karakoram – to understand how the stories told there are intimately related to gender identity. In the book, I focus on the expedition narratives and other accounts centred on three of the highest mountains where important developments in climbing happened: Annapurna, K2, and Mount Everest (figure 1.2). The majority of widely read expedition narratives have been written about these mountains, all of which have been and remain significant objectives for climbers around

Figure I.2 | Map of the Himalayas and the Karakoram, with 8,000-metre peaks.

the world.[3] The chapters of *False Summit* are arranged by mountain, rather than historically, in order to highlight the importance of each mountain as natural and cultural sites where issues about gender are constantly being played out. I did not want to create another history of mountaineering where imperial masculinity is a dominant discourse and then, "later," women and climbers of colour enter that discourse, while Sherpa life remains a backdrop within that history.[4] *False Summit* investigates why the story of mountaineering has remained within a heroic frame for so long, and so part of its argument is about the pervasiveness of that story, and its tendency to repeat during different climbing eras.

I look to climbing narratives about expeditions – rather than the accounts by famous climbers of their climbing lives, or memoirs about rock climbing – as places to think about gender, for two reasons. The first is that memoirs and general accounts of high-altitude[5] expeditions to the Himalayas and the Karakoram form the most widely read and most enduring body of writing about mountaineering.[6] Most of the classics of mountaineering that inspired others to climb, and that remain in print, are about this type of climbing, from the "golden age" of first ascents in the 1950s, to the advent of alpine climbing in the 1960s and 1970s, and the commercial era of guided ascents beginning in the 1990s.[7] There are so many classic expedition narratives (and disaster narratives) about Mount Everest, K2, Annapurna, Nanga Parbat, and other mountains in these regions in part because expedition narratives helped to fund the cost of expensive "siege-style" operations, where hundreds of porters helped large teams establish camps and inch their way up glaciers and mountain faces. Climbers who wanted to be known as superstars in the 1960s and 1970s had to go to the Himalayas and the Karakoram and climb more difficult lines and big mountain faces in order to further their careers and push the boundaries of the sport. Expedition accounts of these climbs, such as Tom Hornbein's *Everest the West Ridge* (1965, 1980), became best-selling classics that inspired climbers to climb in the Himalayas as they would in the Alps, the Urals, or the Rockies: alpine style, with minimal equipment and small teams. The commercial era, ushered in on Mount Everest by the 1990s, brought its share of narratives that explored the controversy, most notably Jon Krakauer's best-selling memoir, *Into Thin Air* (1997). Part of the argument in this book is that the formation of masculine identity in climbing is made through such accounts, in a relatively unbroken line, from the earliest works about George Mallory, to Krakauer's lament for the loss of Mallory's heroism in the mountains. The heroic era of general mountaineering is long gone, but as new generations of climbers try ever more dangerous and extreme versions of climbing (and other activities, such as BASE jumping) on big walls, boulders, and ice faces around the world, the connections between gender politics and heroism in the books and films about more recent exploits continue to be informed by the establishment (and critique) of heroism in expedition accounts and memoirs about high-altitude climbing.

The second reason why nonfiction genres about high-altitude climbing demand consideration has to do with the work of nonfiction as a mediation between climbers and the social world they inhabit, on and off a mountain. Richard Mitchell makes this point in *Mountain Experience* when he says that "in simple terms, the identity a climber obtains within the climbing community is achieved in two ways – through performance and negotiation" (1983, 82). Climbers perform on mountains, but that performance is bound up with what Mitchell calls "debriefing," when the performance is assessed by other members of the community. The assessment involves negotiation between the climber and the community in publishing of expedition accounts that rely on diaries, or other types of conversations about the quality and style of the climb (76). Mitchell understands these negotiations to be social, because they are publicly shared:

> As a social phenomenon the climb is not over till the tale is told. The meaning of mountaineering events emerges in the reflective discussion and debate that follow them. Debriefing is the occasion when one's private physical accomplishments become public social topics of interest. It is here that the climbing community decides if a particular ascent is a noteworthy deed or a mediocre accomplishment. The past event is reinterpreted, clarified, and judged ... During debriefing significant accomplishments and misdeeds become public information, and the climber accrues or loses status accordingly. This is prime time for identity negotiation. (72)

It is key that the "tale" is what makes a climb social, and that the identity of a climber involves public negotiation using nonfictional genres. To be in a climbing community involves climbers negotiating who they are, and what their position in their community will be, just as much as they describe their significant climbs, or recount accidents and disasters. It is why nonfictional writing and documentary filmmaking, both of which are supported by those who attend mountaineering film and book festivals around the world, are key to understanding how mountaineering identity is connected to the act of climbing. Mountaineering texts and films do several important things for climbing. They provide information about climbing routes and logistics, and are essential to promoting the work of climbing to the general public, which can result in direct economic benefits for climbers through product endorsements, film screenings, and book sales. The hundreds of books written about classic high-altitude expeditions to the highest mountains in the world have a cultural function as well: they are a means of telling climbers about each other, and of working out what a "good" climber is supposed to be like. Expedition accounts about the highest mountains have made the mountains, as well as the climbers who attempted them, legendary. They are part of the business of climbing, which is why there are literally hundreds of memoirs in print by climbers about their adventures, and why many well-established climbers go on to profitable careers as motivational speakers and coaches, if they survive their adventures in the mountains. And when there have been disasters in the mountains, written accounts have played a vital role in constructing what happened and analyzing who, or what, might have been to blame. Mountaineering writing, therefore, is central to the idea of climbing as social, rather than as an individual pursuit. Unlike most other strenuous physical pursuits, as Bruce Barcott has claimed, "mountaineering is the most literary of all sports" (1996, 64) because writing about climbing is so central to the activity. It is why mountaineering has inspired a large body of literature that is widely read, with its own literary festivals, publishers, and writing clinics exclusively dedicated to producing this genre of writing for a public that is clearly eager to read it and to see their favourite authors give readings in public venues. For all these reasons, it is important to think about mountaineering writing as central to building and maintaining ideas about climbing, identity, and the relationship of human beings to the natural world.

Memoirs, expedition accounts, documentaries, and climber biographies, rather than fictional genres, play a central role in climbing cultures. They play such a role because they are about creating identity through narrative, and they contain truth claims. Critics of life writing, the discipline devoted to studying personal forms of nonfiction, have argued that in the case of autobiography, the "truth" of an identity in a life story emerges between an author and a reader, what Sidonie Smith and Julia Watson have called "a shared understanding of the meaning of a life" (2010, 16). It may seem obvious that autobiographical narratives need to be true. But what the "truth" means is a bit more complex than it might first appear. Truth can be about facts, but it also can be related to how an event is experienced, or whether the author of an autobiography is seen to be a credible person. The question of what truth is in an autobiographical narrative ultimately relates to the discourses of authorization and validity that are applied to it: as Leigh Gilmore has said, "'What is truth'? cannot be separated from the process of verifying that truth" (2003, 107). What is "true" in someone's life story has as much to do with audience expectations and narrative convention as it does with facticity.

In the case of biography, the biographer has to construct an idea of the biographical subjects from interviews and documents; but what emerges inevitably is an interpretation of who that person is or was, a process that Richard Holmes has called "inventing the truth" because biographers must work with unreliable source material and create a believable identity for their subject nonetheless (1993, 17–18).

Classic memoir and biography have a strong connection to constructing the identity of their subjects as a way to both record history and to interpret who they are within history. Smith and Watson point out that this can take the form of chronicle in personal narratives of many kinds, but that the author's own needs to perform or construct their identity within history may come from other motives, including "justifying their own perceptions, upholding their reputations, disputing the accounts of others, settling scores, conveying cultural information, and inventing desirable futures" (1993, 13). Memoirists and biographers are not, therefore, just recounting facts, but are situating themselves (or their subjects) within cultural and temporal contexts for many reasons. Often, these motivations are connected to the conventions of adventure stories as a way to connect the exploits of climbers to other kinds of accounts of male heroism. Some of these stories have become adventure classics in their own right and have inspired generations of climbers to go to the mountains. For example, Reinhold Messner in *The Crystal Horizon* recalls being inspired as a child to climb by hearing his mother read a German translation of *Storm over Mount Everest*, an account for children of the British expeditions to climb Everest. Messner has said that he remembers it as a thrilling fairytale that inspired him to climb (2013, 3).

Memoirs by famous climbers thinking back over their careers certainly can feature some or all of the more general aspects of memoir as a genre because of the role memoirs have as documents of a climb, and a way to create climbing reputations. An example of the role memoirs play in this respect involves a mountain that is not discussed in this book: Nanga Parbat, the ninth-highest mountain in the world. Nanga Parbat was already important in medieval Europe, particularly in the area that would become Germany. Later, the mountain played a central role in the development of "the German imagination" (Ireton and Schaumann 2012), when the already-existing idea of mountains and mountaineering became part of German Romanticism. Nanga Parbat continued to be important to the identity of German people in the twentieth century (and is still important to contemporary Germany) through dozens of expedition accounts widely read in Germany, *Bergfilm* (mountain films) by noted directors and actors, including Arnold Fanck, Luis Trenker, and Leni Riefenstahl (Höbusch 2016, 52–3) and in the wide circulation of adventure stories for young Germans (13). The obsession that German climbers, German governments (including the regime in Nazi Germany), and members of the German public had and still have with Nanga Parbat as a national objective form the backdrop to Reinhold Messner's memoir *The Naked Mountain*. Messner's memoir situates his interpretation of German climbing history on Nanga Parbat as a history of iconoclastic climbers like Willy Merkl or Hermann Buhl, who defied authority and climbed Nanga Parbat in their own style. Messner does this as way to defend his own anti-authoritarian climbing style on the mountain, because he claims that he is part of an honourable tradition on Nanga Parbat. Such a defence provides the explanatory frame for Messner's controversial actions and decisions on the mountain in 1970, and the question of whether Messner's choices led to the death of his brother on the peak (2003, 81–2, 295–6). Memoir in this case becomes part of a national imaginary, forms part of an argument about what happened during a climb, and serves to build a climber's reputation. In this respect, the truth claims within memoirs about climbing are of political importance as well as documentary significance.

The work of memoir has another function too: it connects the identity of the climbers within it to adventure rhetoric. Henrich Harrer's *The White Spider* (1959) about his climb of the Eiger, Gaston Rebuffat's classic *Starlight and Storm* (1956), Jon Krakauer's *Into Thin Air* (1997), *Touching the Void* (1989) by Joe Simpson, Maurice Herzog's *Annapurna* (1952), David Roberts's *The Mountain of My Fear* (1968), and Hermann Buhl's *Nanga Parbat: Pilgrimage* (1956) – to name a few of the most prominent examples – regularly appear on lists of the greatest climbing books of all time because they read as adventure stories, which stress action, immersion, and heroism, even though these books are all nonfictional accounts. And, particularly regarding the memoirs connected to mountaineering disasters, climbing memoirs are acts of witness within adventure, and are all the more thrilling because the stories are real. It is no accident, either, that all of the most famous stories are by North American or European men, because these tales of real-life adventure have helped to form and maintain the discourse of Romantic masculinity, from the early twentieth century to the current time. In the case of Sherpas and other high-altitude climbers and porters in the Himalayas and Karakoram, whose labours have made so many mountaineering achievements possible, there are very few stories in circulation that are written by them or told from their point of view. As Amrita Dhar points out: "High- and low-altitude porters, guides, sirdars, and cooks have continued to render their own crucial service in the mountains. Particularly for the Himalayas, there is no overstating the importance of their work from the nineteenth century onwards. It is important to register the desperate paucity of these voices in authorial positions" (2019, 352–3).

In the case of white, middle-class, and elite women, the narratives they did make are seldom part of the mountaineering canon in their own right. The reception of *Tents in the Clouds* (1956), an account of the first all-female expedition to the Himalayas by Monica Jackson and Elizabeth Stark, is a strong contrast to better-known expedition memoirs by European or North American male climbers. The book records the travel of Jackson, Stark, and Evelyn Camrass in 1955 to what was then an unmapped part of the Himalaya. The climbers named the peak they climbed Gyalgen, in order to honour Gyalgen, their lead Sherpa guide. Mapping the area and climbing Gyalgen was a notable achievement, but their account of the expedition went unnoticed for decades. Climber Arlene Blum, who wrote the foreword to a 1999 edition of *Tents in the Clouds*, has this to say: "I so wish I had known about this book in the 1960s" (1999, 15). But Blum – and the American climbing community as a whole – was unaware of the book and the achievements of its authors, which meant that the book could not inspire other women to take up climbing. Even now, *Tents in the Clouds* is not often cited as a classic of climbing in general. When it is remembered at all, it is mentioned as an example of "female" climbing writing, for it does not engage in adventure discourses of heroism in its account and it is not about "typical" climbers of the time (that is, white male climbers). The same is true of British climber Dorothy Pilley's *Climbing Days*, a 1935 memoir about Pilley's climbs with the literary critic I.A. Richards, who was her climbing partner. The book also contains an account of Pilley's founding of the Pinnacle Climbing Club for women in the United Kingdom. But Pilley is almost unknown today: *Climbing Days* has been out of print since 1965. Her legacy is so obscured that Pilley's great-great nephew Dan Richards, when he accidentally discovered a copy of *Climbing Days*, was inspired to set out to become a climber himself as well as his great-great aunt's biographer (Richards 2016). Pilley, an important figure in British climbing history, is eclipsed by the legacies of other British climbers like George Leigh Mallory, Eric Shipton, Chris Bonington, or Edmund Whymper. The rhetoric of adventure within the stories that are most often remembered has the effect of making them (and their subject matter) exist outside time, and so they remain classic, forestalling questions about the narrow basis for this kind of heroism.

The discursive and negotiated nature of "truth" and "identity" in genres like biography and memoir does need to be kept in tension with the work of what Philippe Lejeune called "the autobiographical pact," an informal understanding that an autobiography has been written by a real person about real events. If there is no match between the author as a real person, the first-person in a narrative, and the proper name on the title page, the work must be fictional (1989a, 16). In a later essay, Lejeune stated that the pact is meant to be descriptive, not prescriptive, of autobiography as a genre (1989b, 119), but the formulation of the pact does highlight the importance that truth-telling can have to some forms of writing about one's life, particularly for readers. The expectation that authors of "true" stories actually do tell the truth is what gives rise to autobiographical hoaxes or imposture, because belief in truth-telling is necessary for a hoax or fraud to do its work (Egan 2011, 151; Smith and Watson 2012, 137).

In the case of writing about mountaineering, sometimes, it really does matter to readers whether an autobiographer has told the truth or not. For instance, it would seem to matter whether or not Greg Mortenson, who wrote the best-selling memoir *Three Cups of Tea* about his failed climb of K2 and his subsequent work to found schools in Pakistan, was lying about his philanthropy or not (2006). In *Three Cups of Deceit*, Jon Krakauer took Mortenson to task for misrepresenting events in the memoir, causing what the *Guardian* called "a dizzying fall from grace" for Mortenson (Shah and Pilkington 2011). The existence of truth claims in autobiography and biography is what gives these genres their power, particularly when they are confessional (Gilmore 2003, 108–10), when they bear witness to atrocity, or when they contain testimony.[8] In the case of mountaineering memoirs, especially about accidents or disasters, memoirs can provide additional facts, but also can impart what an experience felt like, not just what happened. They unite the discourses of confession and adventure narrative.

For instance, the impact of Joe Simpson's *Touching the Void* – a classic mountaineering disaster narrative with the subtitle "the true story of one man's miraculous survival" – comes from its confessional nature, as Simpson recounts what it felt like to be left for dead and to try to survive. But the power of the account also comes from its truth claims, because of the circumstances of Simpson's mountaineering accident. In the foreword, climbing legend Chris Bonington notes that the first-hand nature of *Touching the Void* gives the book an "immediacy and strength" that it would not have had if a professional writer had written the account (2003, 10). Beck Weathers's *Left for Dead* (2000) and Lincoln Hall's *Dead Lucky* (2009), both about their near-death experiences on Mount Everest, cover similar confessional terrain. *High Crimes*, a memoir by Michael Kodas about corruption among Mount Everest guiding outfits, contains Kodas's perspective as a witness to events such as the death of climber David Sharp high on Everest in 2006 to support his contention that "greed and ambition conspire to draw corruption to the wilderness" (2008, 13). Walter Bonatti's classic memoir *The Mountains of My Life* is a discussion of his whole climbing career, but it also contains a section about the controversy related to the first ascent of K2, when members of Bonatti's climbing team accused him (falsely) of trying to sabotage their summit bid (1998, 2010). The truth-telling and storytelling aspects of memoir assist Bonatti in making an argument about events and creating the grounds for his authenticity as a climber. Arlene Blum's memoir *Breaking Trail* looks over her whole climbing career as part of her arguments about sexism in the American climbing scene, which motivated her to lead what she described as an all-female expedition to climb Annapurna (2005, 251, 256), and as a way to write back about accusations made about her leadership during her time as a climber (304–5, 356, 366–8).

Truth claims also play similar roles in mountaineering biography, despite the problems Richard Holmes identifies with working from unreliable sources and the imperfect memories interviewees have about the subject. Nonetheless, Holmes observes, ethical issues remain central to the work of biography, because biographers must always ask themselves this question: "by what right does a biographer enter into another's zone of activity and privacy" (1994, 17). When the answer justifies the violation of privacy, Holmes gives ethically defensible reasons, including a correction of the historical record, the need to highlight what he calls "minor lives" who have been overlooked (18), or a defence of the life and reputation of someone who cannot speak for themselves. All three rationales are present in mountaineering biography, particularly because many world-class climbers lose their lives while they are climbing, and so biography represents the dead. David Rose and Ed Douglas's biography *Regions of the Heart: The Triumph and Tragedy of Alison Hargreaves* (1999) was written as a way to set the record straight about Hargreaves, who had been accused of being a bad mother by the British press because she was a career climber. Since Hargreaves had died while she was trying to climb K2, and was there so that she could get the sponsorship she needed to escape a violent marriage and provide for her children, Rose and Douglas's biography is both an ethical response to the misrepresentation of Hargreaves because she could no longer represent herself, as well as a correction to the historical record and its gender bias (Rose and Douglas 1999, 272–6). Bernadette McDonald's *Freedom Climbers*, a collective biography of the groundbreaking female and male Polish climbers who redefined extreme climbing in the Himalayas in the postwar era, often paying for their achievements with their lives, aims to understand their determination and include the political context of Polish climbing – particularly of Wanda Rutkiewicz and Jerzy Kukuczka – that few outside Poland understood, and that most of the climbers could not discuss because they had not survived (1999, 10–12). Jennifer Jordan's *Savage Summit: The Life and Death of the First Women of K2* (2005) has a similar mission, in that it aims to tell the stories of female climbers who did not survive their K2 climbs or died during other climbs shortly thereafter; Jordan's book works to expose the sexism women faced on K2 and in climbing generally.

Another book by Jennifer Jordan, *The Last Man on the Mountain*, a biography of Dudley Wolfe, the first man who died climbing K2, represents another use of biography as a correction of the historical record. Jordan argues that in 1939, during an American team's attempt to climb the mountain, Wolfe's death alone in a high camp did not occur because (as one of the other climbers said) he was "overconfident, clumsy, fat, slow" and did not belong on an expedition (2010, 280). He died because some of his teammates abandoned him. What was said of him was untrue, because "the adjectives describe a stereotype, not a man," based on Jordan's extensive research (280). Jordan concludes that Wolfe's reputation was tarnished because the expedition leader, Fritz Wiessner, refused to take responsibility for abandoning Wolfe and worked to hide the truth from the American Alpine Club (which sponsored the expedition) and the public (259).

Most nonfiction about mountaineering, then, works in a creative space between adventure narrative, identity work, and history, acting as evidence and as explanation, a way to tell an adventure story, an act of witness, a justification, or a way to consolidate one's reputation. It combines truth-telling discourse with the features of adventure stories. It thrills readers and audiences, and it sends messages to the climbing communities about the worth of what is reported. It is why memoir, biography, documentary, and other nonfiction genres are so well-suited to narrating and assessing climbs, and climbers, and why so many mountaineers write books and make films: the stories of their lives pay the bills, settle scores, create arguments about climbing style, and make their reputations. It does all this, because mountaineering – and especially alpinism – uses memoir, documentary, and expedition narratives as a type of benchmarking within adventure discourse.

Mountaineering and other types of climbing on rock and ice are leisure activities that, at elite levels, can take on the characteristics of a competitive sport, but alpine climbing and elite general mountaineering in particular remains nonquantifiable, without an international body of experts who determine what the worth of an achievement is. There are no Olympic medals, no America's Cup sailing trophy, no Tour de France yellow jerseys to determine who the best in the world in climbing might be, beyond the Piolet d'Or (the Golden Ice Axe) for alpine-style mountaineering – and that award itself has often been controversial since its inception in 1996. For example, when a team withdrew their climb of Cerro Torre for consideration in 2006, one of their members – Rolando

Garibotti – explained in a letter to the sponsors of the award: "it was the essence of the experience [during the climb] that interested us most. An award such as the Piolet d'Or tries to quantify this essence and attempts to judge the quality of the experience ... How could there be any real value to such a subjective judgment? How to judge elusive concepts like elegance and imagination?" (Parnell 2006). Without a purely objective way to assess aesthetic qualities or – as the Piolet d'Or also tries to do – determine which climbers in a given year practise the "best" ethics or which ascents are the most original, climbers receive recognition from the stories that they tell, presented for assessment by their peers and the general public, supplemented by photographs and eyewitness accounts.

What Is Gender in the Mountains?

By now, it should be clear that memoir and biography (and documentary films) about high-altitude expeditions have been so important to the culture of mountain climbing because they do the work of publicity, documentation, and reputation building. They are just as much about the identity and values of climbers as they are about climbing itself. They are one of the ways that climbing celebrity is built and maintained, and in a material way they help to pay for the expeditions and adventures that are their subjects. Climbing life stories are essential to the making of climbing lives. But what kind of lives are represented in climbing, and whose lives are represented? What forms the identities of climbers? The argument of *False Summit* is that nonfiction about climbing shows that gender is one of the most important aspects of climbing identity, just as it is an important part of identity in general, and that gender identity is foundational to how climbers write about themselves, even when it goes unmentioned, and appears indirectly in discussions about climbing style, climbing ethics, or authentic climbing identities and bodies. As we shall see, questions of belonging in mountaineering are – very often – gendered questions, although they are not often phrased that way.

It is important too to keep in mind that gender as a category of identity, expression, and analysis does not exist in isolation from other aspects of who we are or how we are seen. The analysis of gender in this book proceeds from the understanding that issues about gender are intersectional, and so are related to other forms of identification, including nationality, physical ability, class, or race. Intersectional issues to do with gender and race inform the discourse of science in extreme environments, including on high mountains: as Vanessa Heggie has pointed in *Higher and Colder: A History of Extreme Physiology and Exploration*, the story of science in the mountains is "a deeply masculine story" (2019, 12) connected to similar intersectional currents in exploration and science. Women were excluded from "extreme environments" as either research subjects or as researchers until the 1980s. Sherpa men who worked on research sites, like women, had their labour rendered invisible and subordinate, and they too were neither considered to be research subjects nor researchers in their own right.[9] Heggie observes that in the case of Western science of the twentieth century, evidence of this kind of bias is "hardly a dramatic finding" (12). But in the case of climbing more generally, gender issues still need this kind of foregrounding, in part because after more than two centuries of writing about climbing, accounts of mountaineering by cis-gendered women, brown men, and genderqueer people remain relatively rare, and feminist writing about gender issues in climbing is rarer still.

It is not as if there is no work about gender or intersectional work about climbing, however. There is now a body of critical work about masculinity in climbing, and there is a postcolonial critique of climbing that is also focused on the interaction of white masculinity with other kinds of masculinity.[10] But much less has been written about gender as a social construct and a discourse within mountaineering when the focus is not masculinity alone. Most of the gender-focused scholarship about women in climbing has been historical, and so it has sought to incorporate women into the existing historical record.[11] More general works on women in climbing most often do the work of historical recovery within an ideology of liberal inclusion that includes a list of "great" or overlooked female climbers. For example Arlene Blum, in her expedition account in *Annapurna: A Woman's Place*, included a history of notable female climbers in her introduction (1980, xix–iii). Other titles of this nature in English include Cicely Williams's *Women on the Rope* (1973), Mikel Vause's *Rock and Roses* (1990, 1999), Rachel da Silva's collection *Leading Out: Women Climbers Reaching for the Top* (1992), David Mazel's *Mountaineering Women: Stories by Early Climbers* (1994), Rebecca Brown's *Women on High: Pioneers of Mountaineering* (2002), and

Chris Noble's *Women Who Dare: North America's Most Inspiring Women Climbers* (2013). This kind of rewriting of history to include women is highly reminiscent of the critical work of collective biography, a genre that flourished in English from the nineteenth century to the 1920s. As Alison Booth explains in *How to Make It as a Woman*, the hundreds of collective biographies of women published in that period contained the life stories of exemplary women such as Joan of Arc, Queen Elizabeth, or Florence Nightingale, or they were large collections of the life stories of lesser-known women whom the emerging middle-class of female readers were to imitate. They functioned as a type of "self-help" that provided role models for young women in the form of "prosopography," which is the collective study of lives for certain qualities.

Their great numbers meant that collective biography was a way to write the lives of women who had been public figures into national history (2004, 2–3). The strategy of collective biography about women is both about a pedagogy of exemplarity, and an attempt to make women's lives more public than they may have been thought to be. It is a hopeful and positive strategy, but what it did not do was directly confront the sexism that prevented equal opportunities for women. Collective biography sought to inspire individual women to succeed, but it did not identify the barriers to success, and it did not challenge the masculine models for success that were in place. The problem with collective biography is that it can resemble prosopography, which can render individual stories as examples of collective characteristics. This can have the effect of erasing other forms of difference from such stories, and individual motivations, too, potentially can disappear within such a form. Sharon Wood, the first Western and North American woman to summit Mount Everest, writes in her memoir *Rising* that she has doubts about the inspirational discourse of prosopography in mountaineering memoir for just this reason. She says in *Rising* that for years she delayed writing about her Everest climb because she wanted to tell a less celebratory, and more complex, story of her own motivations and experiences that resisted the reductive narrative of her position in Everest's climbing history (2019, x–xi, 224).

As important as it is to make sure that women are in the historical record and that the achievements of climbing women of the past and the present are known, it remains equally important to think about what the criteria for the historical record has been, and how gender issues have worked to shape climbing, for all climbers of any gender, in profound ways, particularly in the writing about classic ascents. It is neither possible nor desirable to untangle the work of gender from all of the climbers who have tried to summit the highest mountains in the world, to look at masculinity as a discourse that only belongs to male bodies, or at gender as only about the fact of women's presence and participation in climbing history.

Gender issues structure every climber's identity and every climb: masculinity may be a discourse that cis-gendered women take up, or that some men inhabit differently from others. For example, expeditions in the Himalayas from China, South Korea, or Japan do not receive the same coverage in the English-speaking world or elsewhere in Europe. As a result, narratives by climbers from these countries are published, but are almost never translated into other languages, and so most expedition accounts or memoirs by important climbers are unknown beyond the linguistic borders such publications have to negotiate. The effect of this is to render climbers from Asia as unknown and unknowable, which opens their reputations and their actions to be considered within Orientalist stereotypes, and to think of them as "other" to the history of climbing. When climbers from Asia most appear in accounts by Euro-Western writers, who as a rule do not understand the thoughts, feelings, and motivations of these climbers, they are often othered within climbing narratives and subjected to racist stereotyping and Orientalist discourse, regardless of their gender. Male climbers from Asia are either feminized (they rely too much on guides and ropes), or they are associated with lockstep ideas about climbing style, especially when they are accused of acting too collectively to be good climbers (generally speaking, most climbing accounts adhere to a liberal model of a good team structure as composed of critically thinking individuals, with a strong, yet consultative leader). Other models, including the older tradition of large, nationally organized teams, are often assumed to be passé. For example, in his account *No Way Down: Life and Death on K2* about a 2010 disaster, Graham Bowley sees the Korean team on the mountain as a throwback to the past, without actually knowing anything about the team in question: "There was no doubt a distinction between the Korean and the Western – American and European – teams. In the modern mountaineering age, the Western expeditions no longer climbed for their country – that belonged to a different, old-fashioned era" (2010, 44).

In other words, the Korean team is pictured within an Orientalist trope about Asia as timeless and somehow "behind" the West in development, repurposed to show that they, but not Europeans, are part of a climbing past, and so they cannot "belong" to the mountains in the present. Bowley also represents the Korean team as too large, too inexperienced, too ambitious, and too collective because they had no leader to tell them to turn back (46). Their lead climber, a woman named Go Mi-Sun, is described merely as "a small, stocky, pretty woman" (119), a description calculated to diminish her and her abilities. Bowley did not interview any of the team members to see if his assumptions were correct. He did not have to do so, because climbers from Asia are not often spoken to in such accounts. They are spoken about.[12]

Jon Krakauer does much the same thing in *Into Thin Air*. Krakauer describes Taiwanese climber Gau Ming Ho (commonly called Makalu Gau) as overly ambitious and callous about the worth of human life. Krakauer introduces him that way through the words of Conrad Anker, a highly regarded American climber, who calls Gau's actions during an earlier climb when he celebrated a summit victory after some of his teammates died "pretty weird" (1997, 98). Later on, Gau's lack of emotion about a teammate's sudden death from a fall is interpreted by David Breashears, another American climber, as callous (162). Krakauer also says that "there was a very real fear" that Gau's team would have to be rescued, presumably because Gau was understood to be incompetent, and would thereby jeopardize others' summit (98). Ten years later, Gau said in an interview that Krakauer had never interviewed him and had made false allegations about his abilities and motivation that had damaged his reputation as a mountaineer (Gau 2007).

Even more disturbingly, Krakauer represents Japanese climber Yasuko Namba as the quintessential inexperienced client who represents the commercial era's worst sins, writing that she is taciturn, when her first language clearly is not English (1997, 39), and that she does not even know how to use crampons, which are spikes climbers wear on the bottom of their mountaineering boots (85). Later on during the climb, Krakauer characterizes Namba, who was one of the best-known mountaineers in Japan and who had climbed many other high mountains, as not fitting what Krakauer calls "the meek, deferential stereotype of a middle-aged Japanese woman," because of a conversation he had with her about women's rights. It appears at this point that he is willing to see

Namba in a somewhat different light after talking with her for awhile. But he does not: he sees Namba's confidence as a problem, calling her impatient and technically inexperienced, while a guide "scolds" her as if she were a child (184). *Into Thin Air* ends with the picture of Namba losing her grip on Neal Beidelman, the guide trying to rescue her, and sinking into the snow to wait for death because "she was so little" (301). She is pictured as a victim in a tragic scene that denies her any agency, where her salient characteristics are her small stature and her outsized ambition. Because she is dead, she cannot speak against the way she has been depicted.

Like Gau Ming Ho, or the Korean climbing team on K2 in 2008, Yasuko Namba is pictured unfairly because she was not a white Western climber, and her thoughts and feelings therefore remain unknowable beyond the broadest stereotypes. As a result, like Gau, she is seen in Orientalist terms as passive rather than active, as childlike, and as someone who does not belong in the mountains. She is feminized, and when she does not act according to type, her desire to climb is read as inappropriate. Like Sherpas in earlier expedition accounts, who are sometimes feminized (Ortner 1999, 227–8), or who are assigned similar tropes about impassivity in the face of death (137) or about childlikeness (59), stereotypes about Asian people even in recent climbing accounts like these circulate as they do because there has been little opportunity to think about the discourses of masculinity and European, Western whiteness that keep them so current.

What has connected mountaineering to the world of white, European men for so long? Why does climbing the highest mountains in the world remain a metaphor for masculine stories of sovereignty and achievement? Why there are still rigid ideas of success that rely on those century-old stories, and circulate them in the culture of climbing and its representation? The latest online issues of *Gripped* magazine, *Climbing*, and *Rock and Ice* all feature female climbers doing the hardest classic and sport routes. Accompanying the spectacular photographs and stories, there generally is little or no discussion about how their gender might affect what they are doing, beyond questions of visibility and participation. When gender issues do appear, they often are associated with the sexist "past" of climbing, or a sign of inequality that must be surmounted. For example, a 2017 article in *Climbing* described women's rock climbing as having evolved since the 1990s, when few women were in gyms or on crags. The article suggests that things have changed because "today we feel more empowered to find our own way, break free of the mold, and climb what we want to climb. Women have decided to follow their hearts" (Philips 2017a). Such a picture of female climbers as those who succeed because they dream big and simply try harder is compelling, but it is not complete, because it depends on a liberal ideology of individual success and heroism that makes gender something that climbers themselves need to climb past because "women are making a name for themselves as not only top female climbers, but as top climbers – of either gender" (2017).[13]

Against that positive picture of women who can succeed if they just try is the problem of visibility in representations of mountaineering. Before she begins her historical study of women and climbing in *Annapurna: A Woman's Place*, Blum points out that the barriers to participation she experienced as a young climber did not happen because she did not try hard enough, but because of the sexism she personally experienced, as male climbers did not want women to go on expeditions with them. To make sure that the problem is understood as sexism and not as the need for individual empowerment, she adds that "other women climbers have told me of similar experiences" and then quotes Sir Edmund Hillary, at length, to show that as recently as 1979, he saw the inclusion of women in climbing parties as a detriment to the success of the climb (1980, xviii). In this view, women are not supposed to participate, and so they should not and will not be seen climbing.

It is significant too that the lifetime achievement category of the Piolet d'Or, the alpine climbing award I have mentioned previously, was not awarded to a woman until 2020, when Catherine Destiville won it ("Five Women"; Gardien). As of 2018, only two woman – Kei Taniguchi of Japan in 2009 Lise Billon in 2016 – have ever won the Piolet d'Or as members of a team for a specific climb, although a climb by Chantal Astorga, Jason Thompson and Anne Gilbert Chase also received a Special Mention in 2018 ("2018 Honoured Ascents" 2018; "Piolets" 2016; "Piolet" 2009). Beyond the obvious question of lack of representation, the criteria of Susan Frohlick's ethnographic study of masculinity at mountaineering film and book festivals – important venues for writing and film about mountaineering to circulate at key locations around the world – concludes that male filmmakers and male subjects overwhelmingly dominate the programs. Women are positioned as spectators, not as actors (2005, 178), while the films in particular produce images of hypermasculinity, male bodies that are supremely able, mobile, and white. Brown people and white women occupy at best supporting roles in these stories of mastery (179–80). Frohlick describes the overall effect of these images as a "bombardment" that viewers both do and do not desire because of the excitement the images are meant to impart (2005, 182). They are repetitive, and they exist within an ideology of extreme adventure, performed for a middle-class "soft" adventuring audience (183–4). Frohlick's other studies of mountaineering and mediation, most notably her study of controversies in the Western press about Nepali climber Lhakpa Sherpa (2004) and of the stereotype of the "bad mother" with reference to Hargreaves's death on K2 (2006), highlight the importance of studying the representation of gender in books and films, because of the effect representation has on the circulation of ideas about gender and race in climbing.

In her study of climbing guides, Georgie Abel (2017) also points out how images (or a lack of them) directly affect who is thought to have the "right" body for the mountains. Most climbing guides, Abel writes, do not refer to female climbers or picture them, and non-white climbers are represented very rarely. When other climbers at a pitch assume that Abel's climbing partner should take the lead, ignoring the fact that she is clearly geared up to lead a climb, she wonders why, at first. She asks herself: "Why don't they see me? Then I stumbled upon an explanation. Typically, the people with whom I interact in outdoor arenas are white. Similarly, the industry's media tend to showcase scientists, activists, or athletes as white and usually male. No wonder people don't see me; I am not what they are accustomed to seeing in our field. But I am here, and so are other women – including women of color and those of differing ages, abilities, sizes, sexual orientations, and socioeconomic backgrounds" (2017).

Abel's observations link the representation of climbers to the ability to "see" someone who does not fit what is supposed to be in one's field of vision. Her observations mark climbing as subject to cultural expectations, not as the scene of freedom from culture. And the problem of "seeing" links her experiences as a climber to the problem of representation in mountaineering literature, where gender and other differences are played down so that the path of achievement appears to be level. As we have already seen, the 2019 Banff Mountaineering Film and Book

Festival acknowledges this problem as intersectional in the text accompanying the Climbing through Barriers panel as a problem of visibility, when it says what if "there was no one who looked like you or who you could relate to" in climbing. Lack of visibility, in other words, means that there are no role models for others to emulate, and so the discussion of visibility and barriers must happen first.

Silences around gender in climbing (or the need for gender to remain silent) might seem to signal that gender does not and should not "matter" to climbing. But as Charlotte Austin, an important American climber, guide, and climbing writer has pointed out, gender issues structure the activity of climbing. She suggests that climbers could benefit from being more aware of what gender studies has to say about what they do: "there is research – a lot of research – being done about gender, decision-making and communication ... Consider how alpine climbers have adopted practices and vocabulary first developed by other researchers: We talk about risk tolerance, the expert halo, fear extinction and risk-reward matrices, all of which are terms borrowed from studies done outside the context of climbing. So what can we learn – both about ourselves and our climbing partners – if we look at modern gender research and apply it to the mountains?" (2017).

Austin is thinking here about what climbers could learn from the behavioural sciences about her gender, but her observations can also be applied to the narratives of classic expedition climbing that so many climbers have cited as important to their own development as mountaineers. Gender surely matters to the act of climbing, but it matters to the representation of climbing too. The focus of *False Summit* remains within the terrain of representation, rather than of phenomenology or socio-anthropological studies of mountaineering experiences. The reason for this has to do with the work of genre within mountaineering writing. Phenomenological studies relying on interviews do not address the importance of the written record to classic mountaineering because they tend to emphasize the reporting of experience as evidence of lived bodies, which does not take into account how and why memoirs and expedition accounts work on the level of representation to construct, rather than describe, experience.[14]

Sharon Wood's memoir *Rising*, her account of the Canadian team's 1986 climb of a new route on Everest, is an example of how even relatively overt discussions of gender in mountaineering memoir are complex in the larger web of relationships and expectations on an expedition, and how gender works to construct identity in sometimes subtle ways. Wood's memoir reflects on the expedition that saw her become the first Canadian woman and the first woman in the Western hemisphere to summit Everest successfully. The Everest Lite expedition climbed Everest via the technically difficult West Ridge route plus a new route on the summit cone, with a team of some of Canada's best climbers. *Rising* therefore is a document of the expedition and its use of a modified version of alpine style, but it also addresses Wood's doubts about climbing, and about herself as a climber, particularly because it includes aspects of Wood's life that were not directly about the expedition, such as the failure of her marriage, her celebrity after Everest, and her struggles with depression. The memoir features Wood's thoughts about events that took place decades ago, providing ample opportunity for reflection, and it places concerns about sexism and gender difference within a larger set of concerns about style, team dynamics, and personal motivations. Wood's narrative structure means that she can identify more easily what gender difference did and did not feel like on her expedition, partly because she has the advantage of years of reflection about the meaning of the Everest climb and the impact of the climb on her life. But gender differences and even overt sexism do not, for Wood, consistently appear in ways that are easy to identify, partly because she was very adept at playing the game of machismo in the 1980s. The result, sometimes, is a set of ambivalent feelings about the climb and her own place in it. For example, her teammates call her "Woody," a sign that she belongs because she has a nickname. But the name is male (even if it is most readily associated with a cartoon character), and it so serves to give her enough masculinity so that she can be, most of the time, one of the guys and a full member of the team. In the same vein, the teammates banter with Wood about her desirability on the expedition without ever harassing her, just as they banter with each other about masculinity (2019, 30, 45, 93, 222). Wood usually knows that she belongs on the expedition and deserves to be there (76), but at key points, she realizes what the limits of belonging actually are. On the one hand, her teammates clearly respect her, and she experiences relatively little sexism on her own team as they joke with her and share work responsibilities. She and Jane Fearing – the expedition cook – are sexually harassed by Tibetan yak herders when the team is still at Base

Camp, but they shrug this off (21). Wood and Fearing also enjoy flirting with members of a Spanish climbing team who clearly appreciate them as women, but they remain in control of the situations in which they find themselves (16–17, 63–4), even joking with their own team members about the yak herders later (22).

These are all aspects of the expedition where gender matters, but not all that much. But gender also becomes something that Wood works out with Fearing. They talk about how lonely it feels to live with men (22). They discuss men's and women's shortcomings, and realize that they do not feel completely at ease with men when they socialize (23). It is Fearing's presence that changes something in Wood. As Wood says, "it's not as if I ever saw myself as inferior, but her [Fearing's] presence validates something in myself that I can't quite identify and hadn't known I was missing" (23). At another point, Wood does not always understand how to easily banter with or kid her male teammates (46, 48). She mentions that she had to work hard to earn the respect of some of her team members before they would let her on the expedition, in part because some thought she would be a sexual distraction (62, 74–5), but she herself almost does not allow Fearing on the team for the same reason. Fearing responds that she is used to fending off advances (62–3). The environment even causes them to compete with each other at first: as women in a male-dominated environment, they did not initially trust each other (23), just as Wood instinctually sizes up Annie Whitehouse, a climber on another team, before she trusts her too (60–1). As Fearing herself says, Wood is "cagey" and has learned to pretend to be tougher than she actually is, "like a block of wood" (55). And Wood is tough, which is how she gets along in climbing circles, even when some situations in those circles remind her of the problems of being female in climbing. For example, when she has to figure out whether a snow slope is safe or not, she remembers a sexist lesson about snow hazards where the instructor had leered at her. She then thinks: at least the lesson was memorable, and she can apply it and survive (84).

At other moments, she needs reassurance, and she sees this as something she does because she is a woman, notably when her own teammates tell her to take the chance and be on the summit team. She chides herself as she resists, telling herself that a man would not hesitate to say yes. In the end, it is Fearing who convinces her to ask for what she wants and deserves (128–35). Even when she has earned it, Wood has trouble asserting mastery. There is a long history in mountaineering discourse that points to some of the reasons why it might have been so hard for her to do so – and she was one of the most accomplished high-altitude climbers of her generation, climbing a difficult line on Everest as a respected member of one of the best climbing teams at the time.

Sherry B. Ortner's landmark feminist analysis of climbing in the Himalayas, *Life and Death on Everest* (1999), represents a way to think about interviewing and textual analysis together, within an anthropological framework of mountaineering as a "serious game" with important stakes for each of the actors within the activity. Ortner's study was intersectional, the result of her decade-long research of high-altitude climbing and the position of the Sherpas within Sherpa culture and mountaineering culture. Using interviews and written accounts to create a nuanced analysis of "Himalayan mountaineering [as] both a dream and a practice, both as a form of solidarity and a form of power," Ortner considers how Sherpas and non-Sherpas encounter each other within the activities and discourses of climbing (24). Ortner was the first scholar to think of gender as one variable within a complex set of interactions between Sherpa men, Sherpa women, and non-Sherpa male and female climbers from different points in the history of Himalayan mountaineering, and to think of gender in the mountains as having a history and a set of cultural norms that have been enacted, re-enacted, resisted, and debated. Unlike nationality, which Ortner discards as having little descriptive power (because in her view both non-Sherpa and Sherpa people during the development of Himalayan climbing operated within a dense network of national stereotypes), Ortner sees gender as "highly relevant to this study" because of the male-dominated nature of early mountaineering (32), and because "inter-cultural relations are never gender-neutral" (227). In other words, gender (like class, or ideas about modernity) structures other ideas Sherpas and non-Sherpa climbers have about death, money, and religion, all of which in their turn affect the practice of mountaineering, and its connection to larger ideals. Gender does not have to be discussed *as gender* in order for that analysis to take place, but as the effect of describing another kind of "game," in climbing, for instance of races on the mountain between Sherpa and non-Sherpa climbers, where the non-Sherpa climbers admired the Sherpas and recorded this in their expedition accounts, but also expressed "the nagging fear among the sahibs [an older Sherpa word for male non-Sherpa climbers] that it was really the Sherpas who were climbing the mountain" and not themselves (168). Why would they play this game? Ortner reads this situation as an instance of the game of machismo (for the sahibs, who need to prove their manhood in indirect ways) and a way to assert equality in a light-hearted way (for the Sherpas, who raced as a challenge to the idea of racial inequality). Ideas about class difference and gender combine within a "game" with serious overtones for all participants.

Understanding the history of climbing machismo is important for working out what masculinity means in climbing, where relatively silent competition between male climbers expresses masculinity without it being referred to directly (162–5). In the postwar era, particularly during the 1950s, Ortner says, competitiveness was a way to assert physical superiority in terms of who could climb (particularly in alpine style) faster or better, and this took the form of competitions between climbers and, at times, between climbers and Sherpas to prove the "fact" of non-Sherpa male dominance (165). Sherpas on some early expeditions, meanwhile, treated this stress on competition as a "game," but as game about equality, a way to make fun of the emphasis on speed, and establish their own superiority. The Sherpas playing such a game sometimes mock what the non-Sherpa climbers think they can achieve, or disavow the seriousness of non-Sherpa climbing style or goals, to show the limits of non-Sherpa thinking and assert their own way of being in the mountains (170).

As time went on, Sherpa "competitiveness" appeared to become one of their most endearing traits, one that also helped those who hired Sherpas to achieve their own goals. In another version of this same idea of a game where the stakes are high, Jemima Dika Sherpa (2014) juxtaposes the pervasive stereotypical image of Sherpa cheerfulness and speed with the reality that Sherpa climbers and porters *have* to work hard, and take chances, in order to make money. Machismo and competitiveness are therefore not innate qualities, but strategies that help in making a living. In the case of her cousin, a young porter who died from a fall when he was not clipped into a rope, being fast and working hard was about career advancement, not cheerfulness: "As a young high-altitude expedition worker, the more you carry, the more you are paid. There is a per kilogram equation for payment, and there is value, both in hard cash and in securing future work, in proving you are good. If you prove you're good, you get hired next season, possibly recruited by one of the better companies, climbing literally up the mountain and figuratively up the ranks. The best way to do all this is to move fast and carry a lot. And the best way to do that is to dance, possibly unclipped, across the icefall ladders."

After the golden age, the game of machismo changed, although Ortner still sees it as a re-establishment of masculinity, this time for the counter-cultural climbers of the 1970s. Some male climbers in that period, notably Peter Boardman, reacted against competition as a given and advocated for more cooperative approaches to climbing, but this debate about competition remained part of a debate about masculinity within climbing, rather than as a way to make climbing more diverse. Boardman "disapproved of competition in principle" because he was "in a seventies mode" (1978, 190). He does not discuss competition as a gender issue, but as part of climbing style. In other words, competition is a way to mark out masculinity among differences, but without discussing openly what manliness involves. It expresses aspects of gender without referring to them. It creates social hierarchies that marked out cultural differences as gender differences. It displaces onto the action of bodies the social aspects of what it is to have a body. As Ortner says, "sahibs [non-Sherpa climbers] rarely talk about physicality as such" (1999, 163), with a notable exception that proves the rule: Jan Morris, a well-known travel writer who was the reporter on the 1953 British expedition to Mount Everest tasked with reporting Edmund Hillary and Tenzing Norgay's successful ascent. Morris detailed the ascent and her role in publicizing it in *Coronation Everest*, a text that is still in print. In her lesser-known memoir *Conundrum*, an account of her view of gender and what led her to get hormone treatments and sex reassignment surgery in the 1960s, Morris does discuss what she calls the "speed" of the male climbing body when it is fit as "this feeling of unfluctuating control, I think, that women cannot share" ([1974] 1997, 81). This is not the same thing as claiming that women cannot climb in an essentialist way. Rather, Morris writes that looking back at her time on Mount Everest, "the male body may be ungenerous, even uncreative in the deepest kind, but when it is working properly it is a marvelous thing to inhabit" particularly when it "works" at peak fitness (82). Morris's description of such a body is almost mechanical, and it connects the activity of climbing with the feeling of control and mastery, of oneself and one's surroundings.

This is a concise expression of what being a climber in the golden age was supposed to feel like when everything was "working" and nothing was wrong, or when there were no "others" (Sherpas, women, working-class climbers) to challenge or even unsettle that feeling of mastery. And what it was supposed to feel like was the feeling of masculinity without a thought of the other, and without culture. It is connected to other kinds of privilege which work by remaining unaware that there could be other modes of being. This is, as Ortner points out, one of the few times that a writer talks about "the centrality of the well-tuned male body for mountaineering in this era [the 1950s]" (1999, 163). But potential existed, even then, for physical superiority to destabilize this vision of masculinity, since the Sherpas could and did outperform their "masters" (166). What Morris suggests is that the pleasures of doing this kind of physical masculinity cannot be open to "women" in the same way because women (if they are identified as women) do not have access to either the experience or discourse of mastery.

Morris would probably not see this as analogous to Judith Butler's idea of the performativity of gender as imitation and repetition, a copy of a copy that exposes the nature of identity as non-essential, and so is in need of constant reaffirmation and re-inscription (2006, 138). But there is a parallel between their positions worth noting. If one is not at ease in one's assigned masculinity (as Morris was not: this is the foundation of her "conundrum," as she called it, since she did not experience her gender as other people saw it), then can someone actually *be* masculine in the mountains without mastery? Does the presence of others always set a limit, as the presence of "'identities' that cannot 'exist'" (193) creates a threat that must be neutralized and naturalized? In the case of the mountaineering body, the belief in the importance of mastery, of the body, the environment, and of others within one's field of vision are all key to understanding why this kind of physicality as the signal of masculinity persists – regardless of the gender of the person who takes up this idea of the body – and why it has been so hard for so many mountaineering writers to discuss it critically.

Wanderer above a Sea of Fog and Sovereignty

The relationship of corporeal sovereignty to mountaineering masculinity has a long history. From the early characterization of climbers as men of science in the eighteenth century (Clements 2018, 14–15), to the heroic era of Himalayan first ascents, to the free solo work of Alex Honnold, who says in the 2018 film *Free Solo 360* that "climbing without a rope requires a level of mastery that rope climbing doesn't," the representation of mountaineering remains connected to the idea of sovereignty over one's body and one's environment, a story told over and over in best-selling books and films shown at mountaineering film festivals around the world. It is important to note just how central personal sovereignty is to creating that discourse of "modern man." Sovereignty is usually discussed with reference to the ability of a state to exercise power over people or territory. But as Peter Hansen (2013) has argued, the development of the idea of individual sovereignty, which would become central to the political philosophy of liberalism, was directly connected to the development of mountain climbing. Sovereignty over one's self meant that a man could choose to climb to the summit. And from the summit, a man could possess, through seeing it panoramically, the whole of a landscape, claimed for scientific knowledge, or for other kinds of mastery over the environment (53). And so, discourses of success have come to depend on picturing mountaineering as a metaphor for personal achievement and human freedom, but without discussing that it is "a man" of a certain type who is capable of exercising mastery. Sovereignty has a body in mind, but the properties of that body tend to go unmentioned. This is why the discourse of mountaineering gender has been tied to political exercises of sovereignty over territory such as colonialism, or as the exercise of Romantic ideas about sovereignty when the mountains become places of leisure and adventure for certain classes. Ultimately, sovereignty is the reason why mountaineering came to depend heavily on the gendering of sovereign bodies as normatively white, European, able-bodied, male, and heroic, without mentioning gender very much at all.

Figure I.3 | Caspar David Friedrich, *Wanderer above a Sea of Fog*.

It is possible to see sovereignty structuring the work of masculinity in Caspar David Friedrich's iconic painting, *Wanderer above a Sea of Fog* (1818, figure I.3). The subject embodies Romantic ideas from the nineteenth century about the self and about the so-called mountaintop experience of climbing as part of self-realization and mastery. We cannot see the face of the climber in *Wanderer* because he faces away from us. It is clear that we are meant to share in his view, but not in his experience, which is private. We can see from his clothes that he is a gentleman, or at least an idealist, possibly because he is wearing the outfit of a soldier in the fight against Napoleon (Koerner 2009, 210–11). The wanderer is young and fit, but otherwise he is anonymous. If he is a soldier, he is a metaphorical one, in that he has "fought" the mountain and confidently stands at the top. And he is alone, without even a name, a solitary wanderer, someone who is not tied to the things of the world. He seems to be above civilization and is part of a higher realm, blocking a view of the landscape that only he can see, above any aspect of the social world. He is literally at the peak of success, without any equipment except for his staff, a singular figure at the summit with no one else there who might have helped him or even accompanied him. He does not seem to be tired, cold, hungry, or thirsty. Because his face is turned away from us, we are invited to imagine that we could take his place at the centre of a sublime natural moment: free, peaceful, balanced, taking in the scene without effort or suffering. He is the picture of self-possession.

Wanderer thus embodies a Romantic ideal of mountaineering as a quasi-religious experience, a theme Friedrich explored in other paintings as well. We witness the spirituality he saw in mountain environments, for example, *The Cross in the Mountains* (1807–08). It is an ideal that has endured for almost two centuries. And something else in the painting has endured too: the physical fact of the climber occupies the centre of the composition. It is impossible to look at *Wanderer* and not see that the body of the protagonist marks him as white, European, able-bodied, and male. And yet, as viewers we are not invited to contemplate this fact, even as it structures what we are seeing. What cannot, what *must not* be mentioned occupies the centre of the painting. *Wanderer* has often been thought of as the embodiment of the Kantian sublime, a figure whose judgment is suspended as he confronts the power of nature (Haladyn 2016, 60). The figure might be Percy Shelley's "wise, and great, and good [who] Interpret, or make felt, or deeply feel" the power of Mont Blanc, the highest mountain in the Alps (III, 33–4). Or this is a modern subject, a figure of the self when it is detached from the world, a prefiguring of Hannah Arendt's concept of the citizen as cut free from nationhood, and instead connected to the modern idea of human dignity, encapsulated in citizenship rather than religious belief (Haladyn 2016, 49, 56). All of these versions of the sublime depend on us not seeing who the wise, and great, and good are in any specific way. The sublime is supposed to depend on transcending social conditions. The conditions themselves are not supposed to matter.

But in *Wanderer*, they do matter. The figure is *in the way* of the rest of the scene, in effect preventing viewers from seeing the view as the figure sees it (Haladyn 2016, 49–50). The painting is about a summit experience, but not about the experience itself. It is about *who is there*, and its power comes from allowing us to imagine that possibly, we (whoever that is) could be there too. In similar ways, gender, culture, race – all the markers of belonging that locate mark our bodies as social, all the aspects of climbing that are connected to how our bodies move through the world – matter to mountaineering and structure it as an activity, but often, the literature of mountaineering has little to say about what structures the experiences climbers have in the mountains, and how those experiences are communicated to others. The design of *Wanderer* bears this out, because the position of the figure follows the iconography of the *Rückenfigur* – literally a figure seen from the back in a painting that is meant to be a way for the viewer to participate in the scene (Koerner 2009, 210–12). Participation is key because the figure blocks our view. In other words, he is the view through which we see. We can think about what he experiences. We can desire what he has. We can admire him. We can imagine ourselves in his place. He, and not the mountain, is the point.

And so, what might it mean if we say that this is true, that "we" (and our genders) do matter intimately to the representation of climbing the highest mountains in the world? In effect, I am asking for us to look critically at climbing as gendered because climbing, like gender, is social, and not natural, and because to speak of something like climbing as natural has so often meant a denial of the social forces far beyond us that structure who we are, what we think the world is about, and how much ability we have to move through that world. This is a different thing from simply saying that women, or people of colour, or climbers who are not from Europe, North America, or the former British empire need to be written back into climbing history, although that is an important part of telling a more complete story of climbing. To return to the *Wanderer* for a moment, we must ask, who is that "we" who is invited to take the place of the one who stands at the summit? Who is supposed to imagine

Figure I.4 | Man on top of mountain. Hiker climbed on peak of rock above foggy valley.

themselves looking out at that view? The grammar of the Rückenfigur appears to allow anyone to participate, and so, there would appear to be no reason why a non-European man, a woman, a brown person, even a child could not imagine themselves in that position of sovereignty, and could not take the place of the wanderer, standing at the summit with the right to assert mastery and success. It is ideal material for stock photographs of hiking (figures I.4, I.5).

Countless reproductions of the pose of the wanderer in inspirational graphics like these repeat the iconography of Friedrich's Rückenfigur in order to sell this idea of substitution as a form of equality and justice. But such a vision, seductive in its simplicity, does not get at a central paradox in climbing, and elsewhere as well: the work of substitution only happens when there is an equivalence, an *equivalence that must never be mentioned*. Without that silent logic in place, all who do not possess the

Figure I.5 | Silhouette of a girl standing on a cliff.

right body for the activity must be excluded. In mountaineering, authenticity in climbing is tied to gender in such an intimate way because the right body – the normal body, the authentic body, the sovereign body – is so often a white, male, European body. Anyone who does not have such a body is either not an authentic mountain climber in the first place, or they prove that they can be a worthy substitute. They must become a virtual mountaineering man. They must learn mastery of the role, as they learn the other skills that they need to climb at all. This is very difficult to do, and it is why so many climbers who do not fit into the discourse of climbing excellence are called inauthentic, or incompetent, or their achievements are not thought by others in the community to be serious or important enough. It is why the history of high-altitude mountaineering is a history of decline. It is why those with the wrong bodies for climbing are most often dismissed or even written out of mountaineering representation, because their ways of doing things, of *being* in the world, are of no account. And it is why gender in climbing should matter, even to those who do not care about climbing. Like George Mallory's famous retort "because it's there" to a question about why he would ever want to climb Mount Everest, gender is *there* in mountaineering representations. It is time to pay attention to its constant presence for all climbers, and to take its work seriously.

There are other Annapurnas in the lives of men.
Maurice Herzog, *Annapurna*

And in the lives of women as well.
Arlene Blum, *Annapurna: A Woman's Place*

CHAPTER 1

LEADERSHIP AND GENDER ON ANNAPURNA

Annapurna is a paradox (figure 1.1). It is the place where the Golden Age of Himalayan mountaineering began, because it was the first 8,000-metre peak to be summitted. Even though it is the tenth highest mountain in the world at 8,091 metres, today, few outside of climbing or trekking circles would recognize it or would even know where it is. In what was once a seldom-visited region of Nepal, the Annapurna massif is accessed from the north by a valley that, according to Maurice Herzog, was unmapped and not known even by the villagers of Pokhara, its nearest town, until a French team (led by Herzog) found a route to the peak in 1950. The mountain is very dangerous for climbers – its north face is swept constantly by avalanches, and its south face has the largest and most difficult "big-wall" ice cliff in the Himalayas. Annapurna means "the Provider" or

Figure 1.1 | View of Annapurna massif from Jaljala Pass, Nepal.

"Goddess of the Harvests" in Sanskrit, but it is a hazardous provider to encounter. Statistically it is the most dangerous 8,000-metre peak, with a fatality rate in 2015 of 35 per cent (35 deaths to 100 safe returns). That is even higher than K2's 2015 rate of 26.5 per cent (Carpenter 2015). Annapurna I, the highest point of the 55-kilometre massif, is the least-climbed of all 8,000-metre peaks as a result. Fewer than 200 climbers have summitted it since 1950 (Samuel 2015).

Annapurna's dangers and inaccessibility are responsible for its legendary status in the world of climbing. Its difficulty attracts few climbers, but they are an elite few, many of them important to the history of climbing, and they have made the isolated massif the setting for some of the best-known climbing milestones and expedition narratives in mountaineering history. According to Reinhold Messner in *Annapurna: 50 Years of Expeditions in the Death Zone*, Annapurna has never become a fashionable mountain to climb but it remains a credible goal for climbers who wish to push the limits of climbing because it is more difficult to climb than Everest or what he calls other "easy eight-thousanders" (2000,

149–50). As a result, Annapurna is seen as a relatively "pure" mountain unsullied by alpine tourism, a place where true devotees of Himalayan climbing can go to test themselves. In addition to the 1950 historic ascent that ushered in that Golden Age of first ascents in the Himalayas and Karakoram, Annapurna was the site of the first successful big wall ascent in the Himalayas, accomplished by Chris Bonington's team in 1970, and the first ascent of an 8,000-metre peak by a female-led climbing team, in 1978. More recently, Annapurna's difficult south face has been the setting for a 2013 solo climb by speed climber Ueli Steck (Kiester 2013) and an epic alpine-style ascent of the difficult "Japanese line" on the South Face by Stéphane Benoiste and Yannick Graziani ("Stéphane" 2013).

And so Annapurna is the setting for some of the best-known and best-selling expedition writing in the world – another paradox for a mountain few climbers attempt, few survive, and not many have visited. In the words of *Inside Himalayas*, "why does Annapurna make for such compelling accounts, when so many more people have climbed Everest, K2, and others of the 10 highest mountains? It surely has something to do with the extreme dangers of Annapurna" ("Respecting" 2017). It also has something to do with the compelling account of its first ascent, itself a classic of mountaineering literature: Annapurna became known to thousands of French school children through Maurice Herzog's *Annapurna* of 1951. Other books about climbing Annapurna have also become classics, notably Chris Bonington's and Arlene Blum's. Bonington's account of the first big wall ascent, *Annapurna South Face*, remains in print decades after it was first published in 1970. Blum, the leader of the first female-led expedition to summit an 8,000-metre peak, wrote what remains the only overtly feminist expedition mountaineering account ever published, *Annapurna: A Woman's Place* (1980), a book that also has stayed in print and is widely read beyond the climbing community because of its feminist message. In 1998, on the occasion of the twentieth anniversary of the climb, the book was even reissued with a new preface and afterword by Blum.

Annapurna's reputation as a mountain for "purists" and professionals, and its position as the setting for important mountaineering writing about gender, make it a good place to start an investigation of mountaineering narratives. Annapurna is a place of achievement, heroism, and idealism in mountaineering history. It is, as we shall see, a setting for classic European mountaineering masculinity after the Second World War, the setting for working-class and counter-cultural mountaineering masculinity a decade later, and the place where the North American and European women's liberation movement of the 1970s tried to intervene in the gender politics of mountaineering. In three key expedition narratives about Annapurna – like other accounts of attempts on the highest mountains in the world – it is possible to see how attitudes about gender, class, and race play out indirectly, within a formation that Sherry Ortner has called "bodily politics" (1999, 236). In bodily politics, ideas that mark what bodies are most often are discussed indirectly, as matters connected to climbing and leadership style, rather than overtly discussing abstract political ideas about class, gender, or race. These issues do structure accounts of climbing Annapurna, but they remain embedded in discussions about leadership and climbing style. Both aspects of expedition mountaineering become a way to invoke politics without referring to the structures of expectation that make bodies political. In other words, the act of writing about climbing expresses what marks one's body or how others see bodies but does not discuss such phenomena in themselves. What kind of person someone is becomes connected to expectations within mountaineering circles about climbing style, which itself is connected to ideas about culture. For each writer, the culture of expeditions becomes connected to accepting, invoking, or resisting ideas about how to be a "good" climber, where being "good" is implicitly linked to set of gender, class, and cultural norms.

Annapurna in the Lives of Men: Siege Style

Bodily politics is in evidence in Maurice Herzog's *Annapurna*, the best-selling title about mountaineering for decades after it was published. The story Herzog told about the struggle to summit Annapurna, the heroism of his team, his own suffering as he was carried down the mountain with severe frostbite in his hands and feet, and his famous phrase "there are other Annapurnas in the lives of men," the book's memorable last line, inspired generations of climbers to take up climbing, and connected contemporary climbing achievements with Romantic ideals of struggle, suffering, and purity of heart. In particular, Herzog's portrayal of leadership became a symbol of resilience for the people of France, collapsing national pride into ideas about male heroism and making climbing appear as an alternative to war, where France could forget its wartime defeat and imagine itself victorious on the world stage. Herzog himself went on to become minister of sport in the postwar French government, because of what he and his achievements symbolized for France. At the heart of that resilience and its connection to war discourse is the prominence in *Annapurna* of siege style, a climbing style developed from colonial military campaigns of the nineteenth century. Symbolically, siege style in Herzog's account becomes a kind of grammar of masculinity, because its methods allow men to feel and be portrayed as heroic and selfless, as if they were soldiers. It connects climbing identity to a certain way of being and climbing, and it connects mountain heroism to war heroism. Within bodily politics, siege style allows gender issues to be discussed as matters of climbing style, and it allows Herzog to portray homosocial relations in ways that strengthen the heroic masculinity of the climbers, particularly in the context of leadership at a time of crisis.

In *Annapurna*, ideas about the character of an ideal leader (and ideal follower) are intimately connected to the work of siege style. Practically speaking, siege style involves setting a series of camps on a mountain face and moving equipment and personnel from the base to the summit. The process of setting up and supplying camps requires large expeditions and a lot of coordination to work, and so it requires a leader who – like a great general – can inspire his team to act selflessly, as he leads the charge into "battle" with a mountain. The language of siege style is militaristic – even the title of Herzog's book includes the word "conquest." The culture of siege style is hierarchical, and it understands hierarchy as the response to managing large teams. Progress towards an objective is steady and methodical. It is slow. A siege is not a lightning raid. It is a style associated with Europeans, not Sherpas or other local porters, except when the latter are doing the carrying. In siege style, the leader leads others, including climbers and servants. All are expected to obey orders, including orders not to climb further. Not everyone – and certainly not porters or non-European climbers – can expect to summit within the rules of this style. The efforts of many – as they haul supplies and equipment – make the summit possible, but not for all. Two decades later, in *Annapurna South Face*, Chris Bonington – who had been a military commander – finds the heroic ideal of siege-style leadership to be less satisfying and inspiring than Herzog did, because the counter-cultural ideals of alpine style climbing of the 1960s and 1970s – fast and light ascents with small teams, individual achievement as a goal, a greater assumption of risk, and a party culture – clashed with the ideals of self-sacrifice and obedience in siege style, particularly when working-class climbers on the expedition rebelled against Bonington's attempts to say what the team should do. Later still, Blum's attempt to adopt feminist leadership on Annapurna also ran headlong into gendered assumptions within siege- style culture and alpine style about whether women can climb at all, whether women could be leaders, how a feminist expedition could be conducted and led, and ultimately what the limitations of white, Western approaches to women's rights were in Nepal in 1978. From the heroic era to the advent of women's climbing, Annapurna is where siege style's dominance was first upheld without question, and then questioned, as changing ideas about men, women, and cultural difference began to affect climbing teams and cause leaders to ask whether the culture of siege style suited who they were and what they and their teams wanted to do.

Annapurna and *Annapurna*: The Heroic Era

When the members of the 1950 expedition emerged from their plane in Paris, they were surprised by the size and enthusiasm of the cheering throng that greeted them. All of France thrilled to the story of what the expedition had accomplished. Early accounts of the climb in *Paris Match* sold out immediately, and it took more than 300 lectures by expedition members to satiate the public appetite for stories of the heroic summit bid and the agonizing descent where the injured team members had to be carried by porters for weeks (Roberts 2002, 135–6). The myth of the Annapurna ascent became vital to the post-war French, who badly needed to see French people, and especially French men, in a victorious light: "For the French, still stuck in the humiliation of the Second World War, the conquest of the first 8,000-metre peak ever climbed became at once a matter of incalculable national pride. Indeed, it could be argued that no triumph of sport in the nation's history ever meant so much to its people. Nor was the glory to be short-lived. Fifty years later, Annapurna still occupies a sovereign place in the French soul" (133).

The summit of Annapurna by the French team remains a landmark achievement in high-altitude mountaineering, in no little part due to Herzog's account, because *Annapurna* enshrined the climb in mountaineering history as a heroic effort. In *Annapurna*, Herzog writes that the team had permission to climb Himalayan 8,000-metre peak Dhauligiri, but their attempt on the mountain was not successful. Next, the team focused on Annapurna. They did not have accurate maps of the Nilgiri region where Annapurna is located, and the climbing team members were the first non-local people to enter the region where Annapurna was – including the Sherpas with the team. It took weeks to even find the mountain, and by then there were fewer than two weeks available for a summit bid before the monsoon came. At first, climbing Annapurna did not even seem to be possible. Although the French members of the team were all excellent climbers in the Alps and some of them – particularly Alpine mountain guides Lionel Terray, Louis Lachenal, and Gaston Rébuffat – were widely thought to be the best in the world, none except Maurice Ichac, the expedition doctor, had ever been to the Himalayas before. No Sherpas in the party had any knowledge of ice climbing, and most of them were not comfortable leading a climb in deep snow. Relatively little was known about the correct medical treatment for frostbite or exposure. Even less was known about the problems with acclimatization at high altitudes. Although British climbers on Everest had used supplemental oxygen as early as 1924, the French team had not brought oxygen along and did not have a plan to acclimatize its climbers.

Nonetheless, using the principles of siege style and with significant Sherpa support, the team quickly established five alpine camps and a Base Camp on the mountain. But the effects of altitude meant that many of the team members were too ill to try to attempt the summit. In the end, two of them did: after an uncomfortable night at Camp V, on 3 June 1950 Maurice Herzog and Louis Lachenal arrived at the summit of Annapurna. Lachenal was exhausted and did not want to be on the summit at all, but Herzog – possibly suffering from delirium because of the lack of oxygen – was exuberant and would not descend. In *Annapurna*, Lachenal pleads with Herzog to descend at once because Lachenal sensed that his feet were freezing, but Herzog, lost in what he later wrote was the national and religious grandeur of the moment, had Lachenal snap photo after photo of himself with the French flag held over his head. Incredibly, it does not appear in the famous summit photo of Herzog released to the press that he was wearing gloves. At that altitude, this would prove to be a deadly mistake. At last, Herzog agreed to descend, and the two climbers started down, just as a storm began to break. Both men were beginning to experience frostbite in their hands and feet, and they were probably beginning to suffer from altitude sickness as well. The cold quickly overcame them, and they could barely walk in the storm.

Somehow, both climbers staggered back to Camp V, where Rébuffat and Terray did their best to help them, but they could do little for their teammates at such high elevations. The group waited out the night in the tents, and then started down to the next camp in the morning. Unfortunately, Rébuffat and Terray became snow blind and could not lead the party as the storm closed in around them all once more. The climbers huddled in an icy crevasse for the night with almost no equipment and no food, a situation that was made worse when an avalanche buried their boots, ice axes, and other equipment. When they emerged from the crevasse the next day, they were near death, but they were rescued by Marcel Shatz, another team member who was at Camp IV just below them. The journey down the mountain was agonizing for the team, particularly for Herzog and Lachenal, who were suffering from gangrene where frostbite had destroyed their hands and feet. They both lost toes and Herzog lost most of his fingers to amputation by the expedition doctor as they were carried down the mountain on the backs of porters. When the French members of the expedition finally got back to France, they were hailed as national heroes for the dramatic summit victory and, particularly in the case of Herzog, for courage in the face of extreme suffering. There are several reasons why Herzog, and not Lachenal, became such a well-known hero for France. The first had to do with the legacy of the French resistance movement in the Alps: unlike Herzog, who served as a Lieutenant in the Reserve, or Lionel Terray, who was a member of the Compagnie Stéphane from 1944 to the war's end (Terray [1961] 2001, 80–1), Lachenal did not serve in the resistance movement or the reserves, and professed a horror of war to Terray when they began to climb together (109). Lachenal therefore did not fit the picture of the hero who fought for France. The other reason has to do with Herzog's control of the narrative of the expedition.

Herzog's expedition account turned the drama of the climb into an enduring myth of suffering, heroism, and triumph over nearly impossible odds. Herzog's image of himself as a leader in *Annapurna* plays a central role in this myth. This begins early in the account: before leaving France, the expedition members were made to swear an oath of loyalty to the expedition and the leader. Herzog does not write about what his teammates might have thought of this, and chooses to concentrate on the oath as the moment when he truly becomes a leader of men: "They [the climbers] were pledging their lives, possibly, and they knew it. They all put themselves completely in my hands ... there is no feeling to equal this complete confidence of one man in another, because it is the sum of so many feelings put together. In that moment our partnership was born. It was for me to keep it alive" ([1952] 1997, 6). Herzog assumes that leadership is more than good management. Leadership is about the ability of one man to inspire others, even when the goal seems impossible to attain. It is where Ortner's idea of bodily politics in mountaineering comes into play, because Herzog is clearly a leader of *men*. He writes of the oath as an act of trust, and of feelings connected to trust that move far beyond a business partnership. Although he uses the neutral term "partnership," Herzog's rhetoric of sacrifice and his reference to the trust placed in him makes the moment homosocial, giving it spiritual overtones, and establishing an emotional basis for the relationship between men that, as *Annapurna* will show, exceeds the bonds of ordinary friendship.

The stress on duty in *Annapurna* is due in part to the French team's decision to employ siege style. The success of siege-style mountaineering depends on climbers who are willing to sacrifice their own climbing goals for those of the team. The leader encourages sacrifice in the style of military leaders, which Herzog himself had been during the Second World War (Ortner 1999, 160–1; Terray [1961] 2001, 78–9). Loyalty to the leader and willingness to make sacrifices for the greater good, as in a military campaign, is key to the success of this type of climbing style, which is why Herzog often portrays the other climbers as a single unit who unequivocally follow him. Meanwhile, he alone makes decisions at key points. Herzog frequently uses terms like "attack," "victory," or "retreat" to describe climbing, and he calls a discussion about a climb "a council of war" ([1952] 1997, 68). Words like these show that for Herzog, a mountain climber's loyalty to the climb and the leader is very much like a soldier's loyalty to the cause and his commander. It is easy to view this connection between climbing and militarism as an expression of the need for masculine heroic strength and the need for patriotic self-sacrifice.

The discourse of siege style is also why in *Annapurna* the other climbers rarely stand out as individuals, appearing instead as masculine types who sacrifice for the leader and the greater goal. Terray and Lachenal, for example, are introduced as "a couple of regular steam engines" (2), a phrase that makes them appear to be superhuman, machine-like, and interchangeable. Later in the account, the climber Jean Couzy agrees to carry loads up the mountain and forgo a summit attempt. Herzog makes Couzy's agreement into a general statement about the right way to climb in a group: "it is this admirable spirit of self-denial which determines the strength of a team" (95). Terray also gives up a summit chance, causing Herzog to feel guilty that he may not be as heroic and selfless himself because he wants Terray, the strongest climber, to be his summit partner (133). Therefore, individuality in *Annapurna* is not thought to be a good trait for mountaineers to have, except when the leader possesses it. Loyalty, self-sacrifice, and obedience are seen as better traits, as Herzog points out when he discusses how the climbers had no thoughts of profit. The effect of the description is to make each man seem to be the same, and to be equally heroic: "From the start every one of them knew that nothing belonged to him and that he must expect nothing on his return. Their only motive was pure idealism; this was what linked together mountaineers so unlike in character and of such widely dissimilar origins" (5).

Siege-style heroism may not appear to be overtly gendered except for its use of military discourse. However, in places where heroism fails, gender and race politics do emerge within discussions of style. Lachenal chides Rébuffat and Herzog by calling them "'a pair of sissies'" (87) for not continuing up the mountain more quickly, implying that they are not truly masculine because they are not tough enough. If they – like gay men stereotyped as "sissies" – act like women, they do not belong in the mountains. The message is clear: only tough men have the right to climb. No one else does. Toughness is not the only criteria for what an authentic climber should do. In keeping with a view of many climbers at the time that Sherpas are not true mountain climbers because they only knew how to carry loads (Ortner 1999, 42–3), Lachenal and Rébuffat complain later that they are not "'beasts of burden'" (Herzog [1952] 1997, 105) like the Sherpas and so they should not have to carry loads like them. When Terray retorts that the two climbers are not acting like true Chamonix guides (which both of them were) but like amateurs, he deliberately refers to the class politics of climbing in France, where guides did heavier work than their amateur clients. Lachenal replies to this in gendered terms when he sarcastically accuses Herzog and Terray of being "'supermen, real supermen, and we're just poor types'" (106).

The exchange between the climbers shows that racial stereotypes about Sherpas (they are beasts of burden or mere servants because they are not white and European) and assumptions about class position (guides are also beasts when they are working at home) were closely imbricated with ideas about masculine strength and sacrifice. "Real men" would not complain about carrying loads while others were heroically doing the same, and real men would remember to be sacrificial on the Annapurna expedition for the good of the team, at least in Herzog's account of who they were supposed to be. Weak or selfish climbers, in his view, could not be real men or real mountaineers in a siege expedition. They could be compared to a group of men carrying loads who were not "real" men either because they were not European: the Sherpas. Although it might have been possible to understand the Sherpas as sacrificial and potentially as real men as well, the pervasive belief in *Annapurna* that the Sherpas on the expedition could not climb because they were not "real" mountaineers – rather than training them in the skills of climbing – means that all team members assume that the Sherpas would have nothing to "sacrifice." The Sherpa men must do the jobs of animals and women: they must carry loads and cook, because that is their role. As Ortner points out, for nations that understood climbing in the Himalayas as the sign of modernity, particularly for men, Sherpas cannot be understood as fully modern or as fully masculine, and so they cannot participate in the sacrificial politics of siege style (1999, 44). The sacrifice undergirding this understanding of masculinity in *Annapurna* is specific. It is only the sacrifice of class position in the Himalayas for the good of the team. Only European climbers, at this point in the history of Himalayan climbing, can be seen this way.

Herzog's account of his summit experience conforms to this association of manly heroism with idealism. But his account of the ascent does something else: it equates the (temporary) loss of ideals to the loss of masculinity itself. On the final push to the summit, Herzog underscores his courage and leadership ability. When Lachenal asks if they should go on in sub-zero temperatures, Herzog's "voice rang out" ([1952] 1997, 158) when he says he is willing to go on alone. Although Lachenal simply says that he will follow him, Herzog sees this as a homosocial moment of bonding: "the die was cast. I was no longer anxious, I shouldered my responsibility. Nothing could stop us now from getting to the top ... we went forward as brothers" (158). At the summit itself, Herzog interprets the accomplishment in idealistic terms as a human and a national achievement. As he takes out a French flag from his knapsack and asks Lachenal to take pictures, he thinks: "our mission was accomplished. But at the same time we had accomplished something infinitely greater. How wonderful life would now become! What an inconceivable experience it is to attain one's ideal and, at the very same moment, to fulfil oneself" (159–60). As Lachenal begs him to descend, Herzog keeps thinking of great mountaineers of the past and his own childhood in the mountains of France. When he finally descends (and after he loses his gloves) he tells Terray that his emotion at the summit was not egotistical: "it was a victory for us all, a victory for mankind itself" (164). Even against considerable evidence that Lachenal did not share his feelings on the summit, Herzog still saw his own experience as a paradigmatic experience of brotherhood with his climbing partner and with all humankind. Later, he would describe this experience as a religious one in the book *L'Autre Annapurna* (Roberts 2002, 124). On the summit, Herzog is at his most heroic and is most like a leader. He not only represents all mountaineers in history, but he becomes a point of symbolic condensation of mankind itself. His presence on the summit also symbolizes a national achievement for the men of France, since he holds the French flag in his hands and says afterwards "the victory that we had brought back ... would remain for ever [sic] with us as an ecstatic happiness and a miraculous consolation. The others must organize our retreat and bring us back as best they could to the soil of France" ([1952] 1997, 187). *Annapurna* ends with a picture of climbing as an expression of the highest human ideals when Herzog writes: "there are other Annapurnas in the lives of men" (246).

Herzog's version of the summit and the horrors of the descent that followed placed the event within a tragic frame, where the climber reaches the heights of joy, only to be sorely tested and then transformed by suffering into a true hero. But Lionel Terray's attempt a decade later to emulate the poetic highlight of Herzog's book – when Herzog and his partner Louis Lachenal finally arrive jubilant at the summit – detours away from the intended heroic effect in order to recapture suffering, not triumph, as the ultimate expression of manly heroism. In his memoir *Conquistadors of the Useless*, Terray meets Herzog and Lachenal as they stagger down from the summit, disoriented from the cold and exposure. Terray's self-assurance deserts him as he looks at his friend Lachenal's frozen feet: "Annapurna, the first eight-thousander, was climbed, but was it worth such a price? I had been ready to give my life for the victory, yet now it suddenly seemed too dearly bought" (Terray [1961] 2001, 288). As Terray busies himself with helping Lachenal, his best friend and climbing partner expressed no joy at being on the first team to summit a Himalayan peak of more than 8,000 metres: "those moments when one [Lachenal] had expected a fugitive and piercing happiness had in fact brought only a painful sense of emptiness" (288–9). During the descent of the climbing team, Lachenal would have to have part of his feet amputated. He would never be able to climb seriously again.

Rather than continuing his thought that as a tragedy perhaps the summit was too dearly bought, Terray's response to the story of his friend inscribes the moment as deeply heroic, and as national: "I listened to him [Lachenal] in silence. The willpower and sacrifice of my friends had crowned all of our efforts and dangers. The action of the hero had fulfilled years of dream and preparation. Those whose work, undertaken in the service of a pure ideal, had made it possible for us to set out, were rewarded. And with what typically French panache Herzog and Lachenal had set the coping stone in this great arch of endeavour, showing the world that our much-decried race had lost none of its immortal virtues!" (289).

French "panache" and "action of the hero" hardly seem to be fitting ways to describe how Lachenal, having lost much of his equipment on the descent, had fallen in the snow and how Terray had found him alone, screaming that his feet were frozen. Terray redeems this detour through suffering and doubt as a detour *for masculinity*: it is part of the suffering that a real man must undergo in order to reach his goal. Meanwhile, Herzog was found wandering dreamily in sub-zero temperatures without his gloves. He did not even seem to understand that his hands were frozen irreparably and could not explain why Lachenal was not with him. He could only talk about the summit victory, with his "eyes shining" (287). He too, routes his masculinity through suffering so that, even as he is about to lose his hands and feet, he appears to be more of a man (and more of a Frenchman) for his country and for all mankind. However indirectly, this is how gender is represented in this paradigmatic summitting of a Himalayan peak, as a small detour, or gap, between the horror of the real and the belief in an ideal.

During his own account of the descent, or as he calls it: "the retreat," Herzog suspends this sense of his own power and destiny so that he can more fully occupy the centre of what manhood signifies in Romantic terms, as a journey from childhood to adulthood. Herzog indirectly describes this process as a loss of himself through suffering, when he receives the care of another man and "grows" into a deeper understanding of manhood. As he endures painful injections for frostbite and begins to experience gangrene, Herzog turns to Terray for comfort: "I whispered to Lionel what a fearful ordeal I found it all, and begged him to hold me close ... I howled and cried and sobbed in Terray's arms while he held me tight with all his strength" (Herzog [1952] 1997, 193). When he hears cracking ice at night, Herzog is terrified but is "ashamed at these childish fears" (198). At another point, Herzog sobs in Terray's arms about how he will never climb again, "while Terray soothed [him] with infinite gentleness" (200), placing his head against Herzog's. Later, Herzog would refer to experiences like these as mystical and religious. He understands his suffering to be like the redemptive suffering of Jesus Christ (Roberts 2002, 125–6). Herzog also interprets his suffering as childlike because he cries and is comforted, and because he is dependent and shows emotion. Later, Herzog decides that his injuries make him *more* manly, not less. His behaviour is explained as part of a heroic journey, and so it is not sissy-ness, childishness, or womanly behaviour when he lets himself be comforted. The retreat of Herzog results in greater understanding, not ridicule.

Herzog's insistence on the greater meaning of the events, especially his idea that weakness is the spiritual centre of masculinity, have made the Annapurna expedition into the mythic journey that captivated readers first in France and then all over the world. The book became required reading for French youth, particularly boys, who loved the exploits of the French mountaineers. Maurice Herzog emerged as the paradigmatic hero for France, someone who was universally respected not just as a leader but more particularly as a *French* leader because (like France) he overcame his own suffering. Herzog's vision has proven to be very popular. Fifty years after it was first published, *Annapurna* had been published in forty languages and sold more than eleven million copies (Roberts 2002, 22). The book has had a tremendous impact on young people who want to be mountaineers and who, in many cases, go on to become climbers themselves. Frequently, these climbers also are major authors, arguably because *Annapurna* inspired them to write as well as climb. David Roberts himself, the author of the classic climbing memoir *The Mountain of My Fear* (1968) in addition to *True Summit: What Really Happened on Annapurna*, in the introduction of the latter book, credits his reading of *Annapurna* as a teenager with the beginning of his burning desire to become a mountaineer himself. Joe Simpson, another well-known mountaineering author, writes in an introduction to a recent edition of *Annapurna* that reading it when he was fourteen "led me into what has become a life-long affair with the world's great mountains" (2002, xiii). Reinhold Messner credits *Annapurna* with inspiring him to climb (2000, 24).

Perhaps inevitably, the ideals of Annapurna are now seen as too good to be true. As Philip Clements points out, not all the expedition members wanted nationalism and masculinity to be considered together, but the crush of publicity and Herzog's subsequent control of the official expedition narrative meant that "the expedition's events that did not fit the nationalist agenda were forgotten" when the climbers returned (2018, 10). Decades later, those events did receive a hearing. The publication in 1996 of Louis Lachenal's unedited diaries (and the revelation that Herzog himself had tried to suppress them) alongside the publication of Gaston Rébuffat's criticisms of Herzog in a biography of him called *Gaston Rébuffat: Une Vie pour la Montagne* (1999) make it clear that Herzog's idealist vision of the expedition – and of himself – is open to challenge. In passages from his own (posthumous) autobiography which Herzog had had censored (along with his diaries) until 1996, Lachenal wrote that he wanted to turn back, and that he only went to the summit because he asked Herzog if he would go on without him. Herzog's answer convinced him that Herzog would die if he went on alone. In that moment, Lachenal decided to sacrifice his feet, which he knew had frostbite, to make sure that his climbing partner was safe. This version of the story is at odds with Herzog's, which has Lachenal following Herzog without a qualm. Even before his untimely death in 1955, Lachenal was furious with Herzog for creating the Annapurna legend with himself at the centre, and often spoke to other mountain guides about this. Herzog retaliated by saying in his book *L'Autre Annapurna* that Lachenal was "nutty," and a follower on the summit, while he himself was a leader (Webster 2000). *Paris Match* republished the famous summit photograph of Herzog with a French flag and pointed out that Herzog does not even appear to be standing on the summit, raising the question of whether Herzog and Lachenal had ever reached the top at all (Messner 2000, 58–9). It was discovered that during the ceremony when the climbers were forced to swear an oath of loyalty to Herzog as the expedition leader (the oath that Herzog claimed they willingly took) the climbers also had to sign a contract forbidding them from publishing anything about the expedition for five years afterwards (Isserman and Weaver 2008, 243). As a result, Herzog's version of events became suspect and his leadership was called into question. The suspicion that now surrounds Annapurna as an account highlights the discursive nature of heroism in what was for a long time the most famous mountaineering book published. As other questions are raised about the myth of Annapurna, the ideals of naturalized, Romantic masculinity and homosociality in the mountains can be looked at more critically.

Alpine Style and Counter-Cultural Climbing

First published in 1971, Chris Bonington's *Annapurna: South Face* deals with another pivotal moment in the history of high-altitude mountaineering: the attempt of a difficult Himalayan ice face. Bonington's British expedition of 1970 was the first to attempt a difficult route such as this in the Himalayas with the help of modern climbing techniques and equipment. A lot had changed in the world of high-altitude climbing since 1950. All of the major peaks in the Himalayas had been climbed, including Everest, Nanga Parbat, Broad Peak, and K2. Approach routes in the Himalayas were now accurately mapped. Mountaineers began to look for new challenges at high altitudes, which meant that they tried to climb mountains on more difficult routes. Most important of all, lighter equipment and other technical advances meant that siege-style mountaineering, with its emphasis on lengthy times at high altitude and its reliance on large numbers of Sherpas and other local mountain people as porters, was becoming less popular in favour of the lighter, faster approach to climbing called alpine style. Once again, Annapurna would be the focus of a turning point in the history of mountaineering as Bonington's team tried to adapt alpine-style techniques for climbing big walls that they had learned in the Alps to a high-altitude environment.

The move from siege style to alpine style climbing in the Himalayas has been called one of the most significant changes to mountaineering since the end of the Heroic Era of first ascents and exploration (Willis 2006, xii–xiii). But the change in climbing style also signalled significant ideological changes in the world of high-altitude mountaineering related to the development of youth cultures in different locations around the world. During the late 1960s and early 1970s, youth were at the heart of new political movements in Europe, Britain, China, and the United States, including the American civil rights movement, anti-war movements, student movements for better education on university campuses in North America, and the formation of the Red Guard in China during the cultural revolution. Teenagers and young adults in Europe and North America began to experiment with drugs, question the values of their elders, and openly look for new ways of living and new avenues for religious expression. Nepal became the focus of this particular aspect of the "counter-cultural" movement because it represented an escape from Western society, where hippies and other youth dissatisfied with what they called the establishment could learn about Eastern religions, live in alternative communities, and experiment with drugs. Kathmandu became a preferred destination for these young people (Ortner 1999, 186–8). Because Nepal is also the focus of so much climbing activity, climbing itself began to be seen as another way to reject the materialism of the West. Mountain climbing communities in the west began to adopt counter-cultural values, while at the same time counter-cultural approaches to climbing grew more popular as climbing became less elite. Counter-cultural ideology meant that leadership styles became more egalitarian and collective decision-making was used far more. The relative simplicity of the alpine climbing style, where there was little Sherpa support and teams climbed as quickly as possible, was also attractive to counter-cultural climbers because it seemed to be less materialistic and hierarchical than siege climbing had been. There were calls, particularly by Peter Boardman – a hero of the alpine style movement – for climbers to be less macho and less competitive with each other (Boardman 1978, 190).

The call for male climbers to change their understanding of themselves and to soften that hard, military approach to climbing seems, on the surface, to be revolutionary. What actually happened was a redeployment of masculinity through counter-cultural discourse rather than a break with the ideals of siege style. The Romanticism of the "heroic" era gave way to the Romanticism of the counter-cultural movement, because the Romantic ideology of climbing and its relationship to individual heroism did not end with the advent of alpine style. Climbers still thought of themselves as heroic, but the reasons for climbing did begin to change. As the culture of mountaineering moved towards the ideals of alpine style, expedition accounts shifted away from the use of military metaphors for climbing. References to the need for self-sacrifice gave way to mystical metaphors for the experience, and to the sense that climbers were in rebellion against what they saw as the dangers of civilization. These climbers had a new goal: individual self-realization (Ortner 1999, 188). For climbers who saw themselves as participants in the counter-cultural movement, the adaptation of alpine style underscored the need many began to have for as pure an experience of nature as could be had in the mountains. Peter Boardman's book about his and Joe Tasker's attempt to climb the West Wall of Changabang, *The Shining Mountain* (1978), encapsulated the new culture perfectly. The book opens with a description by Joe Tasker of the dangerous, perhaps impossible, West Wall. Boardman reads it, already dissatisfied with his climb of Everest the year before because he knows it had no technical challenges and was an expedition with too many people on it, resentful too of the publicity and fame the climb had brought him, and of the office work that kept him chained to his desk, "a tiny cog in the wheel of Western civilization" (1978, 11). He thinks of the Everest expedition, where he simply obeyed a leader, even though the British public saw him as a hero. He longs for "two-man expeditions [because] in comparison with the Everest expedition, [they] have a greater degree of flexibility and adventurous uncertainty" (12). When Tasker asks him to go to Changabang to climb a wall alpine style, he accepts because "just two of us would make the dangers and decisions deliciously uncomplicated" (14–15). The climb represents a move away from siege style, Western civilization, and the problems of public fame and image management. Changabang represents a turn back to what Boardman and Tasker see as a purer and more uncomplicated way to climb a mountain. *The Shining Mountain* represents nature and the idea of the east as the alternative to the "culture" of climbing and of the West. It represents too an escape from what Everest, and siege style, had come to mean.

Boardman's decision to embrace the purity of alpine style in *The Shining Mountain*, therefore, is about exchanging one kind of climbing masculinity for another, even though it interprets the adoption of alpine style as a departure. In climbs like Boardman and Tasker's, the moral purity of Herzog's vision gives way to another, more rebellious sense of moral purity, which gave climbers a sense that they were outside meaningless social restrictions. However, most gendered assumptions about climbing did not change very much, and the freeing up of some social customs in climbing did not necessarily alter ideas about masculine supremacy in the mountains. For instance, although the flattening of hierarchy in the counter-cultural era meant that more women did begin to climb and the idea of masculine "sensitivity" did enter climbing discourse, it "is not that 'machismo' disappeared, but that it became problematized in this period" (Ortner 1999, 196). The decision of some climbers to begin to climb without oxygen was based just as much on ideas about machismo (in the need to do something more difficult and daring to prove oneself as a climber) as it was on the need for simplicity and the faster alpine style. As before, central ideas to climbing like brotherhood and manhood were worked out indirectly as the bodily politics of climbing and leadership style.

Annapurna South Face marks a transition from the heroic era to counter-cultural mountaineering in a number of ways that highlight how ideas of masculine toughness and the brotherhood of the rope are retained within alpine style. The climbing team included working-class climbers Dougal Haston, who was known for his hard drinking, partying, and nonconformist behaviour (2001, 5), and Don Whillans, a plumber from England's industrial north who had a reputation for getting into fights (12). Mountain climbing culture in this account is masculinist in its refusal of the trappings of ordinary life, including cleanliness: Bonington observes that this is "one of the big differences between climbers and ordinary mortals, for the climbers rarely washed either themselves or their clothes" (140). To illustrate this point, Bonington repeats what Nima Tsering, a young Sherpa, told climbers who slept in after partying hard the night before: "'You Sahibs are like buffalo; filthy lying, filthy eating'" (141). Nima's comment is reported as amusing – clearly the climbers did not pay attention to what the Sherpa was telling them. This anecdote ends with Bonington saying that the expedition film crew was "more civilized" than the climbers themselves (141), a comment that makes climbers into a breed apart as it shows how they rebel against social restrictions or disregard them.

Activities like this are interpreted in a gendered way when two women come into the camp, for "the presence of Babs and Cynth at Base Camp was also welcome, giving it a more relaxed and civilized atmosphere" (145). Cleanliness and a lack of debauchery are associated with the presence of women, but dirt and debauchery are also what separates climbers from non-climbers. Thus it is implied that women cannot be part of this anti-establishment world. In the only other description of women climbers in the book, Bonington emphasizes the fact that women are not part of the climbing brotherhood when he describes the arrival of a Japanese women's climbing team: "On 30 March another expedition arrived at our camp. This was the Japanese women's expedition to Annapurna II, consisting of nine petite ladies and nine Sherpas to look after them. We entertained some of them with tea, amidst giggles and clicking of camera shutters ... that night Alan Hankinson and Mick Burke made a social call on the girls but were firmly shepherded away by the leader to talk to the Liaison officer" (83–4). With this anecdote, Bonington describes these climbers in an Orientalist way as stereotypical Japanese tourists (they are described as "petite ladies," they snap pictures) and as women who might be sexual objects but ultimately are not to be taken seriously (they giggle, they are called "girls," Sherpas need to look after them). They take photos as if they were tourists, as opposed to the "authentic" mountaineers who – it is implied – would not engage in this sort of thing.

Ironically, the group Bonington was so prepared to dismiss was hardly made up of tourists. One of its leaders who "shepherded" the amorous male climbers away from her group was none other than Junko Tabei, one of the best climbers from Japan who not only summitted Annapurna

III (one of the peaks of the Annapurna massif) in 1970 after her team met Bonington's, but who also became the first woman to summit Mount Everest in 1975 (Unsworth [1981] 2000, 462). Since she had an English degree from Showa Women's University (Horn 1996), presumably she could have spoken with members of Bonington's team or with Bonington himself in some way. But in a clear case of gender and racial bias, Bonington did not choose to think of or portray Tabei and her team as serious and he records no conversations with them. Instead, he infantilizes them. This is in contrast to how he describes the Sherpas on his team, whom he writes about as fellow climbers who look after him simply because they are generous. That is problematic too, but in a different way, since the idea of generosity itself ignores the business relationship Sherpas had with their employers (Bonington 2001, 116–17).[1] It is also a marked contrast to Tabei's own description of their meeting in her memoir *Honouring High Places*, where she merely mentions that Bonington's group is staying at the same hotel as them in Pokhara, which meant that there were fewer porters for her team to hire (2017, 89–90). Later, she only mentions the British team's killing of chickens for food, and the envy of some of her teammates that the British had fresh meat to eat, remarking that Bonington's team was in the same situation as hers (2017, 97). In both cases, she understands Bonington's team to be another team of climbers like her own. She does not understand either team to be inferior to the other.

Bonington's anecdote tells a very different story. Although he admires the physical fitness of these Japanese women (2001, 83), Bonington's rhetoric makes clear that the climbers – because they are women and because they are Japanese – are not colleagues and are merely an exotic social distraction from the real business at hand, the business of men. After this episode, these climbers are never mentioned again, even though they were making an attempt on Annapurna III (not II, as Bonington says) at the same time.

Except for these brief encounters, the society of *Annapurna South Face* is masculine. But anxieties about what masculinity means in times of conflict surface, particularly when Bonington discusses his own leadership. Bonington is not sure of himself as a leader, in part because of the changing culture of high-altitude mountaineering with its new emphasis on collective decision-making and its questioning of absolute obedience, but also because the expedition itself had started as an alpine-style climb and had been forced to adopt the siege style because the wall the team had to ascend was so difficult. Bonington admits that "there is no doubt that the larger the party, the further you are separated from the feel of big mountains" (2001, 25) but explains at length that this could not be an option on this particular climb. For Bonington, this meant that he had to become a siege-style leader who thought more about supplies and the placement of camps than climbing or sharing chores like campsite cleaning, even when other members grumbled about this (104), or that he had to assert his authority and not give in to attempts to change his plans (238).

Essentially, Bonington would be forced to act like Maurice Herzog and adopt his version of heroic and militaristic masculinity when in fact he did not wish to do so. The result is that he worries constantly in the text about his adequacy as a leader: "I often worried about my ability to hold together a group of individualistic and very talented climbers. For the past eight years I had worked as a freelance with very little responsibility to anyone but myself. The last time I had had any kind of command responsibility was back in 1960 when I was in the army, protected by the pips on my shoulder and the might of military discipline. This is very different from conducting a mountaineering expedition, where one's authority rests solely on the loyalty and respect of the team" (28).

Bonington resolves to mitigate this by thinking of himself as a co-ordinator, and of mountaineering as a game rather than a military campaign: "as leader, it seemed to me I had to be a diplomat and co-ordinator of ideas rather than a disciplinarian ... yet at the same time I realized that I should have to make decisions at times that might be unpopular ... we were not fighting a war, but rather were playing an elaborate, potentially dangerous game; therefore each individual had the right to decide how far he should drive himself and the level of risk he was prepared to accept" (28). By turning the expedition into a "game," Bonington invokes discourses of leisure that could potentially diffuse the militaristic and heroic masculinity that the siege style of mountaineering would require him to perform.

But, perhaps because game-playing itself is often a mark of masculine heroism, he is not very successful in changing the discourse he must adopt. Many of the conflicts in *Annapurna South Face*, including the agonizing moment when Bonington realizes that he has spent too much time carrying loads and does not have the strength to get to the summit (195), are expressions of Bonington's desire to be a different kind of leader with a different type of style. Given Bonington's ambivalence about siege-style mountaineering, it is perhaps fitting that the two climbers who most represent the advent of the counter-cultural climbing aesthetic, Dougal Haston and Don Whillans, are the climbers who do reach the summit of Annapurna. They were known for being working-class climbers who could not be accepted by the British mountaineering elite. They needed Bonington, who was middle class enough that he was initially thought to be too "posh" to climb with them in Scotland (Willis 2006, 8), to be the type of leader who could legitimate what they were doing for the elite members of the Alpine Club, who were essential at the time for climbers who wanted to develop their careers (36–8).

For their part, they translated their working-class culture into a counter-cultural mountaineering style: "they had longish hair and beards, wore grubby bellbottoms, smoked grass and listened to rock and roll" (154). Like Lachenal and Rebuffat before them, they rebelled against carrying loads on Annapurna, but unlike them, they argued that they needed to save themselves for a summit attempt. They rejected Bonington's argument that in siege style, only a few climbers – chosen by the leader – could climb to the top (176). In a film made of the climb, *Annapurna the Hard Way*, and in *Annapurna South Face* as well, Haston and Whillans appear to be rebellious, authentic, plainspoken men who summitted Annapurna because of their talent and grit, and who can shed tears too as they draw close to the summit (181). Millions of people in the United Kingdom followed the climb and found them, with Bonington, captivating because they were not like the elite heroes of the past. They seemed real, and they connected counter-cultural rebellion with climbing in a way that resonated with the British public (193).

Feminist Mountaineering: *Annapurna: A Woman's Place*

Sherry B. Ortner has described *Annapurna: A Woman's Place* as "one of the most extraordinary mountaineering books ever written" (1999, 228) because of its unusually detailed look at the problems of gender and race politics. More than forty years after it was first published in 1980,

Annapurna: A Woman's Place still has the most sustained discussion of gender politics that can be found in any expedition account. The account was intended to be a feminist document of its time, and it still has that status today. Arlene Blum, the leader of the expedition and the author/ compiler of *Annapurna: A Woman's Place*, produced a chronicle of the climb designed to be a very strong political statement about female mountaineers in history and the sexism that women in mountain expeditions have faced. Features such as its introduction – where Blum details how men have tried to exclude women from climbing – and what David Mazel has called the "egalitarian communalism" of the expedition and the more "open and inclusive feel" of the expedition account, mark the 1978 climb of Annapurna as an important turning point in climbing history, and establish *Annapurna: A Woman's Place* as an important feminist expedition account (Mazel 1994, 18–19).[2]

Annapurna: A Woman's Place is also an account about continuity and "a woman's place" within climbing history: Maurice Herzog wrote the foreword, where he discussed the emotional impact of the book, his feeling that women should be climbers because "the reasons given to prove women's inferiority are simply not credible" (1980, xi) and, in an echo of his famous words "there are other Annapurnas in the lives of men," says of the American Women's expedition, "they too, have conquered their Annapurna. I am convinced that this success will lead to further triumphs by women in the fields of adventure, exploration, and discovery" (xi–ii). Herzog's foreword does important political work, because it situates the achievement of the 1978 climb within the climbing history of Annapurna, and it contains a statement about the importance of women's climbing to the success of women in other areas of life. It is a feminist statement, by the person credited with the first ascent of the peak. Herzog's foreword connects *Annapurna: A Woman's Place* to the earlier ideals of his own *Annapurna* and updates the idea of achievement to include the achievements of women in climbing. In this sense, Herzog realizes Blum's own feminist ideals about achievement and inclusion.

The value of *Annapurna: A Woman's Place* is that it moves far beyond a simplistic discourse about women overcoming androcentrism in climbing, and addresses issues connected to more general problems within feminism of the period. Blum's text is actually about "feminisms" that in some respects complement each other, and in other respects are sharply divergent. There are points in *Annapurna* where differences between the female climbers, as well as differences between climbers and Sherpas, so divide the team that the expedition threatens to fall apart. In keeping with the style of expedition accounts like Rick Ridgeway's *The Last Steps* or Peter Boardman's *The Shining Mountain*, Blum does not shy away from those moments: she records them. The result is a text that tracks the successes and failures of different strands of feminism during the climb as it documents the first successful ascent of Annapurna by an all-female team, the first ascent of Annapurna by an American-led team, and the deaths of two climbers who tried to make a second summit attempt. This is all the more interesting because the women who were part of the American Women's Himalayan Expedition to Annapurna in 1978 were not activists in the women's movement of the 1970s. None of them were feminist activists or intellectuals in the strict sense of the word. Nonetheless they were participants in the women's movement of the 1970s because they attempted to break down barriers that existed for women in the climbing world, and they tried to do this by changing how climbing itself was conducted and written about. *Annapurna: A Woman's Place* is a unique document for this reason because it shows how non-activist women from a variety of cultural backgrounds tried to integrate feminist approaches and principles into a pursuit that is known for its machismo culture. The problems within the expedition with different approaches to women's climbing, the incorrect assumptions the team made about sisterhood in a developing country, and the backlash against the expedition at the time and decades later all highlight how unique *Annapurna: A Woman's Place* actually was, and how good it still is at illustrating the possibilities and the limits of feminist ideals when second-wave feminism was at its height.

Leadership: Liberal Feminism and Its Limits

In her introduction, Blum presents the project of the Annapurna climb as explicitly feminist. She details the sexism that prevented her from joining an expedition in Afghanistan (1980, 1) and recollects Sir Edmund Hillary's view that women should not climb but stay at home instead while their husbands go out climbing (3). She writes about common expectations in mountaineering that women should sleep with all men on a climbing team and she addresses arguments that women are biologically unfit for climbing (2–3). She moves on from this discussion to a short history of women in mountaineering to prove that women can climb, and discusses recent achievements in the Himalayas, including the first ascent of an 8,000-metre peak by women unaccompanied by men in 1975 (7) and the first ascent of Everest in 1975 by women climbers: Junko Tabei of Japan and the Tibetan climber Pan Duo,[3] who was climbing for China. She makes sure to include Reinhold Messner's sexist and racist assessment of Tabei, which is that, more important than her strength or experience as a climber, Tabei has "Oriental" grace and above all, is a good wife and mother (7). This record of discrimination contextualizes the decision in 1975 by Blum, the Polish climber Wanda Rutkiewicz (who later had to withdraw from the expedition), and the British climber Alison Chadwick-Onyszkiewicz to organize an all-women's expedition to the Himalayas, the expedition that eventually became the 1978 American Women's Himalayan Expedition to Annapurna.

Blum's intention in the opening chapters of *Annapurna: A Woman's Place* is to make mountaineering itself a political act and to point out how the often-invisible politics of that act had worked to marginalize the achievements of women climbers or downgrade their contributions. But here is where *Annapurna: A Woman's Place* becomes a very complex narrative about feminism and mountaineering. Although the undertaking of an all-women's expedition was radical for 1978, Blum's own politics is centrist because she finds an answer to the problem of sexism in mountaineering in the ideology of American liberal feminism. According to Zillah Eisenstein, the values of liberal feminism from that period included independence, equality of opportunity for men and women in the public sphere, and the preservation of individualism (Eisenstein 1981, 4–5). Therefore, following the lead of Betty Friedan, Kate Millett, and Germaine Greer, liberal feminists believed in the need to work for change within political systems, preserved the public/private split in their thinking about women's roles, and did not (at least at first) have an analysis of patriarchy that would theorize fundamental differences between women and men as part of fundamental inequalities between both genders (Whelehan 1995, 28–9). The belief many liberal feminists had in the right of all women to equality with men also meant, as the expedition t-shirts that the team sold to raise money for the climb rather puckishly say, "A Woman's Place Is on Top," and not just in the home.

Arlene Blum accepted many of the tenets of liberal feminism and repeated them in *Annapurna: A Woman's Place*, particularly in her history of women's climbing. She ends her preface by stating that equal access and individual achievement are paramount in mountaineering because "individual differences are more important than sexual ones [in climbing]. Women do have the strength and endurance to climb the highest mountains, just as men do, and both men and women should have the chance" (1980, 8). She ends the revised edition of the book with an even stronger endorsement of gender equality and complementarity, rewriting the words of Maurice Herzog to make the idea of "other Annapurnas" connect to gender equality: "now the time has come for people to be accepted on expeditions not as men or women but as climbers. Women and men have complementary abilities, and they can and should climb their 'Annapurnas' as equals, with mutual respect" (1998, 246). As we shall see shortly, Blum's belief in the equality of all people on the team becomes an important aspect of her struggle to become a good expedition leader.

The liberal feminist discourse in *Annapurna: A Woman's Place* also contains – in miniature – a significant problem that faced the North American women's rights movement. Many liberal feminists of the second wave who believed in the worth of the individual and the need for equality did not understand that they themselves contributed to inequalities based on race, class, and sexuality differences. Sisterhood, in other words, is not innately transcultural and does not automatically traverse class boundaries or other aspects of power and privilege.[4] For example, like many liberal feminists at that time, Blum's understanding of sexuality in the first edition of *Annapurna: A Woman's Place* does not appear to include recognition of lesbian identity or politics. At the time, some radical feminists in the North American women's movement were not just "lesbian feminists," who saw lesbianism as a political strategy in the fight against patriarchy, but identified themselves as lesbians in terms of their sexual preferences too. Lesbians were not initially well received by leaders of the American women's rights movements. Betty Friedan's well-known denunciation of lesbians as "the lavender menace" at a 1969 National Organization of Women (NOW) convention was merely the most public response of many straight liberal feminists who thought of any kind of difference within women's liberation as a possible threat to the success of the whole movement, and who tried to emphasize the sisterhood of all women without talking about the differences between women within second-wave feminism (Eisenstein 1981, 176–7; Aron 2017).

Although Blum is no Friedan and was not overtly seeking to exclude lesbian experiences in climbing, she may not have recognized what their absence might have meant, because liberal feminism during the 1970s tended to obliterate or disregard other approaches to women's liberation (Eisenstein 1981, 4). When Blum writes that the climbers read an article about their expedition called "What Will Their Husbands Think" and have a good laugh about it, she also mentions that in fact most of the expedition had left husbands or lovers in order to do the climb (1980, 79). This assumption probably does not include female lovers: the sexuality of climber Piro Kramar, who had a female partner at the time of the expedition, is not discussed in *Annapurna: A Woman's Place*, but the boyfriends or husbands of all the other climbers are mentioned. While Kramar may have chosen to remain closeted or at least private about her sexuality given the climate of the time, Blum's reaction to Kramar's need for privacy at some points during the expedition indicates that she saw this as a personality trait (and an annoying one at that) and nothing more. For instance, when Blum says that Kramar did not want to share her personal diary with the rest of the group and guarded her privacy, she describes this as a problem for expedition records, because "Piro ... guarded her privacy to the point of seeming emotionally detached" (1998, 7–8). It does not occur to Blum that, perhaps, Kramar did not want to share her diary because she did not want to be outed and did not want her sexuality to be discussed in the expedition account. On another occasion, Blum sees Kramar's withdrawal from a discussion as a refusal of her leadership, and – unlike her assessment of other team members – does not look for other reasons why this might be the case (1980, 41). Blum's reaction appears to be similar to the initial incomprehension of many liberal feminists at the NOW conferences in the early 1970s when lesbians demanded to be heard and represented in their own right (Aron 2017). Two decades later, these attitudes changed, for activists and for climbers: the second edition of *Annapurna: A Woman's Place* includes a mention of Kramar's partner, Barbara Drinkwater, in her biography at the end of the book (1998, 234).

In a similar way, in *Annapurna: A Woman's Place* the expedition also faces the problem of cultural difference and feminist transnationalism, just as the larger feminist movement has had to do. For example, when Base Camp manager Christy Tews beats a male Japanese climber in sumo wrestling, she is angered by accusations from the Japanese team that she is really a woman in a man's body. Blum sympathizes with Tews, and says that "women who are stronger or smarter or taller or better at things than men often must pay a price" (1998, 130). But Blum only thinks about the treatment of Tews in terms of gender inequality. The fact that Tews – a Western white woman – beat a man at a sport that is central to Japanese masculine culture has political overtones beyond those of gender that could explain the reaction of the Japanese climbers. Blum's belief in the universality of gender inequality could mean that the role that cultural differences played in the conflict is not explored here.

The liberal feminist view of transnationalist feminist analysis also explains why one goal of the expedition members – to train Sherpanis (female Sherpas) to climb so that they could be empowered – was never realized. The expedition members had made the liberal feminist assumption that as all gender relations are comparable, so all kinds of oppression are universal. But the climbers at that time knew relatively little about Sherpa culture and its view of gender relations (Ortner 1999, 5). In her interviews with Sherpa women, Ortner discovered that Sherpa women encountered similar barriers to climbing that non-Sherpa women did: it was assumed that they were too weak to climb and so were not trained to do so (239), or they were expected to do cooking and load-carrying jobs as family members of the Sherpa leader, or *sirdar* (238), but not to become climbing Sherpas. At the same time, beginning in the 1970s, some Sherpa women did begin to climb with their husbands, who taught them mountaineering techniques. To some extent, the formation of these partnerships worked against the changes in gender roles that came to Sherpa cultures because of mountaineering. Sherpa men became more "macho" because of the work they had begun to do, and they were away from their families for extended periods when they were on expeditions. Ortner suggests that some women became climbers not to adapt to Western ways, but to resist what the climbing economy was doing to Sherpa relationships (242).

Arlene Blum and the other participants in the American Women's climb of Annapurna did not know about the impact of expeditions on Sherpa ways of life, and would not have known that Sherpa women experienced gender difference, family ties, and cultural difference in ways they themselves could not immediately perceive. To Blum and some other expedition members, Sherpa women could simply be "freed" by other women, but this way of thinking was not intersectional, and did not consider the economic power the climbers possessed. As Blum points out, she learns the hard way that her feminist beliefs are too utopian when she is forced to fire Sherpanis who want more pay for laundry work and who say that they don't want to climb: "We had wanted to help the Sherpanis, teach them to climb, give them a new opportunity. Instead, here they were, leaving feeling cheated and betrayed, and we felt the same. Our frames of reference were too different. We had probably been naive to try bringing such changes into their lives" (1980, 89). The results of the difficulty that Blum and the rest of the team had with understanding Sherpa issues in any terms other than gendered ones meant that Sherpa discontent was high for much of the expedition. Indeed, as *Annapurna: A Woman's Place* details, the working relationship between Sherpas and climbers became so tense that the Sherpas mounted a strike for better treatment during the expedition (162–72). Some climbers complained that Sherpas were making obscene comments about them and thought of them as sexualized objects (110), while others complained when Sherpas wanted to break trail and deny them the chance to lead (118). For their part, Sherpas who spoke later about the expedition pointed out that there were two expedition members who had sex with Sherpa team members, and so they did have reason to think that team members had amorous intentions. The Sherpas also knew that not all team members wanted them there, and that caused tensions (Ortner 1999, 230). Although some of the problems with Sherpas on the expedition were about gender differences, others (such as the issue of Sherpa pay) were about working conditions and the class differences between the men who climbed for hire and the women who paid them. The intersection of cultural differences, economic inequality, conflicting ideas about gender roles, and the idealism of transnational women's solidarity created many problems within the expedition.

In a 2017 article by Katie Ives for *Outside* magazine, some of the team members – including the Sherpas Chewang Rinjing, Mingma Tshering, Llakpa Norbu, and Lopsang Tshering – reflect on what cultural and gender differences meant on the expedition. The interviews reveal much about the complexities of the intersections between cultural and gender difference, particularly in the case of Sherpa attitudes to women, and how feminist expedition members responded. For example, Blum says of the attempt to hire Sherpani women to train them as climbers: "I liked the idea of having Nepali women as team members and having our Sherpas be women. However, the Sherpa union did not want that at all ... Now, of course, there are Nepali women's expeditions. But the idea was probably ahead of its time for Nepal in the mid-seventies" (Ives 2017).

Blum admits here that her idea was utopian because, as she wrote in *Annapurna: A Woman's Place*, the team members were naïve about cultural differences. She also places her idea within a progressive historical frame, but without mentioning why there was conflict with the Sherpani women at the time, and what changed it. In *Life and Death on Mount Everest*, Sherry Ortner interviewed Sherpas and Sherpanis about the hiring process for expeditions. She found that one of the problems with inviting Sherpanis on expeditions like the Annapurna 1978 climb involved the connections between families where "it became the practice to use Sherpa women ... as 'local porters'" to keep such positions within the family (1999, 237). Blum would have understood Sherpanis as employees who could become "team members," and she thinks of the problem as a "union" problem. But as Ortner heard, Sherpa family relations are an important factor in who can be hired, and for which job. Blum's instructions to Lopsang to hire women sounded to him like instructions to hire his female relatives as cooks in order to give them opportunities to do what had been the work of Sherpa men, but the expedition members saw this as problematic because they associated cooking with women's work (238). Blum's reflection does not include thinking about the problem involved with bringing Western feminist ideas of sisterhood and equality to a context where these ideas were neither understood nor shared.

Annie Whitehouse, an expedition member who married a Sherpa after the expedition was over, is aware of such challenges: "The Sherpa women were put in a difficult position, because they were picked out to excel but they didn't have the background yet, the climbing ability. Arlene wanted them to be different – or to perform differently than they were able to. I think she was generally good about trying to consider Sherpas members of the team, although it's always different when someone's getting paid" (Ives 2017). Whitehouse recognizes the gap between what Western expectations were for the Sherpanis, and what they might have been able or even wanted to do. It is important, Whitehouse points out, to remember that the Sherpas were team members who were also employed. Although the women on the expedition did not understand themselves to be wealthy employers, in the context of Sherpa culture, they were. Although they experienced gender discrimination as women and they wanted to work with Sherpas in a more egalitarian way, they did not know and did not find out how equality in a Sherpa context might work. As Whitehouse says, Blum "wanted them to be different," rather than see what might make the issues different for Sherpa women.

The interviews with Chewang, Lopsang, and Mingma reflect this complex relation. On the one hand, economic relations matter to the Sherpas, who as Sherry Ortner has pointed out, often become involved in the climbing industry because of the economic opportunities it gives them (1999, 67). Lopsang, the sirdar of the Sherpas on the Annapurna expedition, says that he was glad to be offered the job of sirdar not because he would be employed by women, but because "it was an opportunity to earn money," a clear statement of the economic relations Sherpas had with their climber employers in the 1970s. For him, the gender issue is irrelevant and the fact that the climbers were Western is more significant, as it is for Mingma, who says "whether the expedition would be different or whether the climbers would be able to make it to the summit – I never thought of these things beforehand. They were a group of mountaineers, as simple as that" (Ives 2017). What is more difficult for the Sherpas looking back on the expedition were the objective hazards of the job and the problems of family separation. Mingma says in his interview that his son was born while he was on Annapurna, and he wondered sometimes whether he would make it back to his family (2017). When Chewang summits Annapurna, he talks about the joy of that moment, but in the context of his family responsibilities and his ability to provide for them, saying: [when I summitted] I was so happy, so relaxed, that I felt I would forget even my wife and children for a moment. I knew that finding work on expeditions would become easier after reaching the summit" (2017).

Gender bias is part of some Sherpas' ideas about climbing with the American Women's expedition team, at least initially. Chewang says that before the climb began, he complained to the team's outfitter that he thought the women might not make it to Base Camp, and he is sharply

corrected. When he is exhorting other Sherpas to climb a patch of difficult ice on Annapurna, he says "I told the Sherpas that they needed to be
braver if they were to succeed. Wangyel retorted, 'I have a family back
home. What if I fall down and break a leg trying to be braver? You think
these women can rescue us'" (Ives 2017). Here, the dangers of climbing
Annapurna and the problem of providing for one's family collide with
ideas about the strength and ability of female climbers.

The experience of losing two climbers on the expedition does mean
that some Sherpas discuss the connection they had with the expedition
team members, as in the case of Vera Watson, who had close relationships with the Sherpas. Of her, Chewang says: "I often remember Vera
Watson. She treated me like family. It feels like her words will stay with
me even in my next life" (Ives 2017). Lhakpa goes with team member
Mingma to see if Watson and Chadwick-Onyszkiewicz were still alive
high on the mountain because "Mingma and I spent a lot of time together
with the women, and we got to know each other well ... Perhaps part of
the reason that we decided to go was a feeling of guilt that we hadn't gone
up with Alison and Vera Watson [when they initially tried to ascend]." For
their part, expedition team members came to respect the Sherpa climbers. They wanted the Sherpas to be named and given credit in the film
version of the Annapurna story but, in the tradition of heroic narratives
like Herzog's where the Sherpas are unnamed, ABC Television refused.
According to expedition filmmaker Dyanna Taylor, "we felt Mingma and
Chewang, who we'd come to care about, should be identified in the summit scenes. But, of course, ABC wanted to minimize the men in the story.
It was much more heroic for them that way." Taylor goes on to describe
how, in the aftermath of losing two climbers, bonds developed between
Sherpas and expedition members that helped them all work through
their grief: "I remember when we hiked out, how powerful it was to dance
with the Sherpas every night by the fire. They included us, teaching us
the simple steps. All of us were grieving." Taylor says in the same interview by Ives that if she could make an expedition film over again, she
would include more focus on the Sherpas, as they and the expedition
team all worked to climb Annapurna I. This in itself would be a direct
critique of macho discourse in the context of the tropes of heroic mountaineering film. Such a film would be an alternative way to think about
mountaineering and cultural difference.

Leadership: The Culture of Siege Style in a Feminist Context

Annapurna: A Woman's Place is an expedition narrative that is firmly rooted in the leadership tradition initiated by Herzog's account, but with some significant updates. The close connection with Herzog's narrative in particular is deliberate. In addition to Herzog's foreword to *Annapurna: A Woman's Place* discussed earlier in the chapter, Blum's preface includes a reworked passage of Herzog's, a move that installs her narrative as part of his tradition even as she makes sure to change its original gender politics: "Maurice Herzog expresses this [the challenge of the climb] well in his account of the first ascent of Annapurna: 'In attempting to do the hardest tasks, all our resources are called upon, and the power and greatness of man*kind* are defined'" (Blum 1980, 8).

Herzog's words reappear and are altered at another key point of Blum's narrative, for the same reasons. The last words of *Annapurna: A Woman's Place* deliberately echo Herzog's famous ending but give the ending a feminist twist: "As Maurice Herzog declares at the end of his book: 'There are other Annapurnas in the lives of men.' And in the lives of women as well" (244). And in the preface to the twentieth anniversary edition of *Annapurna: A Woman's Place* Blum rewrites Herzog's message again and gives it an even more inclusive political meaning: "There are still many 'Annapurnas' to be climbed in the world – such as protecting our natural environment; decreasing the gap between rich and poor; providing basic necessities for everyone on this planet; and raising our children to live with love and good values" (1998, x).

Although in places she is more direct than Herzog or Bonington about gender issues, Blum often does write about gender much as they do; that is, she conceptualizes it as a bodily politics related to the problem of leadership and the problem of climbing siege style. Like Bonington had done, Blum makes use of expedition diaries by the other climbers in order to talk about a similar type of conflict on her team between siege-style mountaineering techniques and alpine techniques. And like the climbers who appear in *Annapurna: South Face*, the climbers in *Annapurna: A Woman's Place* experience this conflict as one about gender, but this time the disagreements on the team about climbing style refer to differences within feminism itself, and the problems of siege-style leadership, for women.

The nature of leadership is a major part of *Annapurna: A Woman's Place*. In fact, leadership issues are so important in this text that in the preface to the twentieth anniversary edition of the book, Blum says that she largely wrote *Annapurna: A Woman's Place* to help herself understand the challenges she faced as an expedition leader (1980, ix). She now leads seminars on leadership, including a workshop called "Climbing Your Own Everests: Leadership Skills to Meet the Challenge of Change."[5] This is related to the problem of siege style. In *Annapurna: A Woman's Place*, as in Chris Bonington's text, the expedition considers climbing alpine style but decides to try siege tactics because alpine style might prove to be even more difficult and dangerous (1980, 75). And just as siege style forces Bonington to become a different kind of leader, so Arlene Blum has to emulate the masculine heroic model of leadership that siege style requires. This is against her nature, in part because the militaristic style in this kind of leadership is not what she, as a woman, had learned: "Although my upbringing and experience had taught me to be moderate and soothing, I was learning the hard way that these traits are not always compatible with effective leadership. Although I didn't yet sound like an authentic army general, I was moving in that direction. The trick was to move just far enough ... the expedition needed a strong leader but not a dictator" (36).

The ideology of siege-style climbing, with its stress on unquestioning obedience to the leader, is at odds with the feminist principles of the climbers, who often want to make group decisions. In interviews with Katie Ives, team members understand that siege style has an accompanying ideology of heroism and mastery, and that the Annapurna team wanted to challenge that ideology. Expedition psychologist Karin Carrington discusses this as a tension between collaborative decision-making and hierarchical decision-making: "What is an alternative way of leadership that draws on the strengths of women to be more collaborative and at the same time provides the security of a decisive voice – in this case, Arlene's – to make the calls in extreme circumstances? How does Annapurna become a woman's place and not just a replica of expeditions that have been all-male in the past?" (Ives 2017). Dyanna Taylor adds about this problem that "Some of us wanted to be totally independent of men and the leadership styles of men. But there wasn't much documentation we could fall back on. The expedition format was designed by men" (Ives 2017). Team members understood clearly that siege-style climbing was masculinist, and they wanted to resist that style, but as climber Margie Rusmore adds, alpine style was not the norm in 1978, and siege style seemed to offer more safety. As a result, the team struggled with collaboration and the extensive consultation their model of decision-making required, while Blum at times had to default to hierarchical decision-making to settle a question because the expedition was conducted in siege style, a format "designed by men," and that did not work well with the group goals. The group attempted to use a consensus-based model that looked much like the structure of early feminist consciousness-raising groups, and had mixed results (McGlen et al. 2005, 9).

For example, when Blum tells the group that the Sherpas Ang and Lakpa will be among the climb's leaders who will establish Camp I, the group rejects this decision and has a discussion about the decision's problems. At one point, the climber Annie Whitehouse asks Blum to make an executive decision, and Blum observes: "here was the essential paradox again. I was supposed to be the leader and decide what was going to happen, yet everyone wanted decisions to be made democratically" (1980, 116). Blum experiences direct conflict between alpine climbing style, where decisions are made collectively in accordance with counter-cultural values, and siege style, where decisions are made by the leader. In the end, she decides that in this case, consensus decision-making would have been the better course, and she affirms that "it had been worth it to take the time to face each other and expose our vulnerabilities" (119).

But conflict continues throughout the expedition when competing versions of feminist politics become enmeshed with debates about style. The focus of this conflict in the text is Alison Chadwick-Onyszkiewicz. Blum introduces her as "a purist" who believed that the climb should be women-only, without Sherpas (27). This is not a colonial attitude to the Sherpas as mere servants, although Chadwick-Onyszkiewicz does get angry at Sherpa requests for more remuneration and makes little effort to understand why they might be upset (109). Chadwick-Onyszkiewicz's opinions are in keeping with the ideology of alpine style, with its assumption that climbs should be "pure" and as simple as possible so that all team members can achieve individual goals. Her belief that there should be no Sherpas on the climb at all is also in keeping with alpine style's emphasis on small teams and minimal or no Sherpa/porter support. But

Chadwick-Onyszkiewicz's belief that the expedition should be women-only is a feminist interpretation of alpine style that is not liberal, but radical. Unlike Blum's more conciliatory approach towards men on the expedition and in climbing more generally, Chadwick-Onyszkiewicz constantly repeats in *Annapurna: A Woman's Place* a separatist view of climbing that is more in keeping with the separatism of radical feminism during the 1970s, where the presence of any men in the women's movement was thought to prevent women from developing their own ways of thinking and being (Whelehan 1995, 39). At first, Blum shares this view about who should be on the summit team, when she opposes a Sherpa request to summit first and interprets the request as "paternalistic" (1980, 169). Later however, she compromises, and the summit team did include two women and two Sherpas.

But Chadwick-Onyszkiewicz's desire to summit in the alpine style also involved her goal of not only climbing Annapurna but of climbing the middle summit of the massif, which had never been attempted before. In this way, Chadwick-Onyszkiewicz is much more like climbers Haston and Whillans on Bonington's expedition in that she has little patience with siege style or with its hierarchical way of decision-making. As Margie Rusmore says in her interview with Katie Ives, "Alison might have been ahead of her time in a lot of ways. She probably would have thrived on an alpine style climb more than siege style. She didn't want to have this lumbering beast that was the expedition" (Ives 2017). She preferred the riskier approach, and its Romantic associations with achievement, creativity, risk and simplicity: "The route straight up from camp is the most aesthetic line," Alison said. "I'd rather go that way. If two of us [Chadwick-Onyszkiewicz and Vera Watson] could climb that hard rock together, it would be more an achievement than my Gasherbrum climb" (Blum 1980, 206).

After a debate about the safety of this, Blum reluctantly lets Chadwick-Onyszkiewicz and Watson do the climb to Camp V to start the summit attempt, without oxygen. At this point, siege style gives way to alpine style in the narrative because Blum has no authority over the summit team: "I [Blum] had to admire Alison's single-minded dedication – not just to climbing the mountain but to doing it in a certain style" (206). In her interview with Katie Ives, she elaborates on her decision, saying "Alison adamantly wanted her attempt. She had wanted it to be all women. I felt I didn't have the right to tell them not to go. I just remember feeling that we'd already achieved our goal. The team goal. The longer we stayed there, the more dangerous it was. Which ended up being true" (Ives 2017).

Tragically, Chadwick-Onyszkiewicz and Watson fell even before they reached the high camp, and they were killed instantly (Blum 1980, 230). Although it is not the style of climbing that kills them (if there had been Sherpas with them, they would not have been able to stop the fall because they would have climbed on a separate rope), Blum questions her leadership ability because she let them go. She has to be reassured on this point by other members of the team (234–5). In the end, Blum finds some healing with the rest of the group when they chip Watson's and Chadwick-Onyszkiewicz's names onto a memorial stone at the foot of Annapurna.

Backlash: Galen Rowell, David Roberts, Beverly Johnson, Reinhold Messner

The American Women's expedition faced a significant amount of controversy at the time not because they had tried to train Sherpanis to climb, but because male Sherpas had helped the team achieve its goals and reach the summit. The criticism of the team for not being all-female reveals a double standard for men and women: the 1953 British expedition to Mount Everest was not criticized for the presence of Tenzing Norgay on the summit team, for example. The team had already faced significant sexism as they organized the climb. In her memoir *Breaking Trail*, Arlene Blum describes the problems she encountered on the American Bicentennial Expedition to Everest team, when she and the other female team member were denied the chance to set the route through the dangerous Icefall section (2005, 240) and, as another expedition member wrote later, were denied places on the summit teams for the same reason (251–2). Blum's experience on Everest leads her, with Wanda Rutkiewicz and Alison Chadwick-Onyszkiewicz, to imagine that an all-women's expedition could summit an 8,000-metre peak when they met during a climb of Noshaq in the Himalayas, where Polish female climbers set an altitude record (169–70). The American Alpine Club (AAC) initially refused to approve Blum's permit to climb Annapurna, expressing doubts that a women's team should be approved, and challenged her position as expedition leader (256). But the worst backlash against the climb was yet to come.

After she returned from Annapurna, Blum wrote an article about the climb for *National Geographic*. Before the article went to press, the magazine received a letter from a woman unknown to Blum (282–3) that said the presence of Sherpas on the summit team meant that women had not climbed Annapurna because the Sherpas must have led. It also alleged that "women slept with men who were plied into sexual relations with booze" during the climb (282). These accusations were meant to undermine the work of the expedition, since they supported the idea that women on mountaineering expeditions are expected to have sex with team members (Ortner 1999, 228–30) and combined it with the idea that women's desirability was a distraction from the business of (male) climbing. Later, Blum discovered that the author of the letter was well-known American climber Galen Rowell, who had signed it with his girlfriend's name. Rowell remained publicly critical of the expedition and told Blum, when she confronted him, that women did not belong in the mountains. He also admitted that he was the anonymous commentator for an article by David Roberts, where he blamed the deaths of Vera Watson and Alison Chadwick-Onyszkiewicz on Blum's decision to allow them to climb without a Sherpa to accompany them (Blum 2005, 302–5).

David Roberts, a respected climber and climbing writer in his own right, is the author of the memoir *Mountain of My Fear* and an outspoken critic of Maurice Herzog's leadership during the first ascent of Annapurna. In a 1981 article about the Annapurna women's expedition and the state of women's climbing for *Outside* magazine called "Hazardous Routes: Why Has the Course of Women's Mountaineering Led to Tragedy?" Roberts assessed the recent achievements of female climbers, and linked them to climbing deaths, including the deaths of the two climbers on the Annapurna expedition. Roberts argues that "for women climbers, both their triumphs and their disasters take on the proportions of symbolic acts ... women climbers face additional problems when they climb *as women*" (1981, 31) because their actions will face additional scrutiny, presumably, from the male-dominated climbing community.

This in itself does not constitute a backlash against the idea of women's climbing, as Roberts himself has argued (Ives 2017), but *Outside* magazine – without Roberts's permission – blurbed the article on the magazine cover as "Has Women's Climbing Failed?" The implication was that it had because as climbers, women were failures. The core of Roberts's argument is that the deaths of those on the American Women's Expedition might have happened because Blum had allowed them to climb without a male Sherpa (1981, 32). In 2017, Roberts says in an interview with Katie Ives that he did think Blum's decision to send Sherpas to find the bodies of Watson and Chadwick-Onyszkiewicz was also dangerous and that Blum "defaulted to the men on the team" (Ives 2017). For her part, Blum and expedition member Irene Miller contested Roberts's view in a letter to *Outside* magazine (2005, 304) and she argued with Roberts at a 2005 Banff Mountain Book Festival panel (366–7).

What makes Roberts's article a part of a backlash against the Annapurna expedition and the idea of women's climbing was that some of those he interviewed – notably Galen Rowell and John Roskelley – either did say that women should not be climbing big mountains, or, in the case of Beverly Johnson, they cast doubt on feminist approaches to climbing. As Margie Rusmore observes, the article reflected a fear of change in the climbing community, as women began to tackle significant objectives: "I think the response that our expedition got generally reflected changes going on in how we as a culture viewed women. Women were having a little success climbing, and it was starting to make men nervous. It was as if they thought, You girls can climb, but don't take on the biggest mountains. You leave those for us" (Ives 2017).

Roberts's article is significant because it contains in one place most of the objections to women climbers and female leadership that were part of the mountaineering community at the time. The article ends with a quotation from Beverly Johnson, an American rock climber who in 1981 was the first woman to complete a solo ascent of El Capitan in Yosemite National Park, a major achievement. At the time, Johnson was probably the best female rock and big-wall climber in the world. But she did not see herself as breaking trail for women in the male-dominated climbing scene. When Roberts asked her about feminism and the politics of climbing as a woman, she disavowed both, responding "I'm sort of an antifeminist. I do think women are weaker [than men]" (Roberts 1981, 87). Johnson added that "if you had to pick a fire crew ... you'd pick the guys first" because men are stronger, and because "you'd have a better chance of getting somebody who'd used a shovel before" (87).

Beverly Johnson's dismissal of feminism and her statement that women are "weaker" and less capable than men in light of her own achievements sums up the difficulty of women in mountaineering during the alpine climbing era of the 1970s and 1980s, and the backlash women encountered in climbing circles when they did decide to go to the Himalayas. In Roberts's article, Johnson associates climbing ability, including rock climbing, with sheer physical strength. Her position about gender difference is essentialist, because to say that only physical strength is what is needed to climb mountains ignores other skills climbers need, including endurance, balance, and the ability to plan and carry out an expedition. The differences between women and men are not seen by Johnson as cultural, but as biological, and in this response, they are absolute. Johnson believes that men are culturally suited to manual labour because she assumes – without providing evidence – that men would have experience using shovels, and women would not. The implication here is that women occupy a domestic sphere where presumably they know how to use mops and brooms, but not shovels. That space is naturalized: it is where women "belong," and so is not the product of social forces that might assign certain kinds of women to the domestic sphere, and certain men to the kind of public sphere where their strength would be an asset.

Finally, Johnson thinks that American feminism's emphasis on equality (in the late 1970s) must mean "people are making such a big deal out of making everybody the same," when to her, this is clearly not the case (Roberts 1981, 87). Leaving aside Johnson's understanding of the American women's liberation movement's goal as gender similitude rather than equal opportunity or recognition, her comments show clearly that female climbers who wanted to be taken seriously at the time had to take on traditional masculine ideals about toughness and strength, whether they wanted to or not. Like Margaret Thatcher, the first female prime minister of the United Kingdom, who said in 1982 "'I owe nothing to women's lib'" (Holehouse 2013), Johnson understood her success to be an individual achievement, and did not see gender issues as relevant to her life or career. Such an attitude appears to meet with the approval of John Roskelley, well known as one of the most misogynist climbers of his generation because he advocated that women should never climb with men on the same team, arguing that the presence of women distracted men from their task (Wren 1987). Galen Rowell, who had already tried to discredit the Annapurna climb in his letter to *National Geographic*, disputes in the same article whether Dianne Roberts, who was part of the American team on K2, should have been "allowed" to climb high, although she had carried loads as heavy as those of the male team members, demonstrating her strength and commitment in the process. Rowell concludes that Roberts was not a true climber and should never have claimed to be "representing women." Without providing specifics, he opines that the presence of Roberts contributed to "group instability," an expression of a common belief that climbing was a man's sport, and the presence of women was an intrusion and a disruption (Roberts 1981, 86). The article's last words about women's climbing are Roskelley's: he would climb with Johnson, he said, "because she'd just get on with the job" (87). It is implied that feminist climbers, or even female climbers who were aware of their gender, would not.

Given that mountaineering is about the use of the body, and gender identity and roles are intimately connected to bodies and what we think about them, it might seem odd that Johnson so easily dismisses gender issues in favour of a discussion of individual achievement. But is this really the case? Sherry Ortner's "bodily politics" includes the idea that struggles actually about gender identity or gender difference are played out indirectly as controversies about the uses of the body in mountaineering culture. Registers like proper climbing style, heroism, and good leadership become the way that gender issues are voiced and worked out during the transition from the golden age of mountaineering to alpine climbing. In other words, gender politics is discussed, but as style, whether style refers to the siege style of placing camps and working in a hierarchical team where the leader makes decisions, or to the "freer" or "purer" (but still masculinist) alpine-style ascents of the 1960s and 1970s, where lighter equipment, smaller teams, egalitarian leadership, and faster ascents become important. Style in mountaineering is saturated by politics, including gender politics. It becomes a way to put into words what cannot be said about bodies.

Bodily politics displaces issues about gender onto controversies about climbing leadership and style, which is how Roberts can assess Blum's leadership style but not discuss directly the gender politics involved in doing so, other than saying that female climbers invite scrutiny when they foreground gender issues themselves. It is a politics that makes its meaning gendered by what it does *not* say about manliness, and by what – in contrast – it shows about how to be a real man, or (much less often) a real woman in physically and emotionally-trying conditions. Like Eve Kosofsky-Sedgwick's characterization of "closetedness," a condition that says through silence (about sexuality for instance) what "cannot" be said out loud (1990, 3–6), bodily politics in mountaineering constitutes a set of gendered assumptions about what good mountaineers are supposed to do and it informs whatever is said about anything else. Mountaineering discourse is less about "rules" than it is about the "style" of a climb, which "evolves out of an ongoing process of discussion and negotiation" in the climbing community (Mazel 1994, 17–18). Roberts's article contributes to that negotiation: some of the people interviewed for it formed a backlash against the presence of women, and female leaders, in the mountains. It is significant that more than twenty years later, at the 2005 Banff Mountain Book Festival, there was finally an open and direct discussion of gender bias (and anti-semitism, which Blum also discussed in the same panel) in climbing circles. Why did this happen so recently? The work of "bodily politics" was still working to prevent discussion of gender in an activity structured by gender bias for so long.

The backlash against the Annapurna expedition, and the idea that women could lead expeditions on big mountains, continued long after Roberts's article was published. In his writing about Annapurna published only five years before that Banff Mountain Book Festival panel, Reinhold Messner contributes to it. Messner is arguably the most iconoclastic living high-altitude mountaineer who climbs in the alpine style. His achievements – discussed in more detail in chapter two – have helped to push mountaineering in the Himalayas to new levels: he was the first to climb an 8,000-metre peak in the alpine style in a single push; he was the first to climb Everest without supplemental oxygen; and he was the first person to climb all fourteen 8,000-metre mountains. Messner's climbing philosophy has been to increase climbing risks while simplifying the logistics of the climb itself, and to oppose the commercialization of high-altitude mountaineering entailed in the growth of guided climbs.

Messner measures the quality of climbing by its challenge and originality. In *Annapurna: 50 Years of Expeditions to the Death Zone*, Messner affirms his belief that Annapurna is one of the most difficult mountains to climb and adds that it should remain this way or climbing itself will become impure. As he says, "the eight-thousanders first became a vanishing point for national pride, then an exotic destination for millions, and today they are a 'heroes' playground,' because their 'challenge' has not been completely expended" (2000, 68–9). Messner, therefore, wishes to restore a heroic element to mountaineering that he believes is being lost as climbing these mountains becomes more popular and less risky. And for him, national motives or other social reasons to climb are simply not heroic enough. To this end, he defends Maurice Herzog against the accusations that have been made about his leadership in the name of heroism itself, and ignores the nationalist overtones of Herzog's own account. According to Messner, "the ascent of Annapurna is and remains Herzog's own personal feat of heroism" (24), a statement that reinstates heroic discourse at the heart of mountaineering. He ends his retelling of the expedition story with this poem to Herzog: "*Maurice Herzog./What a career!/What a personality!*" (64) in order to literally underscore Herzog's heroic status, despite the criticism of his leadership that has been in evidence since 1996.

Messner goes on to describe the other expeditions on Annapurna that he sees as ground-breaking within his criteria of pure mountaineering and heroism in climbing new routes. These include the climb of Bonington's team, a traverse of the whole Annapurna ridge, and his own first ascent of the northwest ridge. Messner's decision to discuss only the climbs of Annapurna that were notable for their first ascents means that he leaves out any other criteria for achievement. National or even cultural achievements do not matter; there is no mention of the first Japanese team to summit, or who the first Sherpas were. There is no discussion of gender either, except in the abstract language of masculine toughness, when he and his climbing partners come across one of the dozens of corpses on Annapurna and photograph it. Although Messner says of the body "it was as if death belonged here in this bizarre glacial world ... we wasted no time puzzling over who he might once have been, or how he had died" (111–12), for reasons he does not explain, the photograph is repeated later in the book. Why does the photograph appear twice if "death" does not bear thinking about? The corpse serves as the reminder to be stoic and brave in the face of death, but because the gaze of the living climber cannot ever be returned by the body itself, the image of the corpse, or its sign, the grave marker, appears repeatedly in Messner's *Annapurna* as the sign of difference that must be surmounted by manly stoicism.

The tendency to surmount difference by means of a particular type of mountain masculinity and its endorsement of toughness is particularly important for Messner's treatment of the American Women's Expedition to Annapurna. Although he could leave out a discussion of the expedition as he leaves out others, he does not. Rather, Messner includes it much as he includes the unknown corpse which he says does not matter but which he cannot ignore. In *Annapurna*, he includes a photograph of the memorial to Vera Watson and Alison Chadwick-Onyszkiewicz with the caption "Memorial to the Dead at Annapurna Base Camp" (167). He never identifies the women by name. And in his list of expeditions to Annapurna, Messner says that Ian Clough from Bonington's climb "is tragically killed on the descent" but of Chadwick-Onyszkiewicz and Watson he says only that on that climb "one English woman and one American woman fall to their deaths" (154). Messner also includes a photograph of Wanda Rutkiewicz, the woman who originally had the idea to do an all-woman's climb to Annapurna. Messner's caption identifies her as "the most successful female high-altitude mountaineer to date" before he says that the photograph was taken just before her death on the mountain Kanchenjunga after her ascent of Annapurna in 1991 (171). Like the other narratives I have examined, Messner's treatment of women in *Annapurna: 50 Years* shows that gender is often represented indirectly as part of bodily politics, but in this case bodily politics only revolves around the twin signs of death and heroism. Messner's book, therefore, is more than a call to value climbs for their difficulty and risk. It also contains a backlash discourse against the achievements of women climbers in its own use of bodily politics because of its insistence on a narrow type of heroism as its criteria for climbing success. The only other option in this representational system is to be represented as a corpse that must resurface in order to recall the importance of masculine values to mountaineering.

Other Annapurnas, Other Lives

For more than fifty years, the mountain Annapurna has been the site where a complex history of gender in mountaineering writing gets written as a "bodily politics" that does allow gender to have a central place in the creation of mountain masculinities and sometimes mountain feminisms, even within the most romantic documents of mountaineering.

Discussions about siege-style climbing or the purity of alpine style are also discussions about the politics of using these styles, and about what kind of social organization they imply. In a post-feminist climate where so many discussions about the power of women seem to have altered the politics of feminism beyond recognition, the narratives of Annapurna climbs have something valuable to tell us about how politics does enter at least one form of everyday life, even when political talk seems to be silenced. The struggles of women on Annapurna in their attempt to live out feminist ideas of the 1970s within mountaineering clearly demonstrates the strengths and the limits of American feminisms in that period in the heady times before the final defeat of the Equal Rights Amendment in 1982, when feminists all over North America thought that they could challenge any injustice they experienced in their daily lives, anywhere in the world (Mathews and de Hart 1990, viii).

Decades after the American Women's expedition to Annapurna, *Annapurna: A Woman's Place* still has the power to let people imagine what it would look like to climb mountains – and write about them – differently. Journalist Shawnté Salabert links Blum's book to further possibilities for mountaineering writing:

> One day in 2008, I came across a book called *Annapurna: A Woman's Place*. It was an odd size, a strange blue color, and I got completely lost in the story. This was the first time I'd ever read an adventure book in which women were the protagonists. The overriding feeling I had was one of possibility. It made me want more. What I would like to see on bookshelves now are stories from people of all sorts of backgrounds, people who face gender barriers but also financial barriers, racial or cultural barriers. It's going to take a while for adventure writing to become more diverse in a really meaningful way, to untangle this web that's been woven over so many years of what mountaineering looks like. (Ives 2017)

If we look closely at the rhetoric of mountaineering expedition memoirs of Annapurna, it is possible to see how the Romantic ideals in Herzog's often-repeated statement "there are other Annapurnas in the lives of men" can be given a politics and a history – and even, when Arlene Blum rewrites them, to become a call for political change that extends beyond gender to the stories of many kinds of people, on many Annapurnas.

And they [the Americans] failed in the most
beautiful way you can imagine.
Reinhold Messner, *K2: Mountain of Mountains*

"I'm sorry Rick – I apologize, for your sake."
"Sorry? About what?"
"Well, I'm sorry that I'm not a woman."
John Roskelley to Rick Ridgeway, stormbound in a
tent on K2, 1978

CHAPTER 2

K2: THE GENDERED ROPE

Rope

In a British "how-to" climbing guide from 1950 by Showell Styles called
The Mountaineer's Week-End Book, there is a concise description of the
importance of rope to climbing: "the mountaineering boot ... may be
taken as the badge of the mountaineer in the general sense. The rope is
the badge of the climber. The coil of slim, strong fibre slung across his
shoulders is the most important item of the climber's equipment ... it
is the thing on which the whole theory of an ascent, whether on difficult rock or an Alpine Peak, is based" (168). In climbing, the rope is the
most important safeguard when the ascent or descent becomes difficult:
it links climbers to each other and often to a rock face, secured by bolts
or other fasteners. When a climber falls on a rock face, ridge, or into a
crevasse on an ice field, the rope (if it holds) is what can keep the climber

from injury and death. But even in the brief description above, the rope signifies much more than this. Styles makes sure to say that the rope is the "badge" of the climber because it is literally the sign of difficulty and skill. This safety device is what distinguishes its user between someone who is a casual "mountaineer" and someone who can do difficult climbs in any conditions. It is also the "thing" which, in Styles's words, creates theory. Styles meant that the existence of the rope made it possible to imagine how to do a climb. But if we think of this description through Bill Brown's "Thing Theory" essay (2001), as a thing, rope is specific in its reference to an object, while it remains abstract as a concept because it cannot be reduced to its "thingness." Therefore, a rope is not just an object with meaning found only in itself. It is also indexical because in its existence as something more abstract it points beyond itself to a future climbing activity, or it signifies the idea of the activity itself and the subjectivity of the one who performs it. In the case of rope, whenever it appears in a climbing narrative, it has to be there because it is part of climbing, but it also contains important social information about climbing. In Brown's words, the thing-ness of an object contains this paradox within itself because it "seems to name the object as it is even as it names something else" (Brown 2001, 5). The thing is beyond theory even as it constitutes the matter of theory. The word "thing" itself is both a material sign that reminds us of the physical world in which we live, and a sign that signifies an absence of a particularity. It makes ideas (which are not things) thinkable even when ideas work to dematerialize, or forget, the existence of things (5–6). The rope, then, is more than a necessary object such as a boot or an ice axe. In mountaineering, a rope is an object with practical uses, but it also is the visible mark of social distinction and belonging. Its significance moves far beyond its status as a thing, and it becomes the sign of a host of social ideas about what climbing is, who gets to climb, and what good and bad climbing might be. These are ideas connected to climbing as a culture as well as an activity. Contained within this formation are ideas about gender and its politics.

During the 1950s, the idea of rope centred on its connection to some of the highest ideals ever expressed about mountaineering in the phrase, "the brotherhood of the rope." This phrase has been attributed to Charles (Charlie) Houston, and associated with his 1953 American expedition to K2, the expedition which led to one of the most famous rescue attempts in the history of mountaineering. All climbs on K2, before and since that 1953 expedition, have been measured by this idea of brotherhood, and what climbers will (or should) do in order to save each other.[1] When it is invoked, "the brotherhood of the rope" is an expression of the highest ideals of climbing, but it is also a sign of failure, especially for subsequent expeditions to K2, because the high ideals of Houston's team have never again been matched. This is a brotherhood, therefore, that exists to remind people of the loss of a certain kind of masculine ideal of heroism and selflessness. It is an ideal which is meant to be unattainable. But the operational effect of this phrase as a deep sign of mountaineering culture also highlights that culture's gender politics. "The brotherhood of the rope" is obviously a heavily gendered phrase. This phrase has contributed to the effect of rendering unthinkable the participation of other kinds of climbers, such as women, working-class men, or Indigenous people in this ideal realm. When these others appear as climbers within the culture of mountain climbing, sometimes the operational effect of this phrase has been that of exclusion, marginalization and the silencing of those who could not be thought to be "real" climbers (Slemon 2008, 241–2). As Miriam O'Brien Underhill points out in her essay "Manless Climbs," leadership of the rope also determines who leads a climb, and during the 1920s and 1930s when she began to climb only with women, many male climbers believed that women were not capable of taking on the responsibilities, and reaping the rewards, of leading out on a rope ([1971] 1992, 4). Although O'Brien Underhill's climbs with women in the Alps were called la cordée feminine [women's rope] in the 1930s in a way which promised to un-gender the idea of the rope or at least make it possible to imagine that women could climb mountains (Mazel 1994, 12–13), most women remained marginal to the activity of mountaineering, particularly with regards to the world of high-altitude climbing. Although the first all-woman's Himalayan expedition occurred in 1955, just two years after Houston's expedition, women climbers and all-female rope teams would not appear in the Himalayas or the Karakoram until two decades later.[2]

And so, for all its idealism, "brotherhood of the rope" did signify a community of men, and only of a specific kind of community at that – a community that cannot be reconstituted or repeated, no matter how desirable this may seem. The idealism in the phrase that inspired climbers for decades afterwards also contains within itself many of the assumptions about gender, class, and race common at the time and which, in a more muted form, persist today in mountaineering circles. The examination of rope, therefore, is a good entry into understanding how gender politics worked and works in climbing accounts about K2 specifically, and in high-altitude climbing more generally. As what is perhaps the most difficult and dangerous mountain to climb in the world, K2 has been the testing ground not only for the limits of human endurance at high altitudes, but also for what climbing is thought to represent. The idea of rope is tangled up with these ideas about what masculinity and femininity have come to mean to mountaineering itself.

It is not known exactly how the phrase "the brotherhood of the rope" began to circulate beyond the 1953 American expedition, but the phrase is found in the French climber Gaston Rébuffat's 1956 classic account of climbing, *Étoiles et tempêtes* [*Starlight and Storm*] as the "*fraternité de la corde*," where it appears as the heading for a chapter on rope and climbing techniques. Before moving on to think about different accounts of ascents of K2, Rébuffat's use of the term to signify masculine friendship *through a thing* is worth considering because rope has so often symbolized an otherwise unarticulated masculine bond. Rébuffat was one of France's best-known mountaineers and rock climbers. He was a member of the successful French ascent of Annapurna in 1950, in addition to being credited for many first ascents in the Alps. The pictures of Rébuffat in a sweater challenging a vertical wall with strength and grace have become associated with the essence of what it is to be a climber, and they inspired (and by the 1970s, irritated) generations of mountaineers after him who either found his style inspirational, or saw it as affected (Roberts 1992, 147–8). Of the twenty books Rébuffat wrote, *Starlight and Storm* is one of the best known, and one of the most lyrically Romantic accounts of climbing ever published. Part of the romance involves Rébuffat's evocation of the community of climbing as something achieved between men during times of suffering and difficulty. The suffering makes the adventure seem worthwhile, he suggests, because the friendships formed as a result of it become precious. At the top of the Eiger, the deadliest north face in the Alps, Rébuffat recounts the sense of *fraternité* [brotherhood] he and his team all felt after a hard struggle: "Through this ascent, this snow and this storm, we had come to recognize from the bottom of our inmost hearts a sense of fulfilment: of a life closely linked with the elements, a sense of comradeship, a taste of things which, once you have tasted them, can never be replaced" (Rébuffat [1954] 1957, 147).

This is a classic "mountain-top" account of a summit: achieving it results in a heightened sense of one's presence in the natural world, an experience difficult to recount because it is almost mystical or religious. Most importantly at the summit there is a sense of "comradeship" or brotherhood because the goal was achieved, not without difficulty, in the presence of other men. For Rébuffat, it is the rope itself which functions as a tangible reminder of the link between one man and other, and of the community of climbers who understand through experience how important it is. In his irresistibly friendly style, he "invites" the reader, whom he imagines as a young and presumably male would-be climber, to learn about the basics of climbing, now that "he" has experienced something of it. He imagines what this climber might have felt on a first outing in this way:

Clumsily you uncoiled a rope. Feeling happy, rather scared, rather moved, you roped yourself up, or probably you were roped up. Your friend took the lead. Fearfully, you watched him climb, then an angle of rock hid him, and at that moment, you realized better what a rope means. First of all you clutched it more firmly, and when you raised your eyes to watch it rise up the rock face, this nylon thread acquired tremendous value for you, and you understood the full beauty of this link. Then the rope grew taut and you began to climb, and you were at times glad to see this spiritual link before you in concrete form. (152)

The rest of the chapter discusses rope care and techniques before moving on to a consideration of other tools such as the ice axe, crampons, and pitons (metal stakes). None of the other tools receive the same treatment as the rope, which is used to hail the young climber into the fraternity of climbing by pointing out that the reader must be a climber already. Only the rope is treated as the "spiritual thread" between climbing partners as well as the concrete manifestation of safety. The rope, clearly, holds special significance for Rébuffat because for him it is far more than a safety device. It is the mark of spiritual belonging and central to the experience of climbing with other men. It is the index of brotherhood and is spiritual as well as material.

In the simplest terms, as I have said, the rope serves to prevent – or at least attempt to prevent – injury and death. It is literally a climber's lifeline in any difficult situation. But, as Rébuffat observes, the rope is also the symbol of connection between climbers because climbers must move together and cooperate when they are on the same rope. It is a lifeline and a sign of life because it is the visible reminder of connectedness, even when climbers cannot see each other. It proves to a climber that the climber is not alone in either a physical or a spiritual sense within an often-hostile environment. And so, the rope is both symbolic and actual, a potent sign of the activity of climbing but also the guarantee that "you," the climber, are not alone, even when your partner cannot be seen. This is why, in Joe Simpson's classic account of mountaineering survival called *Touching the Void*, the most agonizing chapter involves the decision by his partner, Simon Yates, to cut the rope that connects them, because Simpson, who is injured, is dangling over a cliff out of Yates's sight. Simpson cannot stop his weight from pulling both of them off and so, unable to see where Simpson is and hoping that his actions will save them both, Yates finally cuts what binds them together. When he thinks that his actions have caused Simpson's death, Yates himself questions whether he should have cut the rope at all (Simpson 1988, 88–9). Although both of them ultimately survive (albeit with considerable hardship), Yates had to endure some initial criticism from members of the mountaineering community, who could not understand how Yates could ever have cut the rope because cutting a rope is taboo. Cutting the rope was, for many climbers, tantamount to Yates severing the connection of brotherhood between him and his climbing partner. It was unthinkable, even though it is clear in Simpson's book that Yates cut the rope as a last resort. As Yates has said, once Simpson's account was made public, criticisms of his actions ceased in the mountaineering community because the heroism involved in Yates's decision became obvious (Ritchie 2019).

Rébuffat's chapter title is meant to transmit far more than a description of equipment and how to use it. It is meant to impart the central value of mountaineering as brotherhood and community, not individual achievement. It is also, unavoidably, a symbol of masculine community, a community that – as I said earlier – did not admit women for quite some time, and one that still makes it difficult for women to participate. Women have been central to mountaineering almost since its beginnings, but as Stephen Slemon has noted, mountaineering clubs such as Britain's Alpine Club or the Alpine Club of Canada were in fact slow to admit women to these institutions (2008, 240). He calls this brotherhood a metaphor with real power to exclude "others" from the fraternity, including women, people with disabilities, people without the correct class affiliations for a team, as well as non-white people, including Sherpa climbers and porters. It is "both a grounded and a virtual constituency" (241). In other words, the brotherhood of the rope was taken up internationally as the essence of the highest values that any climber, anywhere, should have, but this ideal cannot be attained even by those who are allowed to imagine that it applies to them. Meanwhile, the continuous articulation of this impossible ideal shows that the community needs the contractions in this ideology to define itself and exclude others at the same time.

When the brotherhood of the rope became central to recalling one of the most famous mountain rescues in history, the 1953 Houston expedition's doomed attempt to save climber Art Gilkey, this phrase began to signify heroism and sacrifice in a more pronounced way. As I mentioned near the beginning of this chapter, this expedition's understanding of the phrase the brotherhood of the rope became known not only as the expression of the care climbers had for each other, but also for the need for climbers to help each other, and even save each other, through selfless acts. Rébuffat's sense of togetherness which was accentuated during difficult conditions on the Eiger in fact depends on hardship to make it work. As he says, if the Eiger had been climbed in good weather, the feeling of comradeship would not have been as attenuated. Therefore, the mark of brotherhood was something that happened during times of trial and disaster on high mountains. It was a way to test men and see if they were found wanting. The fact that it occurred because of a mountaineering accident actually caused by a tangling of ropes makes such a formulation ironic, but it also emphasizes that sense of paradox in the phrase itself. Brotherhood on K2 and other high mountains would prove to be an elusive ideal, even as it was constantly evoked by Charlie Houston, Edmond Hillary, and many others. Its terms of exclusion on subsequent expeditions to K2 also proved open to challenge, as people not included in the brotherhood began to assume their membership in the mountaineering community. The phrase has passed out of current mountaineering usage because it is so blatantly gender-biased. But the ideal it represented still has residual force, as we can see from the initial outrage generated by Simon Yates's very reasonable decision to cut the rope holding him to Joe Simpson. The belief in the brotherhood of the rope, on K2 in particular, is also one of the reasons why female climbers were and are regarded with suspicion on the mountain, because as in the time of Rébuffat, the "brotherhood" is officially open to those who are thought to have the skill and ability to summit, when in fact the brotherhood often stays closed to those who are not male, white, and European.

The phrase brotherhood of the rope is so closely associated with the life and career of Charlie Houston that Houston himself made a film about his expeditions to K2 called *Brotherhood of the Rope*, and his biography by Bernadette McDonald carries the same title. More than anyone else except possibly Sir Edmund Hillary, Houston exemplifies the highest ideals of mountaineering. Throughout his life, he has consciously tried to support the ethical (but not the gendered) sense of the phrase he helped to coin. In *K2: The Savage Mountain*, this sense of ethics is clear. It is why Reinhold Messner says, in the epigraph to this chapter, that the expedition "failed in the most beautiful way you can imagine," since the team did not reach the summit and did not in fact succeed in saving Art Gilkey, but succeeded in an act of heroic selflessness. It is also why, in one of the more lyrical sections of *K2: Life and Death on the World's Most Dangerous Mountain,* Ed Viesturs titles his chapter about the 1953 expedition "Brotherhood" and at length, discusses why he feels that he was born too late to participate in the era of expeditions and adventure which Houston and Bates's account represents for him, when climbing was not subdivided into different specializations, and when everyone knew instinctively what a mountaineer was: a hero (2009, 184–5). Partly because of its long association with the idea of brotherhood, accounts of climbing K2 do contend with these high ideals, with varying degrees of success. In doing so, they bring into view in an unusually direct way the nature of gender politics on this dangerous mountain and the climbers who dream of standing on its summit. It is to the accounts of this mountain and what it means to climb it that I now turn.

K2

At 8,611 metres or 28,251 feet, K2 is the second-highest mountain in the world (figure 2.1). It is only about 200 vertical metres shorter than Mount Everest, but that difference has meant that K2 was not the focus of early twentieth-century British imperial climbing ambition in quite the way that Everest was, even though European climbing parties had attempted the mountain much earlier than they attempted Everest. The mountain still does not have the same fame as Mount Everest beyond climbing circles. But K2 has become the ultimate achievement for mountaineers who want an even greater challenge than Everest presents. Everest's difficulty lies mainly in the danger of the Khumbu Icefall on the Nepali side, and in its sheer size, which makes its "death zone," the place where there is no longer enough oxygen to sustain life, dangerously extensive. Despite those dangers, Everest's status as the world's highest mountain has attracted thousands of climbers to it since the 1980s, adding to its list of hazards the problem of overcrowding on the peak as too many climbers try to summit in the brief period between the winter climbing season and monsoon season. That, and the relative ease with which it can be accessed and climbed, means that in climbing circles Everest is not seen as the crowning achievement in high-altitude mountaineering that it once was. That honour is reserved for K2, which is widely thought to be among the most difficult and dangerous 8,000-metre peaks, as well as one of the most beautiful. K2's triangular shape, beautifully photographed at the beginning of the twentieth century by Vittorio Sela and others, has earned it the name "Mountain of Mountains." Many climbers have remarked how the mountain's "classic" beauty makes it an objective for them: as Jim Wickwire – the first American to summit K2 in 1978 – points out in the 2009 foreword to *K2: The Savage Mountain*, "It [K2] is the perfect embodiment of our mental image of what a great mountain should be like" (Houston and Bates [1954] 2009, ix). Many mountaineers also want to climb it because, arguably, a climb of K2 is the hardest high-altitude test in mountaineering. As Ed Viesturs says, he knows that K2 is an important achievement "from having sat in on the chat of high-altitude climbers all around the world. In their company, if you mention climbing Everest, the remark may elicit nothing more than a shrug. But if you let on that

Figure 2.1 | K2 from the Baltoro Glacier.

you've reached the top of K2, a hush comes over the room. And then, invariably, someone will say, 'Tell us about it'" (2009, 325).

The mountain's technical difficulty, legendary storms, and dangerous approaches that can only be completed after weeks of difficult travel on foot or by riding on camels, coupled with its own extensive death zone and its remote position in the Karakoram Mountains of Pakistan gave it the "Savage Mountain" nickname. The climbing statistics for each mountain show how much more difficult and dangerous climbing K2 is, particularly for women. As of 2011, more than 4,500 people have summited Mount Everest since Tenzing Norgay and Edmund Hillary climbed the mountain in 1953. There have been over 200 deaths on Everest, making the chances of surviving an ascent one in twenty-one. But there have been only 305 successful ascents of K2 since an Italian team stood on the summit in 1954. What is more, there have been seventy-eight deaths on K2 since the first serious climbs of the mountain began in early twentieth century, and so an average of one in every seven climbers who make it to the summit dies on the descent. Due to its hazards and difficulty, K2 cannot be attempted by inexperienced climbers who hire guides to get them up and down the mountain relatively safely, as is the case with Everest. The statistics for female climbers are even more sobering: only twelve female climbers have successfully summited K2. Of these, only five are alive today. The rest either died on K2 or died soon after on other big mountains in the Karakoram or the Himalayas.

Even the source of K2's name shows how remote and unknown this mountain was until the end of the nineteenth century. K2 was named in 1856 when Lieutenant T.G. Montgomerie of the Great Trigonometric Survey of India took the bearings of two large peaks more than 130 miles away. He sketched them and named them K1 and K2 after the Karakoram region (Curran [1994] 1995, 25). The Great Trigonometric Survey generally made every attempt to find out the local names of the mountains it mapped, measured, and named except for Mount Everest, where the local names for the mountain were disregarded (29). Eventually it was discovered that K1 was called Masherbrum by the people in the villages nearest to it, and it was renamed accordingly. But no name for K2 was discovered. According to Curran, Askole, the village closest to the mountain, had no word for the peak because the villagers could not see it from their location. Even remote campsites near the Baltoro Glacier, which flows from K2, do not have good views of it, and there was little reason for local people to travel the barren wilderness of the glacier for weeks just to get a closer look. The surveyor's name was kept (30). K2 did have a name among the Balti people who used the trade routes first across the Karakoram pass and later the Muztagh pass: Chhogho Ri (Great Mountain), which seems to have become Choghiri, but the name never saw usage beyond the Balti or Chinese people in the area.[3] And so, the name "K2" itself shows how the mountain participated very little in the wider cultural life and history of the world until relatively recently. Even this has contributed to its image for mountain climbers as a pure mountain, untouched by any culture. As Fosco Maraini says in his *Karakoram – Ascent of Gasherbrum IV*, K2 as a name signals its otherness. It is "a name that scraps race, religion, history and past. No country claims it, no latitudes and longitudes and geography, no dictionary words. No, just the bare bones of a name, all rock and ice and storm and abyss. It makes no attempt to sound human. It is atoms and stars" (in Curran [1994] 1995, 31). The fact that it was unknown made it irresistible to climbers who wanted to journey to what they thought of as the limit of civilization itself. This is also why K2 is thought of as the ultimate location for the Romantic fantasies of climbers who want to escape what they know and test their limits to the utmost.

Because it is not Everest, but is the image and ideal of a "pure" mountain for any serious high-altitude climber, K2 retains a special place in the history of mountaineering as well as in the current state of climbing in the contemporary, commercialized era. The romance of K2 has attracted some of the most eccentric explorers and best alpinists of every generation from the beginning of its climbing history, including Aleister Crowley, who in 1902 led the first climbing expedition on K2 long before he became an esoteric cult figure, or the explorers William Hunter Workman and Fanny Workman. The latter was a suffragist who famously held up a sign proclaiming "Votes for Women" at the top of the Baltoro Glacier. The Italian Duke of the Abruzzi, whose lavish expedition attempted the spur which now bears his name, took the most famous picture of the mountain in 1909 (65–6). No one tried to climb K2 from 1909 until 1938, when an American expedition led by Charlie Houston made a serious attempt on the summit.

But after the Second World War, when travel to the Himalayas and the Karakoram became easier, like other 8,000-metre peaks K2 became the focus of ambitious national expeditions and the subject of climbers' ambitions. The mountain not only attracted some of the best climbers in the world, but also became the stage for the creation of contemporary climbing culture's highest ideals. Perhaps inevitably, that is how K2 became the focus for climbing's bitterest disappointments. Both extremes are known so well because the many accidents and disasters on the mountain have been well documented in expedition accounts, and have resulted in controversy about the nature of mountaineering in climbing communities and beyond them. As we shall see, key expedition accounts from 1953 until the present have formed and challenged ideas in the climbing community about the nature and meaning of gender identity because so many expedition accounts for the mountain have been written and read. Some documentaries and even mainstream Hollywood feature films such as *Vertical Limit* also form part of this archive about the meaning of gender in one of the world's highest and most inhospitable places. More than any other high mountain, K2 has drawn individuals and groups who, in testing the limits of their endurance, have also tested the limits of gender identity itself. K2 has been central in climbing's own culture of what it means to be a man or a woman. For this reason, it is an ideal place to examine what happens when something as ordinary as climbing rope becomes the symbol for climbing as a deeply, yet unacknowledged, gendered act.

The Early Brotherhood of the Rope: The American Expeditions of 1938, 1939, and 1953

As the third serious expedition to attempt the mountain, Charlie Houston's 1938 American team was expected to simply prepare the way for the German-American climber Fritz Wiessner, whose expedition was already planned for 1939. But the American Alpine club had secured permission to climb K2 in 1938 as well, and so Houston (when Wiessner declined) put together a group of climbers and prepared to make a reconnaissance of the mountain, where, it was hoped, they would find a climbable route to the summit. Although they did not summit, they climbed higher on K2 than anyone had before them, and their expedition remains notable for its lack of conflict. There are some reasons for this. As Bernadette McDonald's biography of Charlie Houston makes clear, most of the climbers in the team were from the same class and racial backgrounds. Almost all of them had attended Ivy League schools in the Eastern United States and there, they had been influenced by the British approach to climbing as a minimalist enterprise. The exception was Paul Petzoldt, a Teton mountain guide who keenly felt the difference between himself and his more elite companions. Houston has referred to Petzoldt as a "blue collar guide" (McDonald 2007, 57). Neither he nor the other team members understood why Petzoldt was often short of money, while Petzoldt himself referred to Houston and Robert Bates, another member of the team, as "Eastern nabobs" (56). As for Houston and Bates, they too quietly expressed doubts about whether a guide of a different social standing would get along with the rest of the team (57). For example, Petzoldt wanted to bring climbing aids such as pitons, but like his British mentors who were "amateur" climbers rather than guides, Houston saw these as "unsporting" and so he would not let Petzoldt acquire any. In the end, Petzoldt scrounged what little money he had and secretly bought hardware himself. Even Houston admitted later that the hardware was key to their success on the mountain (57).

Therefore, class issues did cause some team divisions, but the generally harmonious nature of the group was probably due to the fact that, in other respects, there were minimal differences between them. With the exception of Petzoldt, the similarity of the background of the team members meant that they did tend to agree when decision-making was called for. Years of teamwork in sports and mountaineering pursuits had trained them to be the kind of men who were not apt to become emotional and tear a group apart. Their training at school and in the mountains ensured that Houston's leadership would be respected, and that he in turn would not test the mettle of his team beyond endurance. The harmonious nature of the team also meant, as mostly upper-class white men, they were able to accept and even enjoy their role as sahibs during the more colonial moments of the expedition. They could act democratically when they needed to, and then become colonialist sahibs when this was also required of them. Their relative ease with both styles of expedition leadership contributed to the remembrance of this expedition as a landmark in the history of mountaineering teams, without mention being made of the class, race, and gender advantages in the team that allowed this harmony to be maintained. The idealism of the expedition in its official account has contributed, therefore, to the high ideals of teamwork which the Americans are remembered for, without an attendant analysis of these factors.

Accordingly, *Five Miles High*, the written account of the expedition by Houston and Bates, is marked with the bonhomie and good cheer of an imperial adventure and a Boy Scout club outing in equal parts, particularly during the long and difficult 300-mile march to K2 from the Vale of Kashmir. It is not unusual to see descriptions of camp as "very jolly" (Houston and Bates [1939] 2000, 61) or that their expedition's lavishness was like "Millionaires' Row" (89). The account is also marked by imperialist ideas about the hired help. The Sherpas, who were to help with load carrying and some climbing, are described as seeing "an attempt on a high mountain as a pilgrimage and the white climber almost as a holy man" (32). Mention is made of the way in which "coolies would plead for the privilege of being allowed to blow up the sahib's air mattress" (89), or of "grinning Sherpas" who carry their loads while they are "perspiring cheerfully" (53), despite the fact that later there would be strikes as the hard-working Pakistani porters (who were not going to climb K2 but who carried most of the heavy loads to Base Camp) demanded more pay and better working conditions (152). The team itself is always described in egalitarian terms as its members make their way through spectacular landscapes. They are often described in the first-person plural as they move through the land and up the mountain, seemingly of one accord. The account is also full of idyllic descriptions of the landscape they encounter during their walk to the peak from the Vale of Kashmir, as well as comments about how well the American climbers worked together as a team (59) and how, despite dangerous river crossings and difficult walking, the romance of the trip persisted, because "the mystery of the ages seemed locked in that magic land" (66).

On the mountain itself, decisions about climbing and exploration are made together (184), and most significantly, the decision about who would be on the two-person team that would try to climb as high as possible is reached by a group discussion. During that discussion, one climbing team volunteers to do the support work for another, which means that they are shown to be sacrificing the chance to climb high without a complaint (268). The expedition account, therefore, reads partly as an imperial adventure necessitated by the siege-style climbing system (where Pakistani porters had to be used to carry all the equipment needed to establish many camps on the mountain), but high on the mountain, siege style was not used, and so the official account is also the record of egalitarian teamwork as everyone carries loads, fixes ropes alongside Sherpas, and makes decisions collectively. The 1938 expedition to K2, therefore, is marked by a successful negotiation of the masculine roles required by these climbing styles. It is not yet mentioned in still higher terms, as Houston's 1953 expedition would be, but it is remembered as an expedition that set the standard for contemporary mountaineering practices and communication strategies.

The 1939 expedition, led by Fritz Wiessner, is not remembered in a similar way at all. Wiessner, a German living in the United States at the time when his country entered into war with many of America's allies, was already regarded with some suspicion in climbing circles. Although he himself was a brilliant mountaineer, he had an abrasive personality and an authoritarian style of leadership (Curran [1994] 1995, 82). As Jim Curran observes, "the very qualities he displayed that might enable him to climb K2 could also be the undoing of the whole expedition, particularly an American one, with its own culture of democratic discussion and joint decision-making" (82). This turned out to be the case. Wiessner led a weak and unbalanced team whose members were sometimes chosen for the money they had to contribute to expedition funds rather than for their mountaineering skills. The weakest climber of these was Dudley Wolfe, described in Curran's account as a rich playboy who was "enthusiastic but almost totally without ability" (82–3). He has been described as overweight, and he depended heavily on guides to get him up and down mountain peaks safely, although evidence suggests that he was not as unfit as his surviving teammates led others to believe (Jordan 2010, 279–80). It is inarguable that Wolfe was devoted to Wiessner and desperate to prove himself as a climber.

The team ran into difficulties soon after they approached the Baltoro glacier. One of the team members, Chappel Cranmer, was frozen badly because he spent hours searching for a tarpaulin in a crevasse. Later, he collapsed from what would today be diagnosed as pulmonary edema, a condition resulting from too much exposure at high altitude. Pulmonary edema creates flu-like symptoms that will be fatal unless the person who is suffering from the condition descends immediately. Cranmer recovered but could not be part of the ascent team for K2. Down to five Americans with some Sherpa support, Wiessner pushed on, putting up ropes and searching for a good route to the top of the Abruzzi Spur, a ridge that almost leads to the summit cone and that has been established as the easiest ascent route (as much as this is possible on K2). Wiessner became so obsessed with this activity that he did not notice the rest of his team falling apart in the camps below him. Dudley Wolfe and Jack Durrance, an experienced mountain guide who endured endless criticism from his leader while he worried about Wolfe's ability to continue on, stayed with Wiessner, but relations between the expedition leader and Durrance became strained. Wiessner and Wolfe would not listen to Durrance's entreaties, partly because not as much was known about high-altitude acclimatization as it is today, and so Wolfe continued to slowly climb. Durrance felt too ill to continue and went back down the mountain to Camp II, leaving Wiessner, the Sherpa Pasang Lama, and Wolfe (Curran [1994] 1995, 84–6).

These three established a series of high camps, leaving Wolfe high on K2 in Camp VIII so that Wiessner and Pasang Lama could try for the summit. After a difficult rock climb that has never been attempted again, Pasang Lama and Wiessner could see a clear path to the summit. Wiessner was tempted to unrope and go on alone because Pasang Lama felt that it was too dangerous to continue, but eventually Pasang Lama was able to convince Wiessner not to try for the summit. They climbed down to Camp VIII, thinking to get supplies and other Sherpas for another summit attempt. To their surprise, they found Wolfe there, but he had run out of matches so that he could not cook or melt snow. They went to Camp VII to get supplies, but Wolfe fell on the way, and they almost were pulled off the mountain. Wolfe lost his sleeping bag, and Wiessner had left his at Camp VIII, thinking that he would return the same day. When they reached Camp VII, it had been abandoned: there were no sleeping bags, and the tents were full of snow. Wiessner decided to leave Wolfe there (claiming later that Wolfe wanted to make another attempt at the summit) and climbed down to the next camp with Pasang. But that camp, and the next three, were also abandoned. After a bad night at

Camp II without any supplies, Wiessner and Pasang made it back to Base Camp. Wiessner was enraged when he arrived (86–90). Wolfe was still very high on the mountain, with no food, no way to melt snow for water and not even a sleeping bag to keep himself warm. Today, this would be a death sentence for any mountaineer at high altitudes, and probably no rescue attempt would be made. But three brave Sherpas, Pasang Kikuli, Phinsoo, and Tsering Norbu, decided to climb up to Wolfe and try to save him. They made it to Camp VI in one day, which is an almost super-human feat of climbing in itself. They discovered Wolfe at Camp VII the next day, but he was near death. Wolfe refused to descend with them and asked them to come back the following day. At this time, Sherpas were still accustomed to following orders from their employers, and so they obeyed Wolfe. Two days later, after a storm, they set out to find Wolfe, but they were never heard from again after their morning radio transmission. After a week in the Death Zone, Dudley Wolfe must have died, his body swept off the mountain in one of K2's notorious storms (90). In 2002, his remains were found in the glacier that runs to the Base Camp area of K2 (Jordan 2010, 17–18). Houston's 1953 expedition did find the last camp of the Sherpas, but no bodies were there. The remains of the three rescuers were finally found on the same glacier above Base Camp in 1995 (Curran [1995] 1996, 103). A combination of poor planning, hubris, bad luck, and even bravery had led to Wolfe's terrible suffering, and to the demise of all four climbers, who were the first fatalities in the climbing history of K2 (Jordan 2010).

Accusations began when the remnants of the team returned to the United States. Wiessner accused Durrance of deliberately stripping the camps in order to deny his leader the summit and ensure that the higher climbers would not survive. (It is now known that Wiessner was wrong and another team member ordered the camps to be stripped.) For his part, Durrance blamed Wiessner for poor leadership and said that Wolfe's death was Wiessner's fault. The AAC conducted an enquiry and blamed Wiessner's "Teutonic" leadership style for the tragedy, perhaps because as a German, Wiessner was open to American suspicion at the outset of the Second World War. Wiessner was so angry that he resigned from the AAC. Years later, new information and a reconsideration of evidence led to Wiessner's reinstatement (Viesturs 2009, 174–80).

Unlike Houston's expedition, the 1939 expedition was never seen as successful. It has been viewed as a tragic interlude, and a monument to excessive ambition and a lack of teamwork. It is often contrasted unfavourably with Houston's expeditions, which precede and follow it. It is, however, important to note that Wiessner's expedition does serve as a reminder of a different kind of mountain masculinity than Houston's, one that depended much more on individual achievement, pride, and strength, as well as the hierarchical style that comes with siege leadership, the obedience that Sherpas still gave to their foreign "masters" at the time, and the idea of imperial adventure – with its associated belief in the power of amateur endeavour borrowed from the British – which meant that Dudley Wolfe not only came on the expedition in the first place, but also that he climbed far higher than he should have. Rightly or wrongly, the 1939 expedition became known as the opposite of what mountaineering's highest ideals were about: not "the brotherhood of the rope," but self-interest, group feuding, and poor leadership, with tragic results.

The highest ideals and accolades for expedition accounts are reserved for Charlie Houston's 1953 attempt. *K2: The Savage Mountain*, a relatively short expedition account by different members of the 1953 American expedition, contains within its pages a clear delineation of ideal masculinity for climbers, and it is set during a time when climbing was less commercialized, and more nationalist, than it is today. Its description of Art Gilkey's condition, the attempt to rescue him, and the resulting tragic accident provide the testing ground for brotherhood that the team, admirably, passes. This takes place with a spectacular setting as a backdrop, some Orientalist descriptions of the local people of Kashmir, and a ringing endorsement of Sherpa courage and ability. In this account, at least, the brotherhood of the rope is extended beyond the American climbing team to everyone, Sherpa or Pakistani, in the expedition, because of the values of alpine style leadership that Houston and others worked hard to maintain. In this way, *K2: The Savage Mountain* represents an early account of transnational masculinity, a brotherhood brought together by tragic circumstances. It has proved compelling for generations of climbers and armchair climbers. As Jim Curran says in *K2*: "the 1953 American K2 expedition became a symbol of all that is best in mountaineering. Today the team are still united in friendship and their shared ordeal brought them a depth of understanding and insight" (Curran [1994] 1995, 103).

K2: The Savage Mountain is a narrative about the climb, a report on the expedition, and a climbing history of K2 itself. But it is also a record of the teamwork the Americans practised on the mountain: although Houston wanted to write most of the book himself, in the end chapters are by various members of the team, with lists of food supplies, transportation details, a financial statement, and a medical report placed at the end. After a history chapter, Robert H. Bates describes the selection process for the expedition. Houston and Bates, who were the only members of the 1939 expedition who were also on the 1953 team, decided that climbers had to have expedition experience, technical ability, and good general mountaineering skills. These abilities were necessary partly because the team could not take Sherpas along to assist with preparing ropes and making camps, because of conflict between India and Pakistan, and so they decided to use as porters Hunzas – men who were from northern Pakistan. The Hunzas were strong porters, but they did not have the experience of high-altitude climbing that Sherpas had, and so Houston and Bates knew that they had to choose climbers who could carry their own loads up high, and do the camp jobs and rope-fixing jobs Sherpas usually performed (Houston and Bates [1954] 2009, 17).

Therefore, Bates and Houston also looked for people who were, in today's language, team players. Here is where the ideology of the expedition becomes apparent. Members of this team had to "act cohesively, and there is no place for the brilliant climber who thinks only in terms of success" (16). The climber therefore had to have "that indefinable quality *good personality*, and be able to keep his good nature and add to the humor of the party when bad weather, danger, or hardships strain nerves" (16). These twin ideals, selflessness and cheerfulness, were the hallmarks of a certain type of climbing masculinity of the era. As I discuss in the chapter about Annapurna, the capacity to be selfless, to work as hard as a Sherpa, and to remain cheerful at all times were vital to the prevailing siege style of the era. Siege style required strong leadership, but it also required that many of the climbers on an expedition would work for the good of the team and carry many loads to stock camps, even if these climbers would never have a chance to see the summit. Since siege style developed from military campaigns and depended on vast quantities of equipment, it usually featured hierarchical leadership and a colonialist attitude towards the hundreds of Sherpas and other local people working as porters, required to carry loads to Base Camp and sometimes beyond it. But in the case of the 1953 American expedition, the lack of Sherpa support meant that higher on the mountain, the slow, steady, militaristic pace of siege style would have to be foregone for a lighter, more team-based approach. Therefore, Bates and Houston required men who were tough enough and selfless enough to do load carrying as a team, with the kind of good humour and cheer associated (often inaccurately or without much understanding of their motivations) with Sherpa men (Ortner 1999, 67–9). They would also be expected to make decisions without looking to a single leader to settle disputes when they were high on the mountain. This why Jim Wickwire points out that the expedition "was carried off in the finest style" (Houston and Bates [1954] 2009, xi), where "style" refers both to the lightweight nature of the expedition, and to the conduct of the team members. Since climbing style contains within it social and ethical assumptions about what kind of man is climbing, the decision by the American expedition to create an egalitarian team re-sulted in the kind of masculinity encouraged in the Boy Scouts organiz-ation: to be a man on this team is to be sacrificial, tough, and cheerful. In order to create this team, Houston and Bates minimized conflict by choosing men from similar backgrounds, as Houston had in 1939. Most of the team members were academics, scientists, or professionals. Their transport officer and Base Camp manager, Captain Tony Streather, did not share this background, but he proved to be a strong climber as well. The team also had a Pakistani member, as was required by law, Colonel Atta-Ullah, who also functioned as a full member of the group and who shared their beliefs about the style of the climb. The result was a remark-ably cohesive and dynamic team: the shared values of these climbers contributed to saving their lives on K2.

From its beginning in the lowlands of Pakistan, the expedition forged a nationalist bond between the United States and Pakistan, then a rela-tively new country formed from the Partition of 1949. As Robert Craig recalls, "one of Houston's principal hopes for this expedition was that it should form friendship between Pakistan and America by showing that young country how similar its people are to our own in ambitions, ideals and abilities. We wanted Pakistan to share in our attempt to climb its highest mountain" (26). This rather grand hope of the American team elicited a positive response in Pakistan in a way that would be unimaginable today. Before the climb began, the expedition team was kept busy meeting Colonel Atta's friends, as well as Pakistani leaders. They even met soldiers in the Pakistani army. When they disembarked from a plane that took them to Skardu, the town closest to K2, they were greeted by school children, who cheered, threw flowers, and waved banners urging the climbers to use their influence with the United Nations to hold a plebiscite for Kashmir. Other banners simply welcomed the team to Pakistan. Crowds cheered *"Pakistan zindabad! American zindabad* (Long live Pakistan! Long live America!)" (29). After this welcome, the team met their Hunza porters and began the weeks-long march up to the Baltoro Glacier, and then to K2. As in 1938, the journey is described as a "fantasy," with awe-inspiring landscapes and descriptions of life untouched by civilization (32). But this trip also emphasizes brotherhood almost immediately because "there is a kind of magic which sometimes kindles when men are joined together in a common effort" (32). It is an apolitical brotherhood: immediately after Craig describes the "magic" of being with other men, he says that Balti porters do not just climb for the money alone, but also want to share in the romance of the expedition, a statement that is contradicted a page later with descriptions of "crafty porters" who try to misrepresent their loads, or "laggards" among the Balti porters who have to be encouraged to keep walking (32–3). Balti porters are also described as "itchy-fingered" thieves who are with the team out of curiosity: they do not participate in the ideology of brotherhood as the Hunza porters do (40). In contrast to this, the team's building of a bond is described in rapturous, idealized terms which prefigure the idea of the brotherhood of the rope:

"As we approached our mountain, the magic cement that binds men together, the qualities which make unbreakable friendships began to form. Unconsciously, and imperceptibly, we were forming a team. If we had not it is probable that most of us would not have survived the troubles that we were to face. Perhaps it is these bonds, formed of success and failure, that make mountaineering expeditions – like all ventures of man into the heart of nature – such a rich, emotional experience" (33).

Here is the clearest description yet of the feeling of brotherhood as an unarticulated affective bond that seems unconscious and even magical.

Craig links this directly to mountaineering and other kinds of wilderness adventures, making them the place where men can form homosocial relationships with other men, relationships which can potentially save their lives. Since most expeditions to K2 before and after this one did not experience this kind of bonding, it is hardly the kind of natural event that Craig imagines it to be. The team culture and its early homogeneity are the early framework for creating this kind of romantic feeling the team members have for the mountains and for each other. When the Hunza porters reach their destination and leave the expedition at Base Camp, they are described as "a real part of the team" and the parting is sad, with many cheers of *American zindabad! Pakistan zindabad* (62–3).

The remaining climbers quickly begin to establish camps on K2 on the Abruzzi Route. They work well together until they are stopped by a storm at Camp VIII at about 24,000 feet. As they wait for the weather to clear, they vote by secret ballot for who would be the two men on the summit team because, as Houston writes, "the philosophy of our expedition had avoided one-man decisions, and I was reluctant to choose by myself the men who might have the great chance for the crowning effort" (80). The vote is another indicator of selflessness, since no climber would want to be denied the chance to summit after months of hard work. But even in making this difficult decision, the expedition remains a team which even wanted to make the summit itself a team effort, "for one of our cherished hopes was to preserve the anonymity of the summit pair ... we hoped to report 'Two men reached the top' – no more, no less" (80). After ten days at this camp however, the team's hopes of making the summit diminished. They began to feel hunger and thirst as the storm threatened to destroy their tents, but their cheerfulness remained; Houston radioed to Colonel Atta at Base Camp that morale remained high, even in their worsening situation (82).

Finally, expedition member Art Gilkey developed blood clots in his legs and could no longer walk. Here is where the test of brotherhood begins: the team members immediately abandoned their plans for the summit without a (recorded) qualm, and planned how to bring Gilkey down to Base Camp. The difficulty of the route they had to take meant, as Houston points out, that most likely Gilkey "would never reach Base Camp alive" (84). But the team appeared to immediately decide to rescue Gilkey anyway because "we could try, and we must" (85). This is the core belief of the brotherhood of the rope, that the team must abandon their dream of summiting and band together to save one of its stricken members, much as soldiers band together to save one of their own during a battle. The essence of this ideal is that a man cannot be left to die on the mountain. The reality of high-altitude mountaineering is that when climbers are injured high on a climb, rescue is usually impossible, and dangerous for the rescuers themselves. Nonetheless, the team members agreed once again to be selfless and heroic after several days of discussion because they were "faced with Gilkey's helplessness ... we realized that we *had* to get him down. We didn't know how but we knew that we had to do it" (91). And so, they began to lower Gilkey, wrapped in a sleeping bag and a tent, down dangerous rock and ice cliffs during a storm. Gilkey remained cheerful, uncomplaining, and brave because "he knew also that we would never leave him" (93). At first, the lowering was successful. But at a critical moment, when the team positioned itself across a 45-degree ice face and prepared to drag Gilkey across to the site of Camp VII, one of the climbers fell. Pulling his climbing partner with him, his rope snarled into another climbing rope. All four climbers were swept off the slope, but were stopped by an ice axe belay (where the ice axe acts as an anchor in the snow) that Pete Schoening held behind a large rock for safety. Gilkey and the other four men were held on a single rope in what is the greatest ice axe belay in the recorded history of mountaineering. The four climbers righted themselves and struggled up the slope, while Schoening still held Gilkey. Houston had a concussion and did not know where he was: several climbers were suffering from minor injuries. The team hung Gilkey's litter by two ice axes and then went to set up tents, promising to come back for Gilkey in a few minutes. But when they were gone, they heard Gilkey cry out. Upon returning, they found nothing: an avalanche or rockfall had torn him off the slope. The rescue had failed.

But, as Reinhold Messner says in the epigraph to this chapter, the rescue attempt is widely regarded as a beautiful failure. The team members had done as much as they possibly could to rescue Art Gilkey, and they had done it as a group. They had narrowly escaped an even greater disaster during their heroic attempt. The ideology of the brotherhood of the rope had found its highest possible expression and the source of its greatest and most impossible idealism. As Ed Viesturs writes more than fifty years after Houston's expedition, the ideal of the brotherhood of the rope contained in the account of this failed rescue remains inspirational to climbers because the phrase has material force with residual effects: "'The brotherhood of the rope' that Houston celebrates was no sentimental invention – it was the lifelong bond that their terrible ordeal on K2 forged among its seven survivors. The book affected me hugely" (Viesturs 2009, 226).

The rest of the team made it back safely to Base Camp, where they experienced one more dimension of the ideal of brotherhood. The Hunza porters, who returned to Base Camp to help with carrying loads back to Skardu, greeted them joyfully. Three Hunzas, Ghulam, Vilyati, and Hidayat, climbed up to the team while they were still descending and gave them "an uninhibited heart-to-heart embrace" (Houston and Bates [1953] 2009, 123). In camp, the Hunzas cooked for the team and massaged their tired muscles. For Robert Bates, this calls up a moment of pure connection between the Hunzas, the team, and the community of climber/readers: "At that heartwarming moment differences of race and language meant nothing. We and the Hunzas by the light of a flickering flare shared a great emotional experience as we talked and talked. Those who also have faced hardship and danger can appreciate our emotions and the bond between us all as we lay there" (124).

This is the extension of the brotherhood of the rope from the team to others who can understand. Although the Hunzas are still presented as devoted servants here, brotherhood is represented as a communication that supersedes language and other differences because of the emotional intensity of the events they experienced. Bates says that others who have been through similar hardships will also instinctively understand this connection. Here, unlike what Slemon says, is a picture of brotherhood that includes rather than excludes, although it still sets to one side differences in power and position. The condition of membership is the survival of a trauma, and – at least temporarily – differences in culture and social standing do not matter. It is still, however, an intensely gendered moment. Because they are servants, the Hunzas do what would have been seen by the climbing team as traditionally feminine tasks such as massage and cooking. Some of them enthusiastically embrace the team members in a show of emotion that is not coded as masculine. It is possible that the Hunzas here are pictured as feminized in an Orientalist tradition. But the insistence of Bates on the similarity between the climbers and the Hunzas in that moment can also be read as an act of incorporation, where feminine qualities such as displays of affection and intimacy can be felt between men. No women are actually required to be present. As is the case in the tearful descent of Maurice Herzog from Annapurna, the brotherhood of the rope allows this incorporation to take place, and for men to act in an unmasculine way, but in the service of an even more heroic masculinity. On K2 in 1953, this resulted in the recognition that it was *the rope* that symbolized the coalescing of these values. In other words, discourses of affect not allowed these men congealed around the idea of rope itself and made the experience intensely homosocial: "The terrible days of storm, struggle, and death high on K2 had welded us together with a bond which was hard at the time to appreciate ... when men climb on a great mountain together, the rope between them is more than a mere physical aid to the ascent; it is a symbol of the spirit of the enterprise. It is a symbol of men banded together in a common effort of will and strength – not against this or that imagined foeman of the instant, but against their only true enemies: inertia, cowardice, greed, ignorance, and all weaknesses of the spirit" (136).

It was only in retrospect, Bates goes on to say, that the ideals of the brotherhood of the rope began to take on this quality. But clearly, the rope itself was transformed in the thinking of these men as the means of realizing the very highest of ideals, and to realize them *as men*, all without ever saying that the basis for this heroism is so intensely homosocial. With this ideal firmly established, in true Romantic fashion, it remained an impossible yet tantalizing dream. Houston himself felt very guilty about letting Gilkey die. He suffered from depression and saw visions of Gilkey's blood (something that – along with pieces of rope and clothing – all team members saw as they descended the mountain, but they did not speak about this for decades) because of his experiences on K2 (McDonald 2007, 138).

No other expedition on K2 could ever hope to achieve the heights of heroism that the 1953 American expedition did. When K2 was finally summited the next year by an Italian team, Houston was struck by "global amnesia," and he wandered into a hospital with no idea who he was. The amnesia was brought on by his distress at hearing that the Italians had summited, when he had planned to lead a third American expedition to the peak for the summit attempt denied the team in 1953

(McDonald 2007, 13). The Italian expedition itself was marked by accusations of foul play by team members. The official accounts of the expedition claimed that the summit team of Compagnoni and Lacedelli had summited without oxygen because Walter Bonatti, the most talented climber on the team, had sabotaged their efforts and not supplied them with full oxygen canisters. Bonatti was also accused of being ambitious for the summit himself, and of climbing with his partner, Hunza climber and porter Amir Mehdi (called Mahdi in *The Mountains of My Life*) with a view to beating Compagnoni and Lacedelli to the summit.

The rather complex series of accusations began because Mehdi suffered from frostbite in his feet after he and Bonatti had been forced to spend a night below Camp IX, in the open above 8,000 metres, as they were trying to move oxygen canisters to the lead climbers. The Pakistani press published a complaint where Mehdi claimed that he had been told he would go to the summit, and that he had insufficient equipment, which is why his feet froze, causing a diplomatic incident between Italy and Pakistan. An inquiry was made, and Compagnoni was cleared (Bonatti [1998] 2010, 318–19) but accusations about Bonatti circulated in the climbing community, eventually driving Bonatti into a solo climbing career. In 1966, Bonatti sued for libel in response to a newspaper article claiming that he had tried to sabotage the climb; Mehdi testified, but as Bonatti observed and Mehdi's son later corroborated, Mehdi did not speak Italian well and could not read or write, and so he did not understand how his testimony was used against his climbing partner (Bonatti [1998] 2020, 341–2; Jillani 2014). As Robert Marshall has pointed out in an assessment included in *The Mountains of My Life*, Mehdi was treated as a servant, not as a fellow climber, by all members of the Italian team, including Bonatti, compounding the problems with cultural and linguistic barriers and misunderstandings that already existed (Marshall in Bonatti [1998] 2010, 365). Bonatti eventually won the suit, but then faced public accusations from his former climbing partners in 1984 that he had purposely sabotaged the summit team's chances of success. By 1994, photographic evidence proved that Compagnoni and Lacedelli had used oxygen on the summit, and had not summited K2 without oxygen as they had claimed. What is more, Bonatti did not deliberately supply them with low tanks as a way to ensure that they could not summit (Bonatti [1998] 2010, 379–85). After enduring years of accusations in the press and the inaccurate findings of a public enquiry, Bonatti was finally exonerated: Robert Marshall in *K2: Lies and Treachery* (2009) proved that he had been unjustly accused of sabotage, and that the summit team, and the climbing team leader Ardito Desio, had falsely accused Bonatti in order to make their achievements seem more significant. As early as 1954, the idea of brotherhood in mountaineering was already proving to be hard to sustain, particularly on K2 where it began.

The Rope Frays: Sexism and the Expeditions of 1978 and 1986

Even Charlie Houston, a climber who has never given up on the ideals of brotherhood, has suffered as he found that he could not realize his own dreams. After the 1950s, those dreams of brotherhood became increasingly hard for anyone to realize. As I discussed in the introduction, high-altitude mountaineering in the Himalayas and the Karakoram underwent changes after the "golden era" of the 1950s, when all the major ascents of 8,000-metre peaks had been made. Equipment and access to the mountains improved, which meant that mountaineering was no longer reserved just for the members of elite climbing clubs. More and more climbers were middle-class or even working-class people from Britain, Western Europe, Japan, or North America. They did not begin their climbing lives as soldiers who hoped to escape the devastation of the Second World War, but were instead people influenced by the counter-cultural and political movements of the 1960s. The North Americans among them sometimes began their climbing careers as "dirtbag" sport climbers or alpine specialists who lived meagrely while they climbed new lines on El Capitan or the difficult winter lines of the American and Canadian Rockies. The European and British climbers climbed local crags, went to the Alps or were ski and climbing guides in order to support their climbing careers. As a youth subculture began to develop in Kathmandu, Nepal, these climbers developed new ways of climbing the world's highest mountains, which featured similar beliefs to other young people who were joining the counter-culture, particularly with regards to freedom, individuality, and collective decision-making. As I have discussed in previous chapters, these ways to climb became known as the "alpine style," which featured small teams of climbers with little or no Sherpa or porter support, team members who made decisions together. Climbers like Reinhold Messner proved that it was even possible to climb Everest quickly and without oxygen as part of alpine style, while the efforts of Chris Bonington and his team on Annapurna inspired other climbers to begin to climb far more difficult routes in as light and fast a style as possible.

The advent of the better equipment and the ideals of alpine style from the 1960s to the 1980s also meant that there was a significant change in the mountaineering community culture at the same time. Sherpa climbers and high-altitude porters became more skilful and professionalized, resulting in changes to their work in the mountains. And climbing teams – particularly during the 1970s – began to include women. As we saw in the case of the American women's team and their ascent of Annapurna in 1978, developing feminist movements in some countries meant that the wives of some male climbers began to participate in climbing expeditions, and that other women began climbing in the belief that climbing was open to women. But many of these female climbers, despite the changes wrought by the advent of alpine style, were not received into the climbing community as equals. As Arlene Blum has said in her memoir *Breaking Trail*, she was barred from joining an expedition to Denali in 1969 because it was assumed that a woman would "adversely affect the 'camaraderie of the heights'" and women were thought to be too weak to do the hard work of climbing and carrying loads (2005, 54–7).

One response to the sexism of high-altitude mountaineering in the 1960s was to abandon the ideals of the brotherhood of the rope altogether and to recreate Miriam Underhill's style of "manless climbs" as a gesture of necessary separatism. Wanda Rutkiewicz's all-female climbs in the Himalayas, the Japanese all-female climb of Mount Everest in 1975 that made Junko Tabei the first woman to summit that mountain, and the all-female team on Annapurna in 1978 are example of such responses. Another response was to include women on mixed teams, an experience which was so negative for some women that – in the case of Blum and Rutkiewicz –they were not part of mixed teams for some years. On K2, women were part of climbing parties beginning with the American ascent of K2 in 1975. Their reception, recorded in some landmark narratives from 1975 onwards, indicates how threatening the presence of climbing women could be to the ideal of the brotherhood of the rope. And it shows how the brotherhood of the rope persisted in attempts to protect it from the "invasion" of unwanted others, even when that ideal appears to have been superseded (in theory) by the more egalitarian and freewheeling alpine style of climbing. Alpine style did not guarantee equality for team members, and especially not in the case of women on K2, for decades after the Golden Age of first ascents.

As Ed Viesturs has observed, the transition to alpine style within the rigours of siege style on K2 also had an effect on the kind of climbing narrative that was produced. Unlike earlier exploration narratives that did not discuss team conflicts or individual ambitions, "With the counterculture revolution of the late 1960s and the 1970s came a new trend in expedition literature. In the new narratives, the dirty laundry was not only brought out of the closet, it was put on prominent display" (Viesturs and Roberts 2009, 40). What Viesturs calls "dirty laundry" includes struggles about team dynamics and, as part of that struggle, the place of women on the mountain and the kind of work expected of them. Galen Rowell's *In the Throne Room of the Mountain Gods*, about the 1975 American expedition to K2, had already recounted the struggles of that team, whose bitter feuding contributed to their failure to summit. Rick Ridgeway's *The Last Steps*, the expedition account of the 1978 American expedition to K2 led by Jim Whittaker, provides a similarly detailed look at team dynamics, and particularly of the problems that women on the team faced.

The team assembled for the 1978 K2 expedition included some of the best climbers in the United States. Whittaker had been the first American man to summit Everest, and other male members of the team had extensive climbing credentials on technical rock and ice and on 8,000-metre peaks (Ridgeway 1999, 8–9). There were also three women on the team, all of whom were married to other expedition members: Cheri Bech, who had climbed high on the peak Daulagiri with her husband Terry Bech, Dianne Roberts, the wife of Jim Whittaker who had reached 22,000 feet on K2 in 1975 and was on the 1978 expedition as a photographer, and Diana Jagersky, a non-climber who was the Base Camp manager. Jagersky was not meant to be on the expedition. Her husband Dusan Jagersky was, with his climbing partner Al Givler, supposed to be part of the team. But Dusan and Al died tragically in a climbing accident just before the expedition began. After some deliberation, the team asked Diana to be their manager (36–7). The conflicts on the team were never about Jagersky, who did not go high on K2 and whose authority was not questioned. Bech and Roberts became the focus of intense conflict about what the role of female climbers should be on K2, or any other mountain, even though Roberts herself had asked for more women to be included on the team in an attempt to avoid this kind of behaviour (Jordan 2005, 10).

Roberts had already been the target of sexist beliefs about her ability to climb during Jim Whittaker's 1975 K2 expedition. Roberts was the first woman to ever be at the foot of K2, and she was on the team because Whittaker believed that she would be an excellent climber. She was: she carried loads and prepared camps like other climbers and, as I mention above, got to 22,000 feet on the mountain, but some members of her team thought that she should not be there because she did not have their experience. They also thought that women were either physically incapable of climbing high or that they were sexual distractions from the task at hand (9). In an interview for Jordan's film *Women of K2*, Roberts and Whittaker affirm that these things were said of Roberts, while another climber interviewed for the film, Theo Kreiser, says that he thinks women are a distraction for male climbers on a team (2003). This attitude shows directly that the mere presence of women is a threat to the brotherhood of the rope, even during a period when the alpine style of climbing and leadership was beginning to make climbing more egalitarian and less militaristic in style. The power of this trope ensured that the fragile community it celebrated was to be regarded as always already frayed and constructed by homoerotic as well as homosocial bonds. If women, even a woman as happily married as Roberts was, were nothing but sexual objects who "distract" men, what in fact were they distracting male climbers from? Were they preventing men from being heroic climbers, or were they preventing them from having relationships with each other? In a scene which is the epigraph to this chapter that Ridgeway recounts as evidence that he grew to be John Roskelley's friend, Roskelley even "apologizes" for not being a woman while they are storm-bound in a tent. Presumably, Roskelley is apologizing humorously for not being able to have sex with Ridgeway because they must share a tiny tent together and they have nothing to do but wait for the storm to subside. The storm causes them to become intimate, but as straight men, they cannot express this intimacy other than by joking about it. This episode is clearly homosocial and even homoerotic: Roskelley (as he often does in the book) is giving voice to a desire they both have. But neither of them can act upon it: the trope of brotherhood both enables and frustrates what male climbers can feel for each other. It is this delicate balance that the presence of women who want to be regarded as teammates, not as sexual objects, threatens. Ridgeway's account of the troubled 1978 K2 expedition directly and indirectly explores the assumptions many of the male climbers had at the time about women as climbers and expedition partners, and also about how they felt about each other.

Even during the trek into K2, team dynamics were unsettled, despite the fact that the climbers had agreed to work together because "we all realized that, on big climbs, the glory usually goes to the few who make the summit, while those who work hard to put them there go unnoticed" (Ridgeway 1999, 27). This team pledged to work through their differences with open communication and to respect Jim Whittaker as a leader. They agreed to try to respect the commitment of a combination of siege style and alpine style in the style of the 1953 K2 climb: that all members needed to work hard to get "someone" to the summit of K2 by carrying loads to camps established all the way up the mountain, but that decision-making would be shared. It was also decided that their leader, Jim Whittaker, would decide summit teams based on the strength of the load carriers (131). But the gender politics of the climb itself caused these goals to be altered. During the trek on the Baltoro Glacier, Bech fell into a crevasse and had trouble getting out. Only Chris Chandler, another climber, took the time to show Bech how to use jumars, devices that can help a climber ascend a rope. The others doubted her ability. When Bech carried a ninety-pound pack to help her husband Terry with his gear, instead of admiring her ability to do it, Ridgeway and Roskelley doubted her judgment because they thought that she would burn out. Others remained suspicious of her. Roskelley even said that "every time I go on one of these big climbs with women it's the same story ... I've seen them kill themselves trying to prove they are as strong as men ... people always criticize me for being down on women on expeditions, but I've never yet been on a big mountain with one that's worth a damn" (Ridgeway 1999, 87). Roskelley had in fact seen women die on a recent expedition, and he had decided that it was gender that had created the problem (87–8). Meanwhile, Chandler's kindness to Bech during this incident helped to forge their friendship, which became a romantic relationship on the mountain. The relationship was not problematic for Terry, Bech's husband, but it became intolerable for the rest of the team, presumably because women were seen as a "distraction" by some team members. Roskelley and others assumed that, as a man, Terry Bech *must* be jealous of another man's love for his wife – but in fact, he was not (109). The attitudes to women at the time supported the idea for some members of the team that a female presence created sexual tension, and that any efforts women made as climbers were somehow indications of their weakness as climbers, and their unsuitability for the work they were undertaking. The result, inevitably, was team fragmentation, as Ridgeway himself later admitted in the expedition account. Ridgeway's book provides a detailed picture of the dissolution of this team because of its gender politics.

As the gossip about Chandler and Bech grew, it began to affect the rest of the team. Decisions were made about Chandler's fitness for the summit group – without his approval. The assessments were based in part on his relationship with Bech. In the deliberations, Bech herself is treated as a lesser member of the team. At a number of points, Bech accuses other members of being "machos" and not giving her or Chandler enough credit as climbers (118, 130, 160, 162, 170). Eventually, these tensions and others meant that the team divided into two groups, the group which knew that its members could make the summit, and a support team which worked hard but gradually lost hope that its members could be chosen. Matters came to a head, and the decision was made to have two separate summit teams (184–5). In the end, no members of team B made the summit, and Chandler left the expedition early to avoid a fight with Roskelley (200). Bech climbed to Camp V, which was higher than any woman had ever climbed on K2 before, but exhausted, she could not continue (Jordan 2005, 12).

The presence of Roberts caused another rift. Early in the expedition, Roskelley, Ridgeway, and Lou Reichart (another climber) all agree that Roberts should not be allowed to climb higher than Camp III because they did not want to rescue her. In a meeting, Roskelley voiced this concern. Whittaker responded angrily: "'Look, dammit, Dianne came on this trip to climb as high as she can. She has worked as hard as anyone, deserves the chance to go, and I'm taking her across regardless of your opinion.'" "'I was under the impression Dianne was supposed to be the photographer on this trip, not a climber,' John fired back. 'Everybody here knows the only reason she's along is because she's your wife'" (Ridgeway 1999, 128).

Ridgeway analyzes this as stubbornness on Whittaker's part: "On all other points regarding strategy on the climb Jim had been flexible, listening to everyone's opinions, but when it came to Dianne he was intractable. Dianne herself knew she was the least experienced of us, but she felt she had worked as hard as anyone – if not harder – to make the dream of a K2 summit a reality: she had carried many loads to Camps I, II, and III and she felt she had earned the right to go as high as she could" (128).

But in fact, Whittaker's belief in Dianne as a climber turned out to be correct. Unlike many of the other members of the team, Roberts had experience climbing high on K2, and she carried many more loads than some of the other climbers. Even though she did not want to summit, she climbed more strongly than many of the male team members too, and her efforts did make the summit possible for others. In the end, her ability and efforts were recognized by other team members. When Dianne made a difficult traverse across a snow cliff during a storm to get to Camp IV, high on K2, one of her previous detractors said to Roskelley, "'You've got to admit ... Dianne made a very impressive performance. Believe me, it was rough out there. And she's not a very experienced climber.'" Roskelley grudgingly agrees, and says, "'she did a hell of job getting through that wind. She's got a lot of drive'" (Ridgeway 1999, 196). Earlier, Dianne's letters indicated how much pressure she felt from other team members who did not think that she had the strength or skill to climb; as she writes to her friends, "I guess being 'the wife of the leader' doesn't help much. I wish you two were here so I could talk to you. Can you read between the lines?" (140). Later, she writes about how she wishes she could wear an expensive dress and read an issue of *Vogue*, an indication that she would like to engage in feminine behaviour when it would not be seen as weak (187). Ridgeway highlights Roberts's achievement when he says that the climb gave her the strength to be a climber in her own right, and that she was proud of what she had done: she had carried a load to over 25,000 feet, which few people in the world had ever accomplished (290). The 1978 American expedition did put some of its members on the summit, ending the long struggle of American teams to climb K2. They were only the third expedition to summit the mountain in history. But the cost of the expedition was great: some of its members never reconciled, and the first team to have a significant amount of women on K2 saw this as a threat to the team's well-being rather than a strength. The ideal of brotherhood proved to be too difficult for the team to sustain, even as they sought to uphold it.

Eight years later, the 1986 climbing season on K2 would have many more female climbers, all of whom wanted to become the first woman to summit the mountain. In that intervening time, climbing itself had changed. Reinhold Messner's daring ascents of 8,000-metre peaks without oxygen, porters, or other supports had inspired other climbers to try to climb mountain faces in what he called a purer style. Now, in addition to well-funded large national teams still climbing siege style with fixed ropes, porters, and luxurious campsites, many climbing teams were smaller and composed of climbers from many nations who banded together so that each member could make the summit. These teams climbed as quickly as they could in alpine style, without using fixed ropes, hoping to ascend and descend without having to depend on emergency equipment. Small national teams such as these, particularly those from Poland, were also making their mark on the international climbing scene with their daring ascents in alpine style (McDonald 2011). It was still difficult to approach K2, but it had become easier: an airport had been built at Skardu, shortening the trek to K2 by a week. For the 1986 season, the Pakistani government had approved a record number of climbing permits for the mountain. As a result, there were more people in more teams clustered at the base of K2 than ever before: there were a total of nine permits, including a large South Korean team, a British team, a small team of crack Polish climbers hoping to climb the "Magic Line" (an unclimbed series of difficult ridges to the summit), an international team that included climbing legend and filmmaker Kurt Diemberger and his climbing/filming partner Julie Tullis, and a Polish women's team. Their numbers, and the decision by some teams to climb on unapproved routes without permits, helped to create what is now known as the 1986 K2 disaster.

That year, Wanda Rutkiewicz, one of the best high-altitude climbers in the world and the first Polish climber to summit Mount Everest, was seeking to become the first woman to climb K2. As I discussed in the first chapter, she was a feminist climber who, like Arlene Blum and other female climbers of her generation, had grown tired of the sexism she faced on mixed climbs. In several years, Rutkiewicz had made important ascents of other Himalayan peaks, including Gasherbrum III and Nanga Parbat, on all-female teams mostly composed of Polish climbers (McDonald 2011, 46, 113, 149–50). With Blum, she had planned the 1978 American-led expedition to Annapurna, although she could not go herself. She had even tried to climb K2 with other Poles, and then with an all-female team, although she herself could not climb on the latter expedition because she had broken her leg. This did not stop her from trekking to the peak on crutches and leading the climb from Base Camp on the Baltoro Glacier (125). Unfortunately, despite her dream of forging a team of Polish female climbers, Rutkiewicz's own ambitions and strong personality made her difficult to work with. As Blum observed later, what would be seen in male climbers as strength, heroism, and decisiveness as a Polish climber and leader, was seen as dogmatism and authoritarianism in Wanda because she was a woman: "It was a time when women were not supposed to be dominant, and [Wanda] was pretty dominant. My experience with people from the Eastern Bloc countries is that to get and do things you had to be a little stronger than the next person, and I'm sure she was ... She was probably so focused on her goals she probably didn't notice too much who was in the way. And that's not uncommon of guy climbers too, but I think when women exhibit those behaviors it draws more unfavourable attention than when guys do" (Jordan 2005, 32).

Wanda was not in fact different from other climbers of her time, most notably Reinhold Messner, arguably the most famous climber in the world, who was not known as a good group leader and who developed alpine style for 8,000-metre peaks partly because he did not want to deal with the problems of large expeditions. But expectations of Wanda were different. Already on Everest, she had openly said to her team that she was a feminist and meant to climb the mountain as they did, but she would not carry additional gear because she had a heavy camera: she felt that she was the target of sexist expectations when the men on the team insisted that she take the weight. She summited without the help of her team, and on returning to her tent, she discovered that her sleeping bag had been stolen – this was a potentially life-threatening prank. Kurt Diemberger saved her by offering her his bag (39–41).

In 1986, none of the other Polish climbers on the mountain asked her to be on their teams, and so she teamed up with a French team composed of Maurice and Lilliane Barrard, married climbers, and Michel Parmentier, a journalist who wanted to write about Lillian Barrard as the first woman on K2 and who took an instant dislike to his talented Polish climbing partner partly as a result (McDonald 2011, 194–6). Perhaps, as Polish climber Anna Czerwińska later said, Rutkiewicz chose this team because it was scheduled to ascend first, making it possible for her to be the first woman to summit K2 (194). The plan of the French team was to ascend quickly in alpine style, carrying small tents rather than establishing camps with supplies. They were the first team on the mountain and so could not use fixed ropes or other ways to make the route safe. On 18 June 1986, the team began to move up K2, climbing the Abruzzi Ridge, which by then had become the most common route up the mountain. All went according to plan for two days until a collapsed snow bridge caused a delay. At 7,900 metres, close to the Death Zone, they were forced to bivouac, and the next day they climbed unroped, bivouacking again at 8,300 metres. The altitude was beginning to have an effect on their strength, but the next day, Wanda Rutkiewicz became the first woman to summit K2. Hours later, moving slowly, Parmentier and the Barrards also summited. They spent a last, fatal night high on the mountain and then tried to descend. Parmentier suffered a fall in the Bottleneck, a narrow and steep ramp under a large serac, but he was uninjured and kept going. Rutkiewicz saw the Barrards moving above her and, on her own, she made her way down in a storm, camping at 7,700 metres. Later, she saw Parmentier, who urged her to go down but who later became delirious himself and had to be helped by other climbers. Rutkiewicz herself was rescued at lower elevations by members of a Polish team. But the Barrards were never seen again alive.

Meanwhile, Janusz Majer's Polish team (which included the other three female Polish climbers) was attempting the Magic Line along with two other teams and one solo climber. All teams gave up except for the Poles, who placed three men on the summit. But that team was forced to descend the Abruzzi route because the Magic Line was too difficult, and on the descent, one of the climbers fell off the end of a rope which had been cut by another climber. At the same time, Jurek and Tadek Piotrowski, two of Poland's best climbers who had joined an international team, tried to climb the difficult south face of K2. They ascended it but ran out of food and water and were forced to descend by the Abruzzi route as well, hoping that along the way they would find tents from other expeditions with food and stoves for melting snow. Tadek fell to his death on the descent, and Jurek barely survived (209–10, 212–13). Yet another climber died climbing down solo from the Magic Line. The remaining Polish climbers who were still trying to climb the Magic Line gave up at 8,200 metres, with the exception of Dobraslawa (nicknamed "Mrówka," the Ant) Miodowicz-Wolf, who decided to move to the Abruzzi Ridge with the British climber Alan Rouse, and continue her ascent (212).

With two deaths of American climbers in an avalanche earlier in the season, the death toll began to rise. But controversy about the way climbing was managed on K2 that year had not yet reached its peak. The seven members of the teams which had already abandoned the climbs specified on their climbing permits loosely joined forces and began to ascend along the Abruzzi route, with the help of the South Korean team's fixed lines. As they moved up the mountain with the South Korean team, they faced a major avalanche that destroyed some of the upper camps. Just as seriously, a storm was gathering. At the highest camp, the seven climbers saw the South Korean team summit with the help of oxygen on 3 August in good weather, but did not attempt the summit themselves, presumably because the camp was overcrowded and no one got much rest – none of the seven climbers were using oxygen, and all became overtired at that altitude (Diemberger [1989] 1991, 184–96). On 4 August, five of the seven climbers summited, including Tullis, who became the first English woman and the third woman to summit K2. Mrówka fell asleep just short of the summit. Alan Rouse convinced her to turn around, and they went back to high camp to rest. Julie Tullis fell while she was descending, but Diemberger caught her on their rope and she was saved. Nevertheless, they were forced to bivouac high on the mountain and arrived back at the high camp 5 August. The storm on K2 finally broke, and the climbers were forced to spend five more days at 7,900 metres, close to the Death Zone. It would be a death sentence for most of them, since human beings cannot live for long at that altitude. They ran out of food and the gas they needed to melt snow for water. Julie Tullis died on 8 August from exhaustion. On 10 August the storm subsided, but Alan Rouse became delirious and could no longer walk. At the urging of Mrówka, the other climbers decided to descend, leaving Rouse to die because they could do nothing for him. Two of the Austrians died just as they left the tents, leaving the last member of the Austrian team, Willi Braun, to descend with Mrówka and Diemberger. During their tortuous descent, Mrówka fell behind and she froze to death on the fixed ropes. Braun and Diemberger were rescued as they came lower, and made it to Base Camp, although both of them had frostbite and were almost unable to walk.

With the death of a porter in the South Korean expedition from rockfall, the total number of deaths on K2 in 1986 was thirteen, which more than doubled the number of deaths on the mountain in all preceding years. The analysis, and blame, began to surface in media accounts of the climb almost immediately, and within the controversy it is possible to see what the gender politics of climbing was in the mid-1980s, and how it played a role in the analysis of the disaster. Greg Child and Jon Krakauer, themselves well-known mountain climbers as well as mountain writers by that time, noted in their 1987 article for *Outside* magazine about the disaster that the decision of many climbers to climb in alpine style meant that, unlike the South Koreans who were disparaged by other climbers for their large expedition, there was little margin for error. Climbers did not have enough ropes, clothing, food, or tents to survive high on the mountain beyond a few days, and ironically, they were forced to use the ropes and tents of the South Korean and Basque teams (Child and Krakauer 1987). The Barrards, Parmentier, and Rutkiewicz spent too much time at high altitude, as did the seven climbers following the South Korean team. Their ability to make decisions and stay healthy became impaired as a result. There were also too many teams on the mountain, leading to overcrowding on the ropes and in the high camps. The daring descent of the Polish team from the Magic Line to the Abruzzi led to even greater crowding and stress, as they were forced to depend on the good will of others to survive (McDonald 2011, 214–15). Clearly, the risks of alpine style were very great, and they contributed to the disaster. As Rutkiewicz also recognized, many teams were not true teams, and she felt that the loyalty of climbers to each other disintegrated when disaster struck. She herself blamed Diemberger, the man who had saved her on Everest by lending her his sleeping bag, for not being able or willing to save Mrówka on the descent (215). She did not say this directly, but Rutkiewicz was in fact blaming the disintegration of the brotherhood of the rope, where a team tries to save its members at all costs, for the death of her friend and of others in 1986.

For their part, Diemberger and Braun blamed each other in their memoirs of the disaster: Braun because he said that Diemberger and Tullis should have sheltered the Austrian climbers at Camp IV when there were not enough tents for all climbers, and Diemberger because he felt that the overcrowding could have been avoided by the Austrians when they discovered that they had lost all their camps in an avalanche. Neither of them took responsibility for leaving Mrówka behind, although Diemberger said that the decision not to descend the day before the storm came was a grave mistake (Diemberger [1989] 1991, 184). According to Jim Curran's assessment of the disaster, the brotherhood of the rope (he makes the comparison directly) broke down in Camp IV, so that climbers did not, and then could not, take care of each other. In an interview printed in Jim Curran's *K2: Triumph and Tragedy* Willi Braun says that Mrówka did more than any other climber other than Rouse to save the climbers at Camp IV (Curran 1987, 190), but she was not rescued on the descent because both Braun and Diemberger were too ill to take care of her (204–5).

Curran also observes that there were climbers who were not "real" members of the brotherhood on the mountain. In a curious passage, Curran creates a gendered assessment of Tullis that is meant to call into question her fitness for high-altitude climbing, even as he acknowledges her strength and skill. Diemberger and Tullis were officially with an Italian expedition as the film crew, but as time went on, it was clear that they wanted to climb K2 as well. It would be their third attempt together: they referred to the mountain in mystical terms, calling it their "mountain of dreams." They were not, in other words, like any other team at K2, and other climbers were censorious. Recalling his meeting with Diemberger and Tullis, Curran describes her in this way: "[I] could never decide what to think of her. On one hand she was an apparently bright, attractive and apparently conventional housewife and mother from Tunbridge Wells ... on the other she was a rather bossy 'head-girl' who, through her devotion, almost amounting to hero-worship of Kurt, had come to see herself as a world-class mountaineer in her own right" (51).

Curran mentions that despite her two ascents of the 8,000-metre mountain Broad Peak, her attempt on Everest and two attempts on Nanga Parbat and K2, and despite the fact that she was "strong, fit and very determined, qualities that are as important as any in Himalayan climbing" (51), he feels that she climbs only because of her association with Diemberger, who he calls a mountaineering legend due to his extensive achievements on 8,000-metre peaks. He admits that he is perhaps envious of her and saw her as a rival because she was English, like himself. This is accurate: Tullis had as much or more high-altitude climbing experience than many other climbers in the 1980s. But she was an English woman who had not undergone the rites of passage involving suffering through winter ascents in Wales and Scotland which male British climbers had thought necessary. In Curran's eyes, perhaps she had "cheated," but because she was a filmmaker like him, it is also possible that he was envious of her success and her talent.

Beyond jealousy, however, Curran's assessment of Tullis is interesting for several reasons. He admits that she is a good climber, but he thinks that she is only good because she is associated with Diemberger, which is why he connects her devotion to a male climber as the sign of success, and not her talent or dedication. He belittles her by describing her as a "housewife" and a "head girl," gendered associations that render her childish, in charge in an unimportant way (like a head girl at an elementary or postsecondary school), and domestic at the same time. In his description, her regard for Diemberger approaches fan behaviour, and so it precludes the possibility that they had a true friendship or that she could be a climber on her own. He does not say that they had a romantic relationship, only that they were "a self-contained twosome and their films frequently seemed to be about each other" (52), although clearly, he finds their bond strange.

Ed Viesturs, who was not on K2 in 1986, goes beyond this assessment of Tullis and says "they were an odd pair, the subject of gossip all over the mountain" (Viesturs and Roberts 2009, 293), adding that it was not important whether or not they were lovers or if their spouses knew it, but that "whether the very emotionality of their relationship, like that newly formed between Rouse and Mrufka [sic], interfered with good judgement on this dangerous mountain" (294). Here, Viesturs's opinion resembles that of the 1978 American team members who saw the presence of women on the mountain as sexualized, and as an automatic threat to the brotherhood of the rope and the concentration on the task of climbing within that brotherhood. Rouse and Mrówka were in also in a relationship in 1986, but both had reputations as two of the strongest climbers in their respective countries with extensive high-altitude experience, and both were credited later by Diemberger and Braun for their heroism high on the mountain as they worked to save their teammates. Viesturs appears to be suspicious even of these two climbers, who were inarguably some of the best climbers in the world. This position of Viesturs's underscores his belief, against considerable evidence, that any emotional bond between men and women is bad for climbing, even as he credits climbing with forging strong relationships in the model of the brotherhood of the rope (226). In other words, Viesturs approves of homosocial relationships, but not heterosocial ones. The second is seen as a threat to the first.

What Curran and Viesturs did not realize, but perhaps were reacting to, was that Diemberger and Tullis had tied what they called the "endless knot" of their partnership into the brotherhood of the rope, disrupting the expectations for climbing men and women in the process. Tullis and Diemberger were an unlikely team, since they were older, climbed more slowly than most climbers, and because they appeared to have strong bonds which were not romantic in the conventional sense. They were passionate about the mountains they climbed but were not ambitious in terms of their climbing careers (Diemberger was already a legend in climbing circles anyway). Finally, they were regarded with some suspicion by other climbers because they appeared to be able to succeed *because* of their differences, not despite them. Unlike the American team of 1953, which worked well together because "brotherhood" is about shared beliefs and shared class, gender, and race identities, Tullis and Diemberger worked well together because they shared values but were not alike. Other climbers could not understand how this partnership could succeed and saw its implicit challenge to the brotherhood of the rope and its symbolic economy.

Tullis and Diemberger did understand their partnership in terms of rope, but they used a different metaphor to describe it. In *The Endless Knot*, Diemberger's memoir about K2 and his partnership with Tullis, the figure appears in a diagram as *plebe*, one of the eight auspicious symbols of Buddhism. It signifies the cycle of rebirth and also of life and love ([1989] 1991, 76). The Endless Knot symbolized their own partnership as the recognition and celebration of differences, and the belief they had in the mountain experience as a mystical act. Diemberger understands the differences between Tullis and himself in metaphorical terms, as the difference between mountain animals: "It took a while for us to come to a common understanding: Julie is as strong-willed as a snow leopard, and certainly has the endurance of a Sinkiang camel. For my own part, I can cope with being called the 'Ice Bear': I am every bit as persistent as she is, have equally strong convictions, can override any resistance on sheer obstinacy" (59).

These contrasts create conflict, which creates the metaphor of a knot that cannot be untied: "the result is a Gordian knot of some intricacy!" (59) but their optimistic attitude to life means that "we have always found a solution to the insoluble knot – a mutual comprehension … the intricately interwoven 'Endless Knot,' symbolizing the unity of all things and the illusory nature of time. It could be our sign" (60). Rather than pursuing the metaphor of the Gordian knot to its conclusion – the Gordian Knot is cut because it could not be untied – the solution for Tullis and Diemberger was to change the nature of the metaphor altogether, and to pursue a different path as they climbed. The Gordian Knot becomes the Endless Knot. Differences become the sign of interwoven unity, not a threat to unity. The brotherhood of the rope becomes a mystic symbol which is ungendered. This approach to their partnership and their climbing set Diemberger and Tullis apart, wherever they were. And, like their partnership, *The Endless Knot* also moves beyond common expectations for an expedition narrative. It is a richly illustrated coffee table book, a detailed account of the 1986 disaster with diagrams and charts, a moving tribute to Tullis, a memoir of Diemberger's own experiences on high mountains and, at times, a stream-of-consciousness account of the work of climbing. Before I discuss this unusual book further, it is necessary to discuss the life and background of Julie Tullis, the third woman and second English person to summit K2.

Curran's perplexity about Tullis indicates just how complex a person she was. She embraced domesticity and danger in equal parts, something unusual for female climbers at the time. Tullis combined a relatively conventional domestic life with a passion for filmmaking and mountain climbing, once she met her climbing partner. Even before she met Diemberger, Tullis was a risk-taker in her daily life in small ways (she was a reckless Vespa driver) but her life was defined by two things: her dedication to her husband and children, and her desire to climb difficult lines on the sandstone cliffs near the small town of Tunbridge Wells, in

England. Her husband, Terry Tullis, has said in an interview that "'she was a very normal lady. It [climbing mountains] was just this sort of aberration that she had'" (Jordan 2005, 150). In the 1960s, she and Terry ran a climbing shop and a café to support the family, and until Terry had a farming accident, both were avid climbers. Tullis was also a practitioner of *aikido*, a martial art which combined practices of meditation, strength, agility, and movement. In *The Endless Knot*, there is a photograph of Tullis doing aikido on a glacier as she holds a large, curved sword. It is a portrait of intense concentration: Tullis looks monumental, and calm. This is the side of Tullis that Diemberger noticed when he went on a British climbing trip and saw her climbing a cliff effortlessly: "Julie moved up the rock smoothly, each movement expressing strength and a joy of living, just as an animal in its element expresses itself in movement" (Diemberger [1989] 1991, 17). He was transfixed and suggested immediately to Tullis that she sail across the English Channel to France on a sailboat with him. Tullis declined, but at the urging of her husband Terry she did begin to work on films with Diemberger, and to arrange his lecture tours. Terry probably urged Tullis to work with Diemberger because of his fame in climbing circles. As I mentioned, Diemberger was (and is) a mountaineering legend. He is the only person living who has a first ascent on two 8,000-metre peaks, Broad Peak in 1957, and Dauligiri in 1960. He lost his climbing partner, Hermann Buhl (who pioneered the alpine style of climbing) on the mountain Chogolisa a few weeks after their ascent of Broad Peak (Jordan 2005, 105–7). In Tullis, he found someone who he said "had the courage and the desire to try almost anything. Often, she felt obliged to stay quietly at home because of her family, but not always" (21). Eventually, he asked her to come on a French expedition to Nanga Parbat, an 8,000-metre peak, to do the audio work for a film he was making. Although Tullis knew little about audio work, she agreed to go, and they became what they later claimed proudly was "the highest film team in the world" (44) as well as "the oldest couple climbing in the Himalayas" (48). Both Terry Tullis and Diemberger's wife Teresa had no difficulty with this partnership, and even encouraged it (42, 46–7).

Diemberger could not join the Nanga Parbat expedition until Base Camp, and so Tullis arranged to transport the equipment. According to Jennifer Jordan, she encountered a similar experience to that of Dianne Roberts: the men on the team resented her presence. Porters mocked her attempts to pee on the trail, and the expedition leader forced her to film the ritual slaughter of a goat. The other team members laughed at her revulsion as she did this. She was forced to move her tent needlessly when she was sick, and one of the team members told her that one of the Pakistani officials on the expedition wanted to fuck her, just to see what she would say. Julie was outraged, particularly when the team treated this as a joke (Jordan 2005, 108–10). Later, Diemberger admitted to Tullis that the expedition leader Pierre Mazeaud had not wanted women on the team because he said "they cause trouble. Especially if they are not married [to someone on the trip]" (111). This was Tullis's first experience of sexism on a high-altitude expedition, but it was not her last. Mazeaud did not allow Tullis to climb above 5,000 metres, even though Tullis had summited higher mountains than that in the Alps. This was "a bitter pill for Julie to swallow" (Diemberger [1989] 1991, 30–1). As other women had discovered before her, Tullis had to negotiate the prevailing belief that women were a burden on high altitude expeditions, and that they existed only as sexualized threats to the brotherhood of the rope. But unlike Rutkiewicz or Blum, Tullis did not stop climbing with men, partly because she thought that "all-women's" expeditions relied on male support anyway (Jordan 2005, 116). Instead, she created a partnership with Diemberger grounded in her abilities as a high-altitude filmmaker and sustained by the bond of the Endless Knot.

Tullis went with Diemberger to film the North Ridge of K2 in China in 1983, where she went to 7,000 metres. The following year, she went with Diemberger to film the 1984 expeditions to K2 again, but storms prevented them from climbing the mountain. Diemberger and Tullis decided to climb nearby Broad Peak instead. Tullis became the first British woman to ascend the peak, but on the way down, she and Diemberger were forced to bivouac, and they were caught in an avalanche. The climb made her into a celebrity in the United Kingdom, and it got her an invitation to climb Mount Everest in 1985. In a short space of time, Julie Tullis had gone from being a wife, mother and weekend climber to one of the best-known British climbers in the world (116–20). And then, she and Diemberger decided to go to a K2 a third and fateful time, to work for an Italian expedition in 1986 and to climb what both of them called their "dream mountain" (Diemberger [1989] 1991, 40–1).

The Endless Knot begins as what Diemberger calls "a promise" to Tullis to impart the experience of climbing the mountain and a promise to Tullis's friends and family to tell the story of her attempt to climb K2.

It is, as Diemberger says, a companion book to Tullis's posthumously published memoir, *Clouds from Both Sides* (vii–viii). This is also what makes the book unusual: Diemberger attempts to impart, sometimes in a stream-of-consciousness style, what climbing mountains feels like as a fulfilment of a promise to Tullis. But this promise is a promise to a dead climbing partner who will never receive it. This could very easily overwhelm the narrative and make Tullis heroic, but Diemberger manages to escape this by foregrounding the bodily experiences of climbing and writing as the records of suffering, struggle, and very often, spiritual insight. This is achieved by not leaving out failures in narration. In the section called "The Beginning," Diemberger records the fear of beginning as a material process fraught with difficulty. He mentions that "Julie and I wanted to write it together" (1) but now, he must write alone. His still-painful frostbitten hands mean that he must type with his thumb. He is distracted by builders on a roof outside. A neighbour mowing his lawn irritates him. The letter d on the keyboard gets stuck as he types the word "record" and so he includes this as "recordddddddddddddddddddd ddddddddddddddddddddddddddddddddddddd" (1). His attempts to record what he felt and what his partner, who now cannot represent herself, felt and experienced are literally stopped in the act of trying to record them. And yet, Diemberger records the stoppage as part of the process, and continues, even though the enlightenment he seeks is still interrupted by his irritation at the noises outside.

This kind of foregrounding of physical facts extends to descriptions of Tullis: Diemberger maintains a tension between seeing Tullis as heroic and seeing her as an ordinary person. When he meets her, Diemberger is "held spellbound by her dark eyes" and sees her as "a born explorer" (21). But when they are on their first trip to K2 overland on the Chinese side, he describes Tullis in less idealistic terms. After weeks of travel: "however much she might have longed to be slim, she wouldn't win any beauty contests now ... things like appearance matter very little. Helpfulness is so much more important. Regardless of what she looks like, Julie has lost none of her energy and strength, nor the resilience that I so much admire" (25). Later on, Tullis "mends" a pair of jeans with Pakistani Airlines stickers and jokingly, Diemberger says that "needlework is certainly not one of her strong points! On the other hand, [he admires] her organizational skills" (61). Again, Tullis does not perform tasks traditionally associated with being female, and Diemberger sees this as a sign both of her ordinariness and of her true strengths.

The stream-of-consciousness style of the beginning is replicated in Diemberger's description of the avalanche on Broad Peak, which would have killed them had they not been roped together. Rather than idealized descriptions of brotherhood, Diemberger depicts the accident through his own experiences at the time: "Everything is spinning: down is up, up is down; terrible forces against which all resistance is vain; they toss you, carry, twist you, crush out your breath ... your mouth is stuffed with snow ... you grab another gulp of air, and then you're sucked in again ... moving down Broad Peak ... remorselessly ... That's it ... the end ... I think, but ... no! Don't give up! A pause. Then the tug of the rope again, pulling, pulling ... more of this terrible tumbling ... Oh, Julie! You, too" (51).

The claustrophobic experience of the avalanche appears in the ellipses, which come when Diemberger cannot breathe. The rhythm of the passage is disjointed, replicating how it felt to be dragged down the mountain. Eventually, they stop and Diemberger can see Tullis's body, in another passage meant to represent the experience of finding one's climbing partner:

Julie!
Great God, let her be alive.
I yell: "Are you hurt?"
Seconds of eternity. Answer, please answer.
"I'm all right, but I can't move. Please help me get up."
Her voice. Alive. (51)

The lines read like poetry in their sparseness. There is dialogue, but also Diemberger's panicked internal monologue. The style of the passage is meant to make readers experience the scene as if they were there, rather than describe exactly what occurred. Tullis's version is also there, as she says to Diemberger, "'I couldn't see anything – my goggles were choked with snow. Then suddenly your voice asked if I was hurt, and I knew you were alive'" (52).

There is no heroism here, only survival, as Diemberger merely observes that the rope saved them (as it did not save his earlier climbing partner, Hermann Buhl, who fell to his death unroped in front of

Diemberger in 1957). Diemberger goes on to remember Buhl – the inventor of the lighter, faster alpine style and the only other person to have first ascents on two 8,ooo-metre mountains – and to recall how painful it was to witness his death. Therefore, the presence of the rope, which he calls "nothing short of a miracle," on this climb of Broad Peak is the occasion for a painful memory of a loss that might have been prevented: "And suppose we [Buhl and Diemberger] had been roped? Could I have held him, or would he have pulled me with him into the void?" (55). Here is the meaning of Diemberger's partnership with Tullis: she is the successor to Buhl, and through the rope, she provides Diemberger with the connection which was lacking. But the connection itself is not the signifier of brotherhood. Either the absence of a rope did not save Buhl, or the lack of a rope saved Diemberger from Buhl's fate. Because he does not know which would have been the case, the idea of the rope must symbolize the unknown, the future which cannot come to fruition. Diemberger does not subscribe to the brotherhood of the rope because of this ambiguity. The rope saves him and Tullis, but it does not always save. It makes him "grateful to the fate that has allowed Julie and [him] still to be here, sitting in the snow" (55), rather than proud of his heroism or paternalist towards Tullis. Diemberger and Tullis's refusal to participate in or resist the brotherhood of the rope discourse is, in fact, what causes both of them to exceed the limits that the discourse sets for them.

This is also why, in *The Endless Knot*, K2 holds such a mystical fascination for both climbers. When they see K2 from Broad Peak, they become entranced by it: "would we ever return? It was as if it held us in thrall: Mountain of mountains – yes, we are yours" (65). Diemberger includes an extract from his daughter Hildegard's diary about the mystical meaning of high mountains for the mountain people she studies as an anthropologist, where Anila, a Tibetan nun, teaches her about the power of the mountains and the need to climb them in an attitude of harmony and unification, not for money or fame: "the gap between 'I' and 'it,' between subject and object: it is unification, becoming one with the world, with the lover, with the mountain" (77–81). This becomes the reason Tullis and Diemberger climb K2 many times, because they seek this unification. But their third expedition brings this motivation into contrast and conflict with the motivations of others. Diemberger writes that at Base Camp in 1986, "the convivial picture on the moraine concealed deep division between opposing and conflicting styles of expedition" (85). Unlike most climbers, Diemberger sees that the differences in style signify differences in worldview, and that the result is a lack of community cohesion, and because consensus, rather than respect for differences, is used in order to solve problems (86, 94). The respect for difference that Tullis and Diemberger practise in their partnership, and which is not evident in the 1986 climbs of K2, extends to his view of local porters and guides, whose differences he also respects. He observes that most mountain climbers do not realize that the Sherpa climbers and Balti porters "look at mountains and at mountaineering with different eyes from us" and that their way of climbing was also valuable, and worth understanding (138).

Moreover, other climbers did not see things as Diemberger did. Many climbers thought that, according to Jim Curran, "there was quite a gap between the grand old man, Kurt, and his protégée. It was a bit like guide and client ... they both kept using this 'K2 is our mountain of mountains' as if they owned the thing" (Curran in Jordan 2005, 125), indicating that Curran did not see Tullis and Diemberger as a partnership, and that the mystical relationship they had with K2 did not make sense to him or to others. Others, like Ed Viesturs, thought that the best way to climb an 8,000-metre mountain was to climb as fast as possible and not linger in the Death Zone, and to turn around if conditions deteriorate (Viesturs and Roberts 2009, 27, 298). By contrast, Diemberger and Tullis were seen as "insanely slow climbers" by climbers such as Alan Rouse and Adrien Burgess (Jordan 2005, 130). But Diemberger sees this as good strategy: "on K2 I cannot see any disadvantage in climbing up slowly and conserving energy on the first half of the mountain; in my opinion you then arrive at a greater height in better condition than if you had 'run'" (Diemberger [1989] 1991, 143). Both he and Tullis had adopted this style as part of their approach to K2 as a respectful climb which made room and time for acclimatization and appreciation. According to Diemberger, the ideology of this style of climbing serves to foreground the pleasures of climbing and put in the background desires for fame or monetary gain, much in the spirit of the excerpt from his daughter's diary. Neither he nor Tullis agreed with the desire to climb as fast as possible in alpine style:

Both of us have tried to understand how even among our best friends there is an increasing mania to make an expedition as short as possible, to climb the mountain as swiftly as possible, to start back as soon as possible. More and more people are caught by this disease: do they still love the mountain? They don't seem to "live" it any more – or if they do, they "live" it differently – perhaps only as an extension of themselves. It is understandable that sometimes for tactical reasons you have to move fast on the mountain ... But with them, it seems to become a rule that dominates everything. Do we go to these wonderful places simply to fulfil a duty – and to get shot of them, the sooner the better? (153)

This passage is particularly important because it shows why Tullis and Diemberger climbed so slowly, and that Tullis was not as inexpert a climber as she appeared. She climbed in this style in order to appreciate K2 and to experience the climb as fully as she could. It also shows that Tullis and Diemberger understood style as an ideology, and that their style ran counter to the prevailing alpine style (and its assumptions about gender, body type, fitness, and age).

These assumptions, as the 1986 disaster showed, were not accurate. It is not always the fittest and fastest climbers who survive, since alpine style's requirement of speed means that climbers cannot carry emergency equipment. If disaster strikes, there is little room for error. For example, the slow and heavily supported siege style of the Korean team in 1986 meant that they were acclimatized and had the resources to wait out storms. They lost no team members except for one porter through rock fall. Meanwhile, as Jim Curran (himself an overweight climber) said in an interview with Jennifer Jordan, Diemberger and Willi Braun "'were very fat and very slow'"; this actually conserved their energy when faster, lighter alpine style climbers ran into problems (Jordan 2005, 150). This was therefore also why they survived when faster, fitter climbers did not. As Curran says, "'I think Kurt has the perfect survivor's physique and also fantastic willpower. Stubborn, stubborn old bastard just stuck it out and refused to give in'" (Jordan 2005, 150).

The Endless Knot is a testament to a way to climb differently, a way that does not seek to dominate the mountain by laying siege to it, recreate gender roles which say that women (and older men) should not climb or that there is only one style of climbing that should be followed. The book also contains moments which explain why the experience of climbing was so important to Diemberger: "all of us up here are held within the power of the mountain. We feel it acutely. We cannot know how this will turn out, where this path is leading us – up here. But already we feel joy" ([1989] 1991, 207). Just before they summit, Diemberger writes his own, moving evocation to the rope's connection, a connection which signifies that it is not brotherhood which holds climbing teams together. He and Tullis are linked by the rope physically and metaphysically: "both of you are linked together like floating thoughts, linked by the rope, two islands in space" (207).

Subsequent female climbers of K2 did not experience the partnership Tullis had with Diemberger and – in different ways – they continued to experience the gender politics associated with Himalayan climbing. Such female climbers included Chantal Maudit, a French high-altitude mountaineer known for her love of the mountains, which – like Diemberger and Tullis – she saw as spiritual and creative places. She wrote poetry on her tents, carried stuffed animals on her backpack and, although she was a strong climber, she did not work well in teams. She was openly critical of overtly masculine behaviour in the mountains, although she manipulated men when she could in order to get them to carry loads for her (Jordan 2005, 200–1). She also did not follow the "rules" for correct feminine behaviour in the mountains. She ignored sexual advances from Pakistani men, but would not dress in loose clothing to accommodate Pakistani culture's expectations of women (188). She used her beauty and charisma to manipulate male climbers into carrying gear for her or in order to gratify her sexual desires, then she would discard them when she did not need them (183–4). Although there are male climbers who have used similar tactics, Ed Viesturs's assessment of her was a common one: she was a strong climber, but she flirted with him and although he resisted her charms, he felt that she had used him (Viesturs and Roberts 2009, 294–5). This is Viesturs's basis for his criticism of Tullis, but it shows that he understood Maudit as primarily a sexual object, rather than as a sexual subject, and that he was perhaps anxious to prove he had the focus to climb K2. According to Jennifer Jordan, Maudit did seduce Viesturs on K2 in 1992 but then discarded him (Jordan 2005, 190), which indicates why he might see Maudit as a threat to brotherhood.

Also notable was Alison Hargreaves, a British climber who developed her professional climbing career as a way to support herself and her husband (who was emotionally abusive) as well as their two children. Like Tullis, Hargreaves was not a·feminist climber (Rose and Douglas 1999, 62) but also did not try to use men to help her succeed, as Maudit had (Jordan 2005, 214). She earned her place as a major climber after completing solo ascents of the six greatest faces in the Alps, a feat she completed while her husband and children, destitute, were living in a campsite (Jordan 2005, 230). These facts were not known about her, and the British press castigated her for climbing when she had left small children at home (Rose and Douglas 1999, 230). In 1995, she summited Everest without oxygen and completely self-supported, not even taking water from the members of other teams. This was a feat which made her one of the best mountaineers in the world (Jordan 2005, 240), but in order to make her future secure for herself and her children (she was planning to leave her husband) she decided to climb K2 only weeks later (243). Her diary records that she missed her young children very much, but she continued to climb, hoping that K2 would provide her with the financial security so that she would not need to take such risks (251). On 13 August she summited the mountain, but then encountered a storm. With five other climbers, she was blown off K2 just below the summit. Her remains were discovered the next day more than 1,000 metres below the summit (258–9). In the aftermath of the climb, Hargreaves was subject to intense criticism in the British press for climbing K2 when she was also a mother. She became an archetypal symbol of "bad" motherhood as journalist after journalist judged her and found her wanting. Polly Toynbee, for example, wrote that Hargreaves "behaved like a man," and that this was reprehensible (Rose and Douglas 1999, 273). Eventually, Greg Child came to her defence, saying that male climbers were not held to the same standards (273). It was not until David Rose and Ed Douglas published their biography of Hargreaves in 1999 that anyone realized that Hargreaves was climbing in order to help her children, and that she was trapped in an abusive relationship. The treatment of Hargreaves in the British press indicates that as recently as 1995, expectations for female climbers still depended on stereotypes about motherhood, and about what good motherhood is. Tragically, Hargreaves did not live long enough to engage publicly with this image and help to change it.

In 2004 Edurne Pasaban became the first woman to climb all fourteen mountains taller than 8,000 metres when she summited K2. Since then, five other women have successfully climbed the mountain, bringing the total number of women who have climbed K2 to twelve. Of these, five are alive today: the rest either died on K2 or on other big mountains. As more women have become part of expeditions to K2 and have successfully climbed the mountain, some female climbers have begun to be more vocal about the prejudices they have faced on K2. Heidi Howkins's *K2: One Woman's Quest for the Summit* details the difficulties she had as the leader of K2 expedition in 2000. Two of the male climbers on the expedition did not want to be led by a woman (Howkins 2001, 205). She had already experienced climbers telling her that the presence of women "ruined" all-male expeditions, as other climbers had (208). She deals with different aspects of masculine climbing culture humorously, by referring to difficult climbers by general names, such as "Ego Man," "Hard Man," or "Crazy Man" (209). But without what Wanda Rutkiewicz once called a "Guardian Angel" to protect her, she was referred to as a "cunt," trash was thrown in her tent, and energy gel (called "semen" by another team member) was smeared on the walls (262). Howkins's expedition did not climb K2 due to storm activity, but also because the team dynamics completely broke down the will of the climbers to try for the summit. Jennifer Jordan, who was a member of this team's film crew, referred to the group as "a sad and disparate group of warring and happy egos" (Jordan 2005, xv). In her film *Women of K2*, Jordan filmed the climb of Spanish mountaineer Aracelli Segarra and her attempt to summit K2. In one scene, Segarra climbs a fixed rope, and explains that sometimes male climbers do not want to let her lead out on a rope. In another, the climber Thor Kieser, once the boyfriend of Chantal Maudit until she left him, openly says that women disrupt male friendships on climbing expeditions. Clearly, the residual effects of the brotherhood of the rope are still part of the masculine culture of high-altitude mountaineering. As this chapter shows, the difficulty of gender relations on K2 is not just due to residual attitudes to women. It is largely due to the culture of climbing developed on K2 itself, a culture which in its use of everyday objects such as rope, has embedded deep within itself attitudes about male homosociality. These attitudes cannot be directly spoken about, and so become transmitted, through rope, into an identification of climbing with brotherhood, a brotherhood which cannot admit women, Pakistani porters or Sherpa guides, since these types of climbers pose a threat to the fragility of fraternity. Rope operates as this sign of vernacular gender: it becomes a thing which stands in for what cannot be said about male love or desire. Even as climbing styles have changed from siege style to alpine style, the traces of this brotherhood remain in the continuing suspicion of threats to the idea of climbing and community. When climbers died in the 2008 K2 disaster, it would not at first appear that the brotherhood of the rope was still in force, since two women and a number of Sherpa guides summited on that day and appeared to fully participate in the work of their teams. But as the controversy about that deadly season began to build, it was clear that as in 1986, different teams with different styles and approaches were on the mountain at the same time, and that their failure to work together and communicate contributed to the disaster (Bowley 2010, 44–6). In essence, the brotherhood of the rope broke down, to the sorrow of onlookers like Ed Viesturs, who believed that people had become afraid to help each other as they once had done: "It's a kind of dehumanization, and if it's inevitably the wave of the future, as I think it may be, well, that says something sad about mountaineering. It involves a scenario in which one climber comes across another climber who's in a truly desperate situation. And it's as if the climber who's not in trouble says to himself, *I don't know you. You're not my problem*" (Viesturs and Roberts 2009, 28).

Meanwhile, Sherpas on the mountain in 2008 were working with teams because they desperately needed the money, putting their lives at risk for their families, and endangering themselves as they bravely tried to save climbers (Bowley 2010, 59, 127–8). The journalists Peter Zuckerman and Amanda Padoan's book *Buried in the Sky* is based on two years of research and interviews with hundreds of people, including many Sherpa and Bhote (Tibetan) people, as well as the surviving relatives of the Sherpas who died in 2008, in order to tell more fully and with better context the story of the motivations and heroism of those Sherpas because, as they say, "some stories get buried" (2013, xv). The brotherhood of the rope, particularly in that account, is not about a purely emotional or idealistic relationship for the Sherpas who risk their lives on K2: it is about more and less than that relation. It is about economic need, as Sherpas run expedition companies which help their communities to prosper (27) and compete with the Bhotes for trekking and climbing jobs and still work with them (68–70). But it is also about an ethical and spiritual relation, which is how the Sherpa Chhiring understands his sense of responsibility for his friend and fellow Sherpa Pasang when he was stranded on K2.

The essential aspect of care within the brotherhood of the rope appears in Chhiring and Pasang's account as another approach to ethics, as the Buddhist act of *sonam,* or compassion for others, as Chhiring works to keep Pasang – who had lost his ice axe – connected to him and safe, even when it was dangerous for him to do so. Ignoring Pasang's plea to leave him on the mountain, Chhiring clips their ropes to each other and says to Pasang, "if we die, we die together" (174).

In the aftermath of the 2008 disaster, it is possible to see the brotherhood of the rope operating in the longing of Ed Viesturs for a supposedly simpler time, when men climbed the mountains without the help of technology, and when Sherpa and other local climbers and porters could be imagined to be fully participating in the enterprise of exploration:

> I was sure that it was I who had been born too late, not Scott or
> Shackleton. Even the 1950s, when climbers were making the first
> ascents of the 8,000 metre peaks, loomed for me like a lost heyday.
> Exploration then seemed simpler, yet more dangerous. Off you
> went into some little-known region on the map, or toward the
> top of some yet-unclimbed peak, without being able to send a
> word back home. You returned home months or even years later.
> Now we have sat phones, up-to-the-minute weather forecasts, and
> online dispatches from the field. It seems we are as burdened by
> technology as we are helped by it, and it becomes a crutch to make
> up for missing skills. (Viesturs 2009, 186)

What is significant for me about this passage is what it does not say about the other great change in mountaineering, which is the opening of climbing to other groups than that of white men and the brown men who helped them. Here in this passage, in the wake of the 2008 K2 disaster, the Romantic era persists in the nostalgia not just for technology, but for a kind of manhood without women or "servants" who are there to serve rather than make their own living. Just as advances in technology has made it possible for women to climb in the mountains more easily, so it has brought changes to what was, for less than thirty years, a mostly white male preserve. Here is evidence of gender diversity and intersectionality as a threat which cannot be named but which must nevertheless occupy the centre of representation.

Who, the question was asked, actually "belongs" on the mountain? Were skill and stamina and will enough? Or was the summit like some children's storybook paradise where only the pure of heart and the well intentioned were admitted? Was there a spiritual component to climbing? Vexing questions.

Tim Cahill, introduction to Broughton Coburn, *Everest: Mountain without Mercy*

CHAPTER 3

EVEREST AND AUTHENTICITY

Is It There? The Culture of Everest

The status of Mount Everest as the world's highest point has had the effect of overdetermining its existence, because climbing this particular peak has become a metaphor for and an expression of human achievement (Manzolini 2016, 3–4). As Nick Heil has pointed out, "Everest has come to symbolize something more than mere mountain climbing" and so the attention of the world is trained on it far more than on other mountains (2012a). Its size, and not its technical difficulty, is what makes it worth climbing. That is why by 2013, more than 5,600 successful summits, far more than any other 8,000-metre peak, have been recorded.[1] It is also why, when disasters happen on Everest, it makes news around the world, and why controversies on Everest become the focus of international attention and debate. Even before it was climbed, Everest started out as an object of colonial desire whose summit was coveted by British imperialists only when they realized that it was the highest. When the Great Trigonometric Survey of India, a British colonial mapping project, determined in the nineteenth century that what was then called Peak XV was the highest point on earth, that mountain almost immediately became the flashpoint for colonial, national and commercial interests that obscured alternative ideas about the mountain and what climbing it might mean (Slemon 1998, 16–17). Sherpa and Nepalese names for the mountain are concerned with its identification as a goddess, its height, or as a water source that gives life, not with a single person or a mapping project. Significantly, these names did not become part of the colonial history of the mountain. "Everest" the English word – and neither the Sherpa word Chomolungma nor the Nepalese word Sagarmartha – became the name of the mountain, because what can be named and mapped can become thinkable as an objective. And then, it can be possessed. Everest's newly discovered status was why Andrew Waugh, the superintendent of the Great Trigonometric Survey, decided to make an exception to the survey's policy of using local names for features. He named the peak after his predecessor on the survey, George Everest, even though it was known that locals called the mountain by other names and Everest himself was embarrassed by the honour (Firstbrook 2000, 49). Mount Everest was not even part of the British Empire, but was on the border between two kingdoms that were not British possessions – Nepal and Tibet. This did not seem to concern British imperialists, scientists, and adventurers. What mattered to them was that Everest was located and named within the Empire's system of classification, and so it could become a scientific object for naturalists, geologists, and explorers from Europe. Local people in this context would be servants to that enterprise, not knowledge-makers. It was only a matter of time, as the viceroy of India Lord Curzon saw, before Everest could be visited, mapped, investigated, and then climbed, conquered, and possessed in the name of the British empire.[2] Since 1839, first exploring, and then mountaineering in the Himalayas had been associated with what was called "the Great Game," the espionage and intrigue supported by British imperialists who sought control over countries bordering India, and who worked to limit Russian control over the same regions (Unsworth [1981] 2000, 13–18). As Isserman and Weaver point out, "out of the political and military struggle for control of the colonial frontier ... ultimately came the thought of conquering the summits" (2008, 22).

Once it was "discovered" and renamed, Everest became the focus for a very specific set of imperial, national, and masculine ambitions, particularly in the wake of the First World War. For these climbers and officials, and later for the British public, Mount Everest came to symbolize what was called "the third pole," the British objective after the North and South Poles, both of which the Empire had failed to claim (Firstbrook 2000, 44, 69). The race to climb Mount Everest catapulted Everest itself, and the activity of mountaineering, into the public sphere and into public images of conquest and sport on a global scale in the years after the First World War, converting the older imperialist dream of possession into a dream of recapturing Britain's pre-war dominance on the world stage. But the war took a major toll on the ranks of British climbers, many of whom were injured or killed in the conflict (Unsworth [1981] 2000, 19). When the first expedition was mounted as a joint effort between the Royal Geographical Society and the Alpine Club, many of the younger members of the team were survivors of the war, including George Leigh Mallory. This was probably why Mallory – who had trouble integrating into civilian life after he came back from the war – became fascinated by Everest. It could also be why John Noel, another former soldier, agreed to participate in the British expeditions to Everest in the 1920s (Davis 2011, 95–6, 200).

Since those early attempts on Everest in the 1920s, Everest has been a symbol of Romantic ideas of achievement, dreams of fame, and a testing ground for masculinity (Ortner 1999, 39–40). But, as Tim Cahill observes, the history of masculinity on Everest also has been bound up with questions of authenticity and belonging. Who belongs on Everest? Who do you have to *be* to climb Everest? These questions arose at the beginning of Everest's climbing history. When George Mallory was asked in 1923 by an unnamed reporter in Philadelphia why he wanted to climb Mount Everest, he answered simply and perhaps with no little irritation, "'because it is there'" (Davis 2011, 465–6; Isserman and Weaver 2008, 116–17). Mallory's famous comment has been repeated ever since to show that, like other forms of adventurous heroism, climbing does not need any justification. In this version of human nature, mountaineering for its own sake is connected to Romantic ideas about human

Figure 3.1 | Mount Everest/Chomolungma.

worth and creativity. The activity of climbing mountains, in this view, is not connected to more political concerns. Mountaineering is literally about higher things. Such a view of mountaineering can work to obscure important questions about ethics and justice, because a mountain like Everest has been made to stand in for escape from a world where such questions are central. Many climbers have talked about their motivation as one of escape from materialism, conformity, and the excesses of culture. In other words, for climbers thinking within a Romantic aesthetic, mountains like Everest are "nature," standing outside of and against "culture," which is seen as destructive, corrupt, and detrimental to the spiritual development of humanity (Ortner 1999, 36–8). As an escape from culture and its histories, mountains can be thought of as not "there" within culture in this version of mountaineering (Isserman and Weaver 2008, 384). Mount Everest, inevitably, is "there" at the centre of a history of mountaineering heroism, particularly for British climbers after the

Great War, and then for many other climbers (professional and amateur) seeking to prove their worth on the world stage (figure 3.1).

The memory of George Mallory as the symbol of postwar ideals has proved to be remarkably resilient, decades after he and Sandy Irvine died on Everest. In *The Boys of Everest*, a history of British climbers on Everest after the 1953 first ascent by Sir Edmund Hillary and Tenzing Norgay, Clint Willis details how working-class climbers from Scotland and the north of England "read books about Everest and other Himalayan peaks with the understanding that such expeditions weren't for the likes of them" because they were not elite enough to be considered Everest material (2006, 17). Dougal Haston, Don Whillans, Mick Burke, Peter Boardman, and Joe Tasker, all of whom were working-class anti-establishment climbers, accepted lower middle-class climber Chris Bonington as an expedition leader because he had the connections that allowed them to get the Alpine Club and National Geographic Society permissions and funding needed to go to Everest and attempt difficult routes (36–8). They went to the Himalayas because at the time Everest was their means to climbing stardom. As Willis points out, however, the group's dedication to climbing and decision to use purer style meant that their ideals about masculine hardness and the willingness to die for climbing were not in fact a departure from earlier climbing ideals of heroism and sacrifice, despite the fact that they would not have shared Mallory's upper-middle class British values (225–38). For example, as earlier climbers also believed, women were seen by this group as a distraction from dedication to climbing (345) and climbing itself was about escaping from the bonds of civilization, which included conventional family ties and relationships with women (471). When they appear on Everest, they are there only as representations, as objects of the male gaze, as *Playboy* images (Steele 1972, 178; Hornbein [1965] 1980, 64), and once, as a "stacked" nude snow statue (Hornbein [1965] 1980, 64). Although the culture of alpine climbing might seem to differ from the culture of expeditions during the golden age, heroic masculinity in the alpine era was redeployed as a counter-discourse against modernity, much as Mallory's approach to climbing has been understood to be "contemporary" because he also understood himself as counter-discursive, dedicated to his goal, and was also suspicious of artificial aids such as oxygen apparatus.[3]

And so, at every point in its climbing history, Everest is both "there" and "not there" where ideas of climbing masculinity are concerned. Its height, which literally put it on the map, has had the effect of blocking out the ideology of heroic masculinity that dominates its climbing history and inspires other, more lofty ideas about success and adventure instead. Peter Bayers points this out when he observes that "the seemingly innocuous nature of mountain climbing – that to climb mountains was to climb them 'because they're there' – obscures the ideological context of heroic masculinity and mountaineering adventure" (2003, 2). As a result, Everest has been many things: a watershed for Nepal and Tibet, a goddess to the local peoples who live near the mountain, an obstacle to travel, and an obsession of empires, countries, and individuals worldwide. Because it looms so large in cultural imaginary systems around the world, Everest has been and still is central to the formation of many ideas about selfhood and what it means to be human. And at the present time during the commercial era, its history of climbing idealism is subjected to a relentless critique of Everest as the field of broken bodies, corruption, and damaged dreams. The mountain itself has become part of a narrative of lament for "pure" climbing, for the very heroic narrative of climbing that its own history as a British colonial object helped to produce. The narratives of the 1996 disaster on Everest will show that heroic masculinity and its inherent critique of civilization has changed in the commercial era of Everest. But much of that discourse survives in the critique of commercialism and the rise of the male guide as the new representative of heroic masculinity in this era.

Perhaps inevitably, Mount Everest itself continues to play a special role in climbing history during the commercial era because of its size, the size of the ambitions of its climbers, and the disasters that inevitably result from the attempts hundreds of climbers make on the peak every year. At 8,848 metres (29,029 feet), Everest's height made it an early career-making objective for climbers from the 1960s until the 1990s, when it became possible for non-elite climbers to stand on its summit with the help of guides. Even now, when Everest is no longer an objective for classic mountaineering "firsts," it draws thousands of climbers each year. Therefore, Everest symbolizes climbing in the way that no other mountain can, but it now symbolizes the "decline" of climbing itself. And it remains the focus of public opinion about who should be in the mountains and why.

Everest is "there" at the centre of high-altitude climbing in its three stages: the Golden Era, the alpine era and the commercial era. During the Golden Era of first attempts and ascents from the nineteenth century to the 1950s, Everest remained at the centre of British ambitions to "conquer" it until in 1953 Tenzing Norgay and Sir Edmund Hillary finally stood on the summit. The alpine era of the 1970s ushered in different kinds of ascents of Everest by climbers who wanted to reach the highest peaks by more difficult routes, or who climbed by what Reinhold Messner, the most famous alpine style high altitude mountaineer in history, has called "fair means" – that is, climbing fast without much equipment or the help of oxygen. For a brief period at the end of the Golden Era, Everest played a role as the location of American Cold War-inspired scientific experimentation and American politics in the "race" to climb Everest and not leave the summit to the climbing teams of communist China, which were then connected to mountaineering ambitions and heroism in 1963 (Clements 2018, 22–3). Finally, Everest became the focus of the commercial guiding era beginning in the 1990s, when amateur clients with enough money could pay for a chance to summit the highest mountains in the world. This last part of climbing history has become controversial within and beyond climbing circles because of the problems commercial guiding has brought to the mountain. Articles like Laura Parker's "Will Everest's Climbing Circus Slow Down after Disasters" for *National Geographic* tell a story that is familiar to anyone who reads about mountaineering: Everest has become the symbol of an unregulated climbing industry where it is possible for inexperienced but well-heeled clients to buy a chance to summit with the help of guides, where Sherpa guides and camp workers are underpaid for the dangerous work they do, and where there are too many people on the mountain every climbing season, causing the conditions for yet another disaster if a storm or an earthquake hits (Parker 2015). Everest is littered with trash and the dead bodies of climbers, some of whom died when others could not or did not help them. Both symbolize the decline of Everest, at least in this version of its story.[4]

The commercial era is also marked by a series of disasters on Everest that commentators often say could have been avoided if there were fewer people on the peak, fewer climbing companies trying to generate a profit, and more respect for traditional climbing values. When there is a disaster, Everest receives intense media coverage, touching off a debate each time about who should be on Everest, and what the rights and responsibilities of Sherpa and non-Sherpa guides and outfitters in the commercial era should be. *Into Thin Air* provides the background for much of this commentary. In the years to come, Everest would be the setting for more disasters arguably caused by commercial activity on the mountain, as hundreds and then thousands of climbers, undeterred by Everest's dangers, some perhaps inspired by Krakauer's account, came to try for the summit. There were more exposés of the problems of amateur climbers on a dangerous mountain, and the problems of an unregulated climbing industry and the pitfalls of climbing ambition would be published, revealing a dark side to the desire of so many people's dream of standing at the world's highest point. Media attention remained on the industry that sprang up to fulfil summit hopes, putting human lives at risk in the process. Every time there is another disaster on Everest, these debates about the decline of climbing values and the problem of amateur climbers reignite, sometimes accompanied by outrage about the conditions for Sherpa climbers, guides, and workers (Kodas 2008, Heil 2009, Brown 2014, Stout 2016). The problem, for many, is that Everest has too many unskilled climbers on it, and that the industry that serves them puts profitability and delivering on promises of attaining the summit above client safety, good Sherpa work conditions, and common sense.

All that media attention and endorsement of Krakauer's framing of the problems of Everest has resulted in some skirting of important questions about Everest and its climbing history. Why has Everest become so connected to Tim Cahill's question that heads this chapter: "who belongs on the mountain?" Why do questions about a certain kind of authenticity dominate discussions about Everest, and why is authenticity so firmly connected – as it is in the 2015 *Everest* IMAX film based on a major disaster in 1996 – to ideas about white, male, and non-Indigenous privilege? What is it about Everest that makes it necessary for the story of Everest to be told again and again as a story of white male dominance and mastery? Why is the story of Everest always a story of decline, and what is the story in decline *from*? Cahill's question of why Everest continues to be thought about as a "storybook paradise where only the pure of heart might enter" is central to this concern. Assumptions about purity are at the heart of who is supposed to belong on Everest and to Everest, but what is at stake is more about racial purity, masculinity, and sexism than it is about the condition of a mountaineer's soul.

Belonging: The Body of George Leigh Mallory

If there was anyone who is thought to "belong" on Everest, it is George Leigh Mallory. He is often talked about as the most authentic climber who has ever been on the mountain, an ideal climber ahead of his time and far more skilled than his contemporaries of the 1920s, the mountaineer wanting to climb Everest "because it is there." Inevitably, Mallory's mysterious end on Everest has become part of the legend, for Mallory's "death on Everest would cause an entire war-stained nation to weep" (Davis 2011, 165). To the people of Britain, "it was unbelievable that Mallory, the star of the mountaineering world, could have perished" (Firstbrook 2000, 16). Mallory is also remembered as a modern climber and a modern man. He is described as having "a mental focus utterly modern in its intensity" (178). He has been called "a climber of exceptional grace and strength" who was far better at rock climbing than most of his contemporaries (Hemmleb et al. 1999, 23). He believed in climbing with minimal equipment and initially refused to use oxygen, a stance respected by alpine climbers decades later, and often mentioned as a sign of authentic mountaineering, as opposed to a climbing style more reliant on technical aids (Manzolini 2016, 21). Most of all, Mallory's focus and drive on Everest became legendary to the point where he is now fully identified with the place where he met his end, and with the idea of elemental struggle in the mountains: Mallory was "a man whose name was destined to be forever linked with that of Everest ... a naked feud between man and mountain" (Unsworth [1981] 2000, 41). The myth of Mallory is both Romantic and tragic, a story about his ambition, good looks, and personal style that has made him larger than life as generations of writers contemplated his life and legacy. He has been written of as "the central, tragic protagonist of what Younghusband called 'the epic of Everest' and the first (and still most compelling) celebrity of Himalayan mountaineering" (Isserman and Weaver 2008, 87). He is the only climber to be metaphorically connected to the mountain because "quite simply, Mallory *was* Everest" (Hemmleb et. al. 1999, 24, emphasis in original).

But nothing about Mallory was simple, just as Everest is not simply "there" to be climbed. Mallory was a complex figure, an athlete, and an idealist intellectual who knew many members of the Bloomsbury group when he was a student at Cambridge. He was known for his beauty and was pursued romantically by Lytton Strachey – with whom he carried on a flirtatious correspondence for years (Kennedy 2015) while he was desired by men and women alike. Of him, Strachey had written as if Mallory were a god or a work of art, "'Mondieu! – George Mallory! ... He's six foot high, with the body of an athlete by Praxiteles, and a face – of incredible – the mystery of Botticelli, the refinement and delicacy of a Chinese print, the youth and piquancy of an unimaginable English boy'" (Davis 2011, 175). Mallory in turn formed intense male friendships with romantic overtones while he was at Cambridge. He had a brief affair with Lytton's brother James, posed nude for a portrait by Duncan Grant, and was photographed in the nude by Roger Fry. He later married Ruth Turner and although the marriage appears to have been mostly a happy one, it was marked by Mallory's absences when he was in the army and on Everest expeditions.[5] Playfully, even flamboyantly, Mallory posed in the nude on the 1922 trek to Everest, after fording a stream, an image used on postcards to promote the expedition (figure 3.2). And perhaps all was not as it seemed: Mallory had a secret flirtation by correspondence with a young female schoolteacher, whom he never met (Sawer 2015). He appears to have carried no letters by his wife Ruth on his final climb (unless he did reach the summit and left them there, as he had promised her he would do) but on his body there was a letter from Stella Cobden-Sanderson, an admirer who had met Mallory in New York in 1923 when he was on his American lecture tour (Douglas 2009). Mallory's sensuality and his passion remain part of his mystique and, as we shall see, are essential to his attractiveness, in death as well as in life. But Mallory's attractiveness and his foibles are often sublimated by the needs of others to harness aspects of his story to a narrative about the right kind of masculinity and heroism for Everest. That narrative does not include much about Mallory's infidelity, incompetence, or neocolonial ideas about Sherpas, even though all of these qualities are part of the historical record.

Figure 3.2 | On the trek to Everest, after fording a stream. From left, Howard Somervell, Arthur Wakefield, George Mallory.

Unlike the imperialist members of the Everest Committee or the expedition leaders of the 1920s, Mallory had been profoundly marked by his experiences of trench warfare during the First World War. In common with his contemporaries Siegfried Sassoon and Wilfrid Owen, Mallory did not romanticize the violence and waste of military life. He came to doubt the rightness of British imperialism because of his war experiences, and after he was demobilized he became an idealistic – if ineffective – school teacher, hoping to create a pedagogy that emphasized the development of the imagination, not obedience to authority.[6] When he became involved in the British quest for the summit of Everest, he became heroic in the public's mind, because of his talent and drive to succeed, without appearing to endorse the conquering of Everest for empire. He did not look like, and was not, an aging imperialist scion like the organizers and leaders of the expeditions in the 1920s. He regarded the climbing of Everest as a spiritual or aesthetic quest, not as part of imperial dreams of domination. He truly seemed to love climbing with other talented young men like Geoffrey Winthrop Young, Noel Odell, or Andrew Irvine, perhaps connecting his early erotic fascination with men to the camaraderie of male soldiers in the trenches as they helped each other to stay alive, depending on and drawing strength from each other in desperate situations. At any rate, Mallory was masculine without machismo, tough, yet graceful. He was an ideal figure for British people to admire as he tried to climb Everest again and again. Over time, Mallory's obsession with Everest became a way for the war-torn people of the United Kingdom to reimagine themselves, and their nation, as strong, potent, and modern, even after a war that had decimated the ranks of its young men and changed Britain's sense of itself as an empire. Mallory seemed to be a link between older imperial British ambitions and the age of exploration and colonization, and an emerging sense of Britain as a modern nation. His special combination of qualities made it possible for the British public to imagine conquering the "Third Pole," succeeding where Robert Falcon Scott had failed in the race for the South Pole in 1912. But in 1924, famously, Mallory's last attempt to summit Everest did not succeed.

After he failed to come back to his last high camp in 1924 and was presumed lost, Mallory became a larger-than-life hero for the modern age. Whether it is in Rupert Brooke's erotic photographs of him when they were students at Cambridge, other photos of him climbing with his friends in northern England, or posing jauntily in the Everest expedition photos, Mallory appeared to embody the ideals of his generation and of those after him, in a way that made his death meaningful to millions of British people. He made climbing beautiful, romantic, worthy, freeing, exciting. He looked the heroic part, with his body often compared (as Strachey had done) to Greek statuary. His death high on Everest with his climbing partner Andrew Irvine only added to his legend, because what really happened to them remains "one of the most enduring and puzzling mysteries in expedition and mountaineering history" (Hemmleb et al. 1999, 19). Generations of climbers wondered (and still wonder) whether Mallory's drive and talent got him to the summit after he and Irvine were last seen high on the summit ridge by their teammate Noel Odell. The pull of Mallory's life, his obsession with Everest and love of climbing, in addition to the tantalizing mystery of his death, have made him the inspiration for many important mountaineers, including Reinhold Messner, who calls Mallory "a great hero of mine since the 1960s"

(1982, 40) and whose ascent of Everest without oxygen has been said to have "fulfilled the dreams of Mallory" (Unsworth [1981] 2000, 476). American alpine style climber Tom Hornbein records in *Everest: The West Ridge* that he looked for "Mallory's steps" on the north ridge of Everest, saying that "Everest was more his [Mallory's] than any other man's" (1965, 94). In an interview for the documentary television series *Nova*, climber and filmmaker David Breashears discusses the respect Mallory inspires to later generations of climbers, because he accomplished so much with much less advanced equipment, clothing, and techniques. How did he do this? The answer for Breashears sounds like Tim Cahill's criticism of purity on Everest: "When we modern climbers are going out on these great peaks, 60, 70, now 75 years after Mallory and Irvine perished, we really hold these climbers in awe and have great respect and admiration for them. They had a certain character" (Breashears 2000). It is no wonder that Sir Edmund Hillary, who with Tenzing Norgay was the first to stand on the summit of Everest in 1953, looked for signs of Mallory and Irvine before he did anything else (Hillary [1955] 2003, 229).

Without a doubt, George Leigh Mallory is *the* hero of Everest, a mountaineer whose ethics and drive are never in question, a climber whose physical magnetism is matched by his high ideals. His grit and toughness are indisputable: he went to Everest three times to try to summit the peak and may even have been the first person on the summit, dressed in thin layers of clothing that would be more appropriate for hiking today. His style, fearlessness, and grace mark him as a modern climber, but also connect him to the lost generation of British men who died in the trenches of the First World War. He represents what could be seen as the apex of modernist white British masculinity and its ideals of brotherhood, persistence, understated heroism, and erotic beauty, its hint of imperialism still in evidence, but without its machismo and violence. No subsequent climbers of Everest could ever forget that such a figure had been there before them. And no climber could ever be expected to fully achieve the ideals Mallory represents. Added to this is the mystery of his death and the question of whether he summited Everest, making Mallory an irresistible tragic hero more than a historical person, attached forever to the myth-building work of Everest and its climbing history.[7]

Mallory's mystique and the question of whether he and Irvine had been the first to summit Mount Everest have given rise to lively debate among Everest commentators, and have been the basis for high-profile expeditions looking for evidence. The last person to see Mallory and Irvine alive was Noel Odell, who had climbed to the last camp on the mountain – Camp VI – in support of the summit team. Odell saw the climbers high on the summit ridge at 12:50 pm, but mist hid them after a few minutes, and it is uncertain where exactly on the ridge he saw them climbing. A storm blew up and subsided a few hours later, but Mallory and Irvine never emerged from it and never came back to Camp VI. In 1933 what is thought to be Irvine's ice axe was found lying on the northeast ridge, just before the First Step, a small rock cliff (Clark and Salkeld 2015). The Tibetan side of Everest was closed to non-Chinese climbers by China in 1950, ending British attempts on that side of the mountain for decades, and so no other artifacts were found for some time. But Chinese climbers in a 1960 expedition later recounted seeing a dead foreigner high on the ridge. In 1979, climber Wang Hungbao of China told Japanese climber Ryoten Hasegawaon that he had seen an "English dead" lying face-up, with his eyes pecked out by birds, near his own camp in 1975. This had to be either Mallory or Irvine, but Wang was killed in an avalanche the day after he told the Japanese climber what he had seen. Given that Irvine's ice axe had been found near that point, the corpse the Chinese climbers found was widely assumed to be Irvine's (Firstbrook 2003, 158). Based on the position of the ice axe and the eyewitness accounts, a 1999 expedition led by Eric Simonson and sponsored jointly by *National Geographic* and the BBC set out to find the body of Irvine and, it was hoped, to retrieve the camera that Irvine had with him. Photos from the camera could prove whether Mallory and Irvine had summited or not (Simonson et al. 1999; Clark and Salkeld 2015). In 1984, Everest historian Tom Holzel already had led an expedition to try to find out what had happened to Mallory and Irvine, although poor weather prevented them from finding many artifacts and they did not discover Irvine's body (Arnette 2010). But with geographic information collected by Jochen Hemmleb, the 1999 expedition set out to find Irvine and the summit camera, in order to solve the mystery once and for all (Simonson et al. 1999).

On 1 May 1999, high on the flanks of Everest's north ridge, climbers Andy Politz, Tap Richards, Jake Norton, Dave Hahn, and Conrad Anker left Camp V and fanned out with instructions from Hemmleb about searching for the body of Andrew Irvine, based on Wang Hungbao's account of finding an "English dead" two decades before. Conrad Anker, one of the best-known mixed climbers of his generation, ignored the instructions and explored a lower gully, "going on intuition" (Hemmleb et al. 1999, 119). Very soon, he found a patch of white that was not snow and not rock. It had "a light-absorbing quality, like marble" (Anker and Roberts 1999, 19). He approached and realized that he was seeing a climber's body, and that it was very old. Anker has recounted the story of how he found the body of Mallory several ways. In his memoir, *The Lost Explorer*, he says "it didn't really sink in at first. It was as if everything was in slow motion. *Is this a dream?* I wondered. *Am I really here?*" (19, emphasis in original). In a documentary film called *The Wildest Dream*, Anker appears to re-enact the moment of discovery and then says in a voiceover, "for a moment I thought, maybe I could just keep walking and keep it to myself. But then, that's what we were there for" (2010).[8] Anker radioed the other climbers with a coded message to get them to come to where he was, trying not to alert everyone listening on the radio frequency. The other climbers arrived and still thinking that this body had to be Andrew Irvine's, they began to investigate further, chipping the ice away from it. To their surprise, clothing labels said "G. Leigh Mallory" and not Irvine. The climbers took artifacts and a DNA sample (Anker and Roberts 1999, 22). They looked for the camera Mallory was supposed to be carrying and did not find it. Then Dave Hahn read an Anglican committal service provided by the bishop of Bristol, where Irvine and Mallory had lived, and the climbers gathered rocks to cover Mallory's body. They went back to Camp V (Hemmleb et al. 1999, 123, 128). Two team members came back to Mallory's body later, uncovered it, searched again for the camera, removed more artifacts, looked at Mallory's face and found that he had a head injury (Hemmleb et al. 1999, 162).

But finding Mallory amounted to more than simply gathering artifacts and covering up his corpse (twice) in the name of archeology. Mallory's body itself became the most substantial sign for the climbers who found it of climbing authenticity grounded in the perfection of the male climbing body. Unlike the other, more broken bodies that they saw nearby and that distressed them (Hemmleb et al. 1999, 118), Mallory's body was relatively undamaged, and they found looking at him to be fascinating and moving. Dave Hahn reported that the "contorted condition" of the other corpses in the area proved that people did not die high on Everest of exposure, but of injuries sustained when they fell off the northeast ridge. Conrad Anker noted that other bodies in the area had their heads facing downhill and were in bad condition (Anker and Roberts 1999, 32). But this corpse was different. Unlike the other bodies, it faced uphill. There was little fall damage. The clothes were there but had worn away from much of the skin. Literally, this body appeared to be frozen in the act of climbing, its mummified skin bleached to a white sheen, hands digging into the soil. The effect on those who saw the body was to compare it to heroic statuary, or to see its mummification as evidence of Mallory's physical dynamism or personal style. It was as if Mallory was eternal and had become the Greek statue that he was often compared to during his life. In a remarkable echo of Lytton Strachey's portrait of Mallory years before, Hahn said, "I felt like I was viewing a Greek or Roman marble statue" (Hemmleb et al. 1999, 121), and Richards said that "it looked like a Greek or Roman marble statue" as well (Anker and Roberts 1999, 22), while Anker himself recalls that "what was incredible was that I could still see the powerful well-defined muscles in his shoulders and back" (21). In *Ghosts of Everest*, this moment is presented as if it were unmediated, in a moment of *prosepopoeia*, the address of the dead to the living that requires no interpretation. The address is one of beauty and heroism: "The body itself did the speaking. For here was a body unlike the others crumpled in crannies elsewhere on the terrace ... frozen in a position of self-arrest, as if the fall had happened only moments earlier ... the arms, still powerfully muscular still, extended above the head to strong hands that gripped the mountainside ... The entire body had about it the strength and grace of a dancer. This body, this man, had once been a splendid specimen of humankind" (Hemmleb et al. 1999, 121).

The extraordinary passage brings together several aspects of the myth of Mallory, once the climbers realize that this is who they are seeing. The image of a body "speaking" appears to give Mallory's body agency after death. It presents what Mallory's body has to "say" as unmediated and easily "heard" by other climbers. It identifies him utterly with the mountain to which he is frozen. Mallory's corpse is heroic in death, and beautiful, like a statue of a classical hero. It is like a statue that crosses the line between art and life, rendering those who discover him as modern-day Pygmalions. And what does the body of Mallory say? It "says" to other climbers that it was not broken by the mountain. The "still powerful" hands are understood as indicative of his commitment to climb or to save himself as he fell, and so they show his character as a climber. Mallory's body is also understood to be doing what a climbing body should do, in death. Mallory's legacy *is* his body, because even in death the body is spoken of in terms of strength and grace, as his climbing style had been. Anker mentions the "awe and respect" he felt as he waited for the other climbers to arrive (Anker and Roberts 1999, 20), as well as the desire – shared in the film – to keep the secret to himself. Politz says "there was this intense feeling of reverence" (Hemmleb et al. 1999, 126) as they worked to free Mallory from the ice. As Mallory was spoken of as beautiful and attractive in life, he is attractive here too, in death. The photographs of Mallory's body in *Ghosts of Everest* reinforce this sense of Mallory as a statue, gleaming in the afternoon light. Close-ups of his foot and the boot he still wore highlight the uncanniness of seeing a body that is not desiccated. One is captioned "Fallen hero – George Mallory" (121). The caption connects Mallory to another well-known form of male heroism: the image of the soldier who "falls" in battle.

The climbers themselves identified intensely with Mallory as they gazed at him, personalizing the body and connecting Mallory's era with their own. They started to call him "George" because to them, it was as if he and "Sandy" (Andrew Irvine's nickname) were "old friends" (Anker and Roberts 1999, 34). This is in contrast to the nicknames these climbers gave to other corpses on the mountain, like "the Greeter," so named because his hand was frozen in an upright position (32). But Mallory is different and is not treated as if he were dead. Andy Politz says that "in an odd sense we felt we were working with Mallory the person, not Mallory the body" (Hemmleb et al. 1999, 126). After the funeral service, the climbers do not want to leave the body because "he was so impressive to be with, even in death" (128). Anker reflects that "this man was a fellow climber. We shared the same goals and aspirations, the same joys and sorrows. Our lives were motivated by the same elemental force" (Anker and Roberts 1999, 38). When taken with Anker's decision to ignore what Hemmleb (a non-climber) told him and to look for a body using his "mountaineer's intuition, not the research manual" (32), the discovery of Mallory by fellow climbers results in their interpreting the body as evidence of Mallory's drive and commitment, and then, as evidence of their own their own right to be on the mountain, and to understand climbing culture as a continuous, living history. These climbers cannot afford see themselves as the corpses who fell, who suffered, who are ugly, but as the heroic climber who is beautiful in death and who, in the opinion of some of them, might have made it to the top of Everest.

The pull of Mallory's story, identification with him as a climber, and the continuing question of whether Mallory and Irvine could have climbed the difficult Second Step have even led Anker back to the northeast ridge of Everest in 2010, where he was the star of the film *The Wildest Dream*, a documentary featuring Anker with voice-overs by major actors, including Alan Rickman, Natasha Richardson, and Ralph Fiennes. The film includes a re-enactment of part of the ridge climb with equipment and clothing based on 1924 designs. In the film, Conrad Anker says, "George Mallory and I; our two paths have intersected, seventy-five years apart," another indication of how closely Anker has come to identify with Mallory, close enough even to replicate his clothing and climbing style in an effort to see whether Mallory could have climbed the difficult Second Step with the resources at his disposal. Anker even chose a younger English climbing partner to share a rope with him, as Mallory had chosen Irvine, and segments of the film deal with the challenges of Anker's wife Jennifer Lowe-Anker, treating them as similar to the challenges faced by Mallory's wife Ruth. The close association of Anker's talent and drive with Mallory's, the identification of the challenges each faced and particularly the re-enacted scenes where Anker looks exactly as Mallory would have, have the effect of collapsing historical differences in climbing style, ethics, and goals together.

Anker *becomes* Mallory, and the "brotherhood of the rope" (Anker even uses this phrase) is seen as something that matters as much today as it did decades ago. To tell this type of story about Mallory as a leader and a hero, *The Wildest Dream* omits the complex nature of the large and colonial-style British expeditions to Everest and the more problematic sides to Mallory's character. The film makes no mention of the siege techniques used by British teams which involved large climbing parties and dozens of Sherpa porters making campus and slowly ferrying supplies up the mountain, a British climbing strategy borrowed from the polar explorers (Isserman and Weaver 2008, 112). There are no references to any of the actual expedition leaders: Mallory is imagined as the person who led and planned the entire enterprise, as if he had been the leader of a modern alpine style climb. Mallory and Irvine themselves are presented as a team from the beginning, when Mallory did not in fact decide to climb with Irvine until late in the 1924 expedition, and had not climbed with him until the summit push. Mallory's legendary absent-mindedness and disorganization (one of the reasons why he could never have led an expedition) are not discussed. There is no mention of the Sherpas who played a major role in all expeditions – they even carried oxygen for Mallory and Irvine to their last high camp – and who Mallory thought of mainly as servants, as did all British climbers in his day (Davis 2011, 248, 275, 285, 327). In order to make him thoroughly modern and heroic, what is emphasized in the film is Mallory's talent and drive to succeed, qualities that can be interpreted as ahistorical, and so are found in other authentic climbers of Everest. In this picture of Everest through the life, death and body of George Mallory, heroism has eternal qualities based on physical ability and masculine beauty, is conventionally heterosexual and monogamous, and is easily connected from one generation to the next.

Finding the body of Mallory did not result in a solution to the mystery of whether he and Irvine summited Mount Everest. For one thing, the "English dead" Wang Hungbao had seen was face-up, with his eyes pecked out because they had been exposed. Mallory had been found face-down, with his face protected from birds and the elements, and without the all-important camera. The mystery endures because the body of Irvine and the camera have yet to be found. The documentation of Mallory's body and its artifacts led to controversy instead about the ethics of selling photographs of the body, and about whether artifacts should have been taken and put on display. The only conclusive proof that either or both climbers had summited would be if the photographs from the camera one of them was carrying were developed and would show a view of or from the summit itself. The camera is probably with Irvine, and his body has not yet been found. It is not even clear how Mallory and Irvine met their end, or how high they were when one or both of them fell. What is clear is that the commercialism that accompanies every climb of Mount Everest affected how Mallory's body was treated and how photographs and film circulated. Raw film footage of the attempt to free Mallory from the ice and find artifacts shows that Mallory's body was not treated with the awe and respect claimed by some team members in *Ghosts of Everest* (Davis 2011, 569–70). Although they had given permission for the DNA sample collection and photograph-taking, some members of the Irvine and Mallory families later regretted that artifacts were taken, and expressed anger that some expedition members profited financially from the bidding war for photographs of Mallory's corpse (Douglas 1999; Beaumont and Douglas 2011). Everest legends, including Sir Edmund Hillary and Sir Chris Bonington, publicly expressed their shock and disgust at the sale of photographs to the highest bidder (Davis 2011, 568). Family concerns about disturbing Mallory's body appear even more justifiable in light of the fact that the body was uncovered a second time by other members of the 1999 team, who searched for the camera a second time, found Mallory's wristwatch, removed the boot from Mallory's foot, and dug out Mallory's face from the ice (Hemmleb et al. 1999, 161).

Although the search for artifacts has historic merit to it, the decision to film and photograph the body so that books and films could be made angered Joe Simpson, the author of the landmark mountaineering book *Touching the Void*. In his second memoir, *The Beckoning Silence*, Simpson excoriated Conrad Anker for his description of Mallory's bare buttocks, hollowed out and pecked at by mountain goraks (birds), calling it "graphically tasteless" (2003, 122). "To me," Simpson concludes of the treatment of Mallory's body by the team, "it amounted to little more than modern-day grave robbing," an act of callousness analogous to those climbers who climbed past Indian climbers in distress in 1996 and who did not help them as they lay dying (124). Simpson's critique of Anker as an indicator of the "new" values on Mount Everest that do not pay respect to bodies or to earlier mountaineering values about the need to help others serves to puncture the myth of Mallory as an eternal hero for Everest, and the myth of authentic climbers as those who can inhabit the spirit of Mallory himself. But it does not dispense with the myth entirely. The critique relies on an understanding of climbing ethics that in Simpson's mind, Anker (unlike Mallory) disregards, like those climbers who proceed to the summit without helping others. The same premise is found in Sir Chris Bonington's outrage at selling photos: "'These people don't deserve to be called climbers,'" he told the *Observer* in 1999 (Davis 2011, 568). The premise here is that Everest – and Mallory – should not be treated as commodities to be bought and sold. The values of an earlier time are understood to have been violated, and mountaineering ethics have been disregarded. True climbers would not have treated the body of Mallory in this way. Commercialism has affected Everest, so that Mallory is exploited for profit.

But what this point of view neglects is that the earliest Everest climbs were intensely commercial enterprises and were not undertaken purely in the spirit of altruism. In *Coronation Everest*, Jan Morris observes that early expeditions were "tarnished by no cheap nationalist ambition" because in her view, early climbs were attempts by elite gentlemen and so were of little interest to the public ([1958] 2000, 3). Nationalism may not have been a motivator because the first British expeditions were not underwritten by the government, leaving the Everest Committee to look elsewhere for ways to fund them. Wade Davis describes the expeditions of the 1920s as "surprisingly modern in execution" (2011, 156) because they were financed much as climbs are today, through a combination of fundraising, endorsements, equipment discounts and exclusive marketing rights for the books, films, and lecture-tours that would result. The 1924 expedition in particular was marked by "the modern idea of exploration itself as a resource, as a marketable product available for investment" (Isserman and Weaver 2008, 118). Although there was much high-flown rhetoric about the national and scientific aims of the expeditions, The Everest Committee cut deals for the sale of botanical specimens to the highest bidder, negotiated transportation and equipment discounts, and created a marketing campaign about the expeditions using cablegrams, the exclusive newspaper coverage of the *Times*, photographs and cinematography (Davis 2011, 157). Sunlight Soap was even approached in a deal that would have seen a cake of soap and a company flag placed on the summit, for advertising purposes (158)! Members of the expeditions had to sign a confidentiality agreement that prevented them from communicating directly with the media and obligated them to give lectures and hand over photographs for promotional purposes when the Everest Committee allowed it (459). These commercializing tactics are familiar to anyone who climbs professionally today. The argument that Everest, and climbing culture, are in decline away from altruism and towards commercialism cannot form the basis for a critique of climbing ethics in the past. Everest has long been presented as just "there" to be climbed, an irrefutable symbol of nature that culture threatens to degrade and defile. But Everest has been forced to carry significant amounts of cultural freight since it was identified as the highest point on earth in the nineteenth century. The problem of authenticity and Everest needs to take that significant cultural freight into account, in order to understand why "who belongs" on Everest has been a question that has worked to legitimate the myth of Mallory as the most authentic climber on the mountain, whose legacy can only be passed from one deserving white man to another.

The Flopping Fish and the Cloth Cat: Authenticity in 1953

In *Man of Everest*, the memoir of his life told to and written by James Ramsey Ullman with the help of Tenzing's friend and translator Rabindranath Mitra,[9] Tenzing Norgay relates two stories about the landmark 1953 Everest expedition that show how Sherpa climbers have been made to participate in the Everest narrative of innocence and decline. With New Zealand climber Sir Edmund Hillary, Tenzing[10] was the first to summit Everest, as they said in a statement they signed, "almost together" (Ullman and Tenzing [1955] 2010, 267). Tenzing praises Hillary, calling him a "friend" (265) and is positive about Hillary's climbing ability and generosity (244), but in several places he is sharply critical of the hierarchical, unfriendly, and uncollegial nature of British expeditions (224, 230–4), particularly in comparison to the 1952 Swiss expedition, whose members treated Tenzing as an equal. In *Man of Everest*, Tenzing tells two stories that seek to correct the official record of the expedition written by Colonel John Hunt, its leader. Both stories speak back to the narrative of white, male climbing heroism that informed Hunt's and Hillary's own accounts, providing an alternate way to understand Everest and a view of Sherpa thinking which resists colonial and neocolonial attempts by British expeditions to see the Sherpas in Orientalist ways as childlike and happy servants.

In the first account, Tenzing repudiates the story from Hunt's *The Ascent of Everest*, presumably told by Hillary for that official expedition account, that on the ice cliff now known as the Hillary Step, Hillary helped Tenzing through a crack: "As I [Hillary] heaved hard on the rope Tenzing wriggled his way up the crack and finally collapsed exhausted at the top like a giant fish when it has just been hauled from the sea after a terrible struggle" (Hunt [1953] 2003, 209). The picture of Tenzing as a flopping fish is comic, but its overtones are insulting. It presents Tenzing as an inexperienced climber who has no agency at all. He has to be guided by Hillary up a technical feature, and Hillary, like a sportsman, lands a fish rather than climbs with his partner. It establishes the summit team as an uneven pairing of an authentic climber who belongs on Everest, and a Sherpa servant who is comic relief. But in *Man of Everest*, Tenzing repudiates this version of events and affirms that he and Hillary were a climbing team:

> I must be honest and say that I do not feel his [Hillary's] account, as told in *The Ascent of Everest*, is wholly accurate ... he gives the impression that it was only he who really climbed it on his own, and that he then practically pulled me, so that I "finally collapsed exhausted at the top, like a giant fish when it has just been hauled from the sea after a terrible struggle." Since then I have heard plenty about that "fish," and I admit I do not like it. For it is the plain truth that no one pulled or hauled me up the gap. I climbed it myself, just as Hillary had done; and if he was protecting me with the rope while I was doing it, this was no more than I had done for him ... I do feel that in his story of our final climb he is not quite fair to me: that all the way through he indicates that when things went well it was his doing, and when things went badly it was mine. For this is simply not true ... All the way up and down we helped, and were helped by, each other – and that was the way it should be. But we were not leader and led. We were partners. (Ullman and Tenzing [1955] 2010, 265)

In his own memoir of the climb, Sir Edmund Hillary did not describe Tenzing's climb of the crack in this way, writing that Tenzing "commenced to struggle and jam and force his way up until I was able to pull him to safety" (Hillary [1955] 2003, 224), a description that gives Tenzing a bit more dignity and agency because jamming is a climbing technique. But the picture is still of Hillary pulling Tenzing along. Tenzing's account insists on a brotherhood of the rope, not a guide/client relation.

When Tenzing and Hillary arrive at the summit, Hillary feels relief that the climb is over, and experiences "a vague sense of astonishment that I should have been the lucky one to attain the ambition of so many brave and determined climbers" (227). Hillary is most concerned with the logistics of being on the summit, and with climbing history and route-finding, looking for signs of Mallory and Irvine (he finds none) and seeing a passable route on the northern slopes (228–9). He takes the famous picture of Tenzing on the summit, eats a mint cake with Tenzing, and buries a cross beside the food Tenzing buries as an offering to what Hillary calls "the Gods of Chomolungma." Although Hillary at the time said that he did not have strong spiritual beliefs, and John Hunt himself was initially reluctant to take the cross, offered to him by a Catholic priest (Hansen 2013, 270), Hillary represents this event with national and religious overtones in his memoir. He writes that he "placed the little cross that John Hunt had given me on the South Col" ([1955] 2003, 229). Hillary also writes that when Hunt had handed him the cross before the final attempt, Hillary understood that Hunt meant to connect the Christian faith to his faith that the mountain should be climbed for "many thousands of people" who had put their faith in the team (187). Hunt's gesture, in Hillary's account, imbues the summit push with a national and Christian (even Roman Catholic) significance. On the summit, Hillary sees the food and cross as "strange companions" because they are from different religious traditions, but he also sees them as representing for all people the spiritual peace and strength the mountains can provide. Like Hunt, when Hillary decides to represent what climbing Mount Everest meant, he pictured the act of climbing as a spiritual quest, and expressions of religious faith as part of the same quest. Fifty years later, in 2003, the story of the crucifix was retold by Father Martin Haigh, whose father gave it to John Hunt to put on the summit. Haigh says that "it meant a tremendous amount to Hillary, and to me, and to all Christians" (Hewes 2003). Clearly, as time passed, Sir Edmund Hillary recast the meaning of those actions at the summit. That recasting is significant, since the placing of a cross becomes laden, in Hillary's account, with nationalist and Christian overtones.

But Tenzing's experience of the summit of Everest was different. Unlike Hillary, who thinks of his own place in climbing history when he arrives at the summit and who looks for signs of the most famous climbing team to attempt Everest before them, Tenzing thinks about the important relationships in his life. He wears the scarf given to him by his friend, the Swedish climber Raymond Lambert, and he thinks of him, wishing that he were there to share the moment (Ullman and Tenzing [1955] 2010, 272). Unlike the description of Hillary saying to his friend George Lowe on the descent, "'well George, we knocked the bastard off'" (Hunt [1953] 2003, 211), Tenzing thinks about Chomolungma as he looks down into the valley where he had lived. He describes Chomolungma as a living being, thinking of her as "warm and friendly and living. She was a mother hen, and the other mountains were chicks under her wings." This makes him think that he, too, can protect and shelter those he loves (Ullman and Tenzing [1955] 2010, 270). This version of Everest is redolent with images of familiarity for Tenzing, as he looks at familiar landmarks and where he has lived. It is maternal, and Everest is alive, "warm and friendly and living." Everest here is neither an inert thing, a backdrop for achievement, nor an occasion to think about climbing history. It is a way for Tenzing to reflect on his life and his place in it. He is alive, with a living being who teaches him how to act. He does not feel "terror" despite the wildness of the situation, but rather love and gratitude on the summit of Chomolungma. Tenzing is also able to see the mountains and valleys all around him, but he does not inhabit a discourse of sovereignty over what he sees. Rather, what he sees teaches him. What he feels, he says in *Man of Everest*, is love and thankfulness.

Tenzing had earlier explained that in his region, Chomolungma did not mean "goddess mother of the world" but meant "mountain so high birds can't fly over it" (38), which is his favourite meaning of the word. Chomolungma, therefore, can mean more than one thing. She can be a hen, someone friendly, a very high mountain or, as Tenzing's grandson Tashi Tenzing explains, she can be the location of the goddess Jomo Miyolangsangma, to whom Tenzing offers sweets and his daughter Nima's small pencil that he carried for her to the summit (Tenzing and Tenzing 2001, 84). Everest is gendered female and is maternal, unlike the "bastard" description Hillary gives to his friend Lowe, and its maternal nature can remind Tenzing that he too, can love and protect. Tashi Tenzing also points out that in his view, Tenzing did not experience the summit spiritually in an overt way, but that he did provide a food offering because he was a dutiful Buddhist (84). This is in contrast to Hillary, who sees Tenzing as a very devout Buddhist, equating what he sees as Tenzing's piety with his own religious conviction ([1955] 2003, 229). As I mentioned previously, however, Hillary was not religious at the time, and may have looked back later on and assigned religious feeling to the time on the summit. That may be why Hillary mentioned the food offering, which he sees as the "spiritual" equivalent of the crucifix, but not Tenzing's daughter's pencil, which he might not have seen as a religious offering in the strict sense. According to Tenzing, Hillary sees what he is doing as he buries the pencil, and that is when he hands Tenzing the cloth cat. He buries the sweets, the pencil, and the stuffed toy together, with a prayer of thanks to Chomolungma (Ullman and Tenzing [1955] 2010, 271). He does not know why he is asked to bury the cat, but presumably buries it because he knows that Hillary saw the pencil and the sweets. Tenzing probably assumed the same thing about the cat, that it has some kind of symbolic significance and is meant to be part of his own brief ritual.

These inconsistencies may seem like small distinctions, misunderstandings, or instances of a lack of communication as two men from different cultures who are not close friends recount a single experience. But there is one detail that cannot be reconciled between the two accounts. Tenzing says in *Man of Everest* Hillary handed him that "small cloth cat, black and with white eyes, that Hunt had given him as a mascot" to put beside the other mementos. Tenzing makes sure to say that this is not a mistranslation or miscommunication about what was given to him: "in his story of our climb Hillary says it was a crucifix that Hunt gave him, and that he left on top; but if this was so I did not see it. He gave me only the cloth cat. All I laid in the snow was the cat, the pencil, and the sweets" (271). It is impossible to mistake the precision of what Tenzing says. Rather than a Christian spiritual object that Hillary buries beside Tenzing's food offerings, an object that connects Hillary to Hunt and to a Christian version of British masculinity while it exists *alongside* Buddhism, Tenzing is asked to bury a mascot. It is something he does for Hillary, but Hillary does not acknowledge it. Neither Hillary nor Hunt ever mention the existence of the mascot. It is possible that Tenzing never saw Hillary bury the cross, but what of the cloth cat? Why is it only Tenzing who mentions it?

The cloth cat does not fit the narrative of heroic, white, colonial masculinity that Hunt and Hillary create, not in the way that the cross does. In the "spiritual" version of the story which Hillary tells later, Tenzing is a true believer, whose spirituality is exhibited by his burying of food (his daughter's pencil does not fit this story, although it might for Tenzing). Tenzing's spirituality is understood by Hillary as existing literally alongside Christianity, the former validating the latter's "right" to be on the summit of Everest. The act of burying two religious symbols, in Hillary's version, brings the sacredness of Christianity to Everest, and in some way expresses what he sees as the innate spirituality of the mountains. Because the cross is from Hunt, it also consecrates the summit for the whole expedition, a fulfilment of a leader's request. But in order to make this equivalence work, the cloth cat and the request made to bury it, a request that re-establishes the master-servant relation, cannot be described. The toy is only a mascot. Perhaps to Hillary, it is like the pencil, beneath notice. It is not serious enough a symbol to bear the symbolic freight of the moment. But that is not how Tenzing experiences the same moment. Tenzing's actual feelings about the event also go unrecorded until he provides them later in his own account. For one thing, he does offer a prayer of thanks and he does make a small offering, but it is important here that the pencil is part of that offering, and probably means as much as the food (which could mean any number of things – it could be important because it is his daughter's, it could be important because it is a gift and Tenzing can offer it to Chomolungma, or it could even represent education for girls, which Tenzing – who could not read or write himself – supported). In any case, Hillary sees none of this and appears to understand less. He leaves out what does not fit the narrative. And so, in that moment, Tenzing is mis-seen by Hillary as an innately spiritual person in Christian terms because he is a Sherpa, so that his spirituality – as viewed by someone who is not Buddhist – can serve the needs of the narrative the expedition *must* create, a narrative of utmost seriousness.

This is in keeping with Jan Morris's description of meeting Colonel John Hunt, a "serious and earnest man" ([1958] 2000, 54) who made the frivolous activity of climbing a mountain (as Morris sees it) of "utmost importance" (55). What was at stake was the representation of the British empire in the postwar world. The climb was timed so that the summit would be announced on the day of Queen Elizabeth II's coronation. That timing was designed to make the British empire's goals connect to the ascent of the Third Pole, a connection made evident in the rapturous coverage of the event by the British media (Hansen 2013, 245–6,

Slemon 2012, 37). Even Hillary's explanation that there is a photo of Tenzing and not Hillary himself because Hillary did not know if Tenzing could work a camera (Hillary [1955] 2003, 228) serves to highlight that Hillary thought of Tenzing as someone who could not be shown to work a camera, as if Tenzing could not have been taught. Tenzing himself was not aware of Hillary's reasoning about the camera, and so he did not know why Hillary did not allow him to take a picture at the time (Ullman and Tenzing [1955] 2010, 271). All this combined to make the summit experience about white, British mastery, "the paramount moment in British imperial self-fashioning" (Slemon 2012, 33). White British mastery is what makes Tenzing the object of a photograph and the occasion of a spiritual moment, but only as an object who is looked at. He is not the subject who gets to tell his version of the story to the world until after the "official" narrative appears.

The cloth cat and the flopping fish offer an alternative to the prevailing narrative of Everest heroism, a story that admits Sherpas but only as colonial others to the real work of climbing, only capable of existing alongside neocolonial claims to Everest when they are presented as "spiritual" in a certain way. Tenzing has to tell these stories after the official versions, and in reaction to them. They are not as well-known as either Hunt's or Hillary's versions: Hunt's account became an international bestseller (Isserman and Weaver 2008, 295) and Sir Edmund Hillary's autobiography is still in print. Neither *Man of Everest* nor another version of Ullman's biography, *Tiger of the Snows*, are easily available in print today and so Tenzing's version of events is not as well known. We are fortunate it is known at all: Walter Bonatti's *The Mountains of My Life* and the journalist Shazeb Jillani record the frustration of Hunza climber Emir Mehdi (called Mahdi in Bonatti's account), who was tricked by the leader of the 1954 Italian expedition on K2 into believing that he would be selected for the summit team. Mehdi's testimony about the climb for a subsequent inquiry was even used against his own climbing partner, Bonatti, without Mehdi's approval or knowledge (Bonatti [1998] 2010, 342; Jillani 2014). And what the climbers and porters on the French expedition to Annapurna thought about not having a chance for the summit remains unknown. Both of these examples underscore the ways in which Western European ideas about climbing masculinity continuously work to exclude, misunderstand, silence, or misuse the work and stories of the "others" who made landmark first ascents possible.

As Tashi Tenzing points out, Tenzing's stories – such as his statement about who actually stepped on Everest first – were relatively unknown to the rest of the world. In the case of who summited first, no one paid attention to what Tenzing had said: only when Hillary himself said it in his widely reported statement of 1993 was it believed (Ullman and Tenzing [1955] 2010, 82–3). Because he does not read or write, Tenzing tells his story with the help of an interpreter to James Ramsay Ullman, who transcribes and translates it, mediating it in the process. Nevertheless, Tenzing's version of events can be read into and against the official story of who summited Everest, who belongs on it, and who Sherpa people are in relation to climbing. They provide alternate narratives about the summit day and about what Sherpas on the expedition experienced. Subsequent stories about Sherpa experience, including Judy and Tashi Tenzing's account of Tenzing Norgay and other Sherpa climbers called *Tenzing and the Sherpas of Everest*, Jemima Dika Sherpa's essay "Three Springs" or Sherry Ortner's book about Sherpas called *Life and Death on Mount Everest*, show that the narrative of climbing authenticity perpetuated by Hunt, Hillary, and others, which foregrounds British climbers as sahibs in the colonial and paternalist tradition (Hunt [1953] 2003, 84; Davis 2011, 160; Ortner 1999, 46–8), depends on understanding Sherpas as childish, cheerful, ready to serve and yet in need of British, military discipline because they clearly were not actual climbers and lacked motivation (Morris [1958] 2000, 19; Ortner 1999, 42–6; Davis 2011, 526–7; Jemima Dika Sherpa 2014).

After the famous climb, Tenzing and Hillary were made to perform symbolically as the representatives of national ambition, because they were placed in a glaring media spotlight that upended the Everest Committee's plans for publicizing the expedition and highlighting the work of Hunt, its leader (Cosgrove 2014). The changing nature of sovereignty, Peter Hansen points out, results in conflicting ideas about national belonging for Tenzing, as Nepal and India assert their sovereignty over him, and Britain (including New Zealand) claims Hillary. Tenzing had carried four flags, including the flags of the United Kingdom, Nepal, and India, and showed all of them in the summit photograph (Hansen 2013, 251).

In India and Nepal, Tenzing was celebrated almost as a god, to the annoyance of Hunt, who saw Tenzing as a servant more than as a true climber (Ullman and Tenzing [1955] 2010, 282–5). Nepal and India tried to claim Tenzing as a citizen, while Tenzing himself resisted either ideal of citizenship, understanding himself as a Sherpa who was a citizen wherever he lived and worked, and emphasizing the pan-national nature of the achievement (Slemon 2012, 38–9; Hansen 2013, 273). But both Hunt and Tenzing did fly the Union Jack from their ice axes when they landed in London, where they greeted by the minister for war, overtly politicizing the event (Hansen 2013, 259). Meanwhile, Hillary was heralded on an American tour for allowing his "guide" Tenzing to share the glory, as if he and Tenzing had not been a team (Isserman and Weaver 2008, 299). Hillary received a British knighthood and Tenzing did not, prompting charges of racism and unfairness in the British media. Hillary, for his part, did not want the knighthood, although it was welcomed by New Zealand (Hansen 2013, 252).

As Peter Hansen has pointed out, the treatment of Tenzing and Hillary highlights how ideas about colonial and national sovereignty had changed since the 1920s. In the Cold War period, nationality mattered more than empire, although the vestiges of empire persisted in the newer idiom of the commonwealth and the crowning of its queen. The treatment of Tenzing by the British members of the expedition of 1953 shows that the British saw him as an organizer more than as a climber or a leader, and saw Hillary, another colonial subject, as a climber. But they were forced to reckon with Tenzing's independence from any attempt to make him seem servile when Nepal and India each hailed him not just as a climber, but as the leader of the summit team. When Tenzing even did an interview with *Life* magazine and accepted cash and gifts (Ullman and Tenzing [1955] 2010, 281), it was clear that the geopolitical landscape had changed. Sherpas were no longer going to be seen so unthinkingly as mere servants of empire. As *Man of Everest* shows, Tenzing understood himself to be a climber. He was no servant.

The myth of Everest's decline from a pre-cultural "innocence" is bound up with a long history of attitudes international visitors and climbers in the Himalayas have held about the Sherpa people. British expeditions had conceived of Everest as an objective while India was still part of the British empire. The 1921 expedition leader Charles Howard-Bury was partly chosen because of his experience of colonial India and his ability to control subaltern people. He loved Indian people as long as they remained servile (Davis 2011, 296). During the 1920s and 1930s, British climbers had treated Sherpas – who carried loads, cooked and set up tents for the expeditions – as little more than colonial servants who had to be "handled" by expedition members so that they would perform well (140–1), necessitating the application of discipline when they were "lazy" (Ortner 1999, 48). This early, Orientalist view of Sherpas became combined with romantic ideals about the people of the Himalayas as unspoiled, simple and childlike (43–7). But decades later, Tenzing and Hillary finally stood on the summit as the colonial representatives of an empire that no longer existed. Their ascent had been deliberately timed to coincide with the coronation of Queen Elizabeth II, as Jan Morris details in *Coronation Everest* ([1958] 2000, 123). And yet, the colonial framework of Everest expeditions was an uncomfortable fit, particularly for Tenzing. In *Man of Everest*, Tenzing is critical of British expeditions, praising the Swiss, and especially his friend Raymond Lambert, for their egalitarian politics and willingness to treat Tenzing and other Sherpas not as servants or coolies – as the British did – but as full expedition members (Ullman and Tenzing [1955] 2010, 111, 224). Tenzing recounts how Sherpas almost went on strike in 1953 because the British housed them in Kathmandu in a stable with no toilet facilities (230–1). There were other problems because John Hunt's leadership was formal and military in style, and so he did not treat Sherpas as full expedition members (233–4).

The Myth of Decline in the Commercial Era: Sherpas

The images of Sherpas in most expedition films or written accounts are most often used to provide Orientalist exoticism, a backdrop to the work of climbing. In many such accounts, Sherpas still appear to fulfil the same role of servants who provide "spiritual" local colour as they did in the 1950s. But the history of the Sherpa people in the Himalayas complicates the narrative of Everest's decline and the assumption that as a people they have been "spoiled" by the climbing industry. The Sherpa are an ethnic group from Tibet who migrated to the eastern and then central part of the Himalayan ranges in the fifteenth century. The Sherpa lived in relative isolation, practising a form of Buddhism and tending yak herds and farming in the valleys of the Himalaya, trading with other Tibetans and northern people of India. They lived in small villages connected by footpaths, ensuring that their way of life developed without much outside influence until the late nineteenth century, when the pressures of global politics brought non-Sherpa explorers, military men, and government agents to this remote part of the world (Ullman and Tenzing [1955] 2010, 2–4). At the same time, some male Sherpas migrated to Darjeeling in India to become seasonal labourers, and like others in such a position, presented themselves as coolies who could carry loads, help build roads, or help on climbing expeditions. Sherpas quickly became known for their abilities at high elevations and were sought after by the early expedition teams as load carriers and servants (Ortner 1999, 12–13).

The view of Sherpa porters and climbers as hard and cheerful workers and their position within a colonial system of racist classification mean that the Sherpa have been celebrated and idealized while they have been subjected to marginalization within the history of mountaineering, exposed to very dangerous climbing conditions that they have not always been able to influence, and in general treated as "other" within a mostly Western frame of reference. Until very recently, they were relatively underpaid for the work they did given its risks, or uninsured so that their families had no income if they were killed or injured. The Sherpas who risk their lives to work on climbing expeditions are often treated as if they are invisible (Brown 2014). Their invisibility has extended to how written accounts and films as people of the mountains portray them in Orientalist terms as cheerful, brave, peaceful, and childlike people with interesting religious and cultural customs, the ideal servants whose customs add local colour.[11] Even now, it is a rare expedition or adventure film about Mount Everest that does not begin with a shot of Kathmandu's busy streets, with a few more shots of Boudhanath monastery, prayer wheels, and small villages, before the story moves to the mountains and with the exception of the *puja* ceremony, leaves all Himalayan cultural references behind.

The Sherpa people are sometimes the object of complaints, even lodged by the same people who idealize them, about their supposed stubbornness, passivity, laziness, or superstitious tendencies. Since the early twentieth century, they have been described as supposedly un-moved by death in the mountains, a false supposition connected ob-liquely to the colonialist idea that Buddhists or Hindus do not value life as Christians might (Ortner 1999, 41–2). As invisible as they often are, Sherpas are necessary to the commercial climbing industry on Everest. Very few climbers who attempt Everest would be able to do so with-out the Sherpas who carry loads, fix ropes in the ice as climbing aids, make food, and set up tents. Recently, Sherpas have begun to assert their agency as climbers who deserve better working conditions. In 2013, a group of Sherpas challenged Western climbers on Everest to a fight when the climbers disrupted Sherpa work, surprising people around the world who were used to thinking of Sherpas as peaceful people who are sub-servient (Adhikari 2017). In 2014, an avalanche on Everest killed at least thirteen Sherpa guides and workers, prompting the Sherpa community to petition the Nepalese government to close the climbing season, and to threaten to strike if families were not compensated (Stout 2014). Sherpa self-determination is causing more criticism of the climbing industry, particularly with regards to the ways in which commercialization is caus-ing Sherpa hardship (Parker 2015).

But the conclusion that the commercial era of climbing is corrupt be-cause of how Sherpas are treated does not take into account what Sherpas think that they are doing on Mount Everest and other high peaks. Nepal is one of the poorest countries in the world, and the regions where the Sherpas live are among the poorest of all. As it did for Tenzing Norgay, the climbing industry brought welcome revenue to some Sherpa, and has opened up economic opportunities that many Sherpa and Sherpani (female Sherpa) would not have imagined a century ago. It is also evident that the commercialization of the climbing industry on Everest has made profound changes in Sherpa social and economic organization, as they adapted to a mountain tourist economy. But this has not resulted in an eradication of Sherpa culture. Rather, it led to a strengthening of some of its elements: "tourism in Khumbu, unlike tourism in some other parts of the world, has not fostered a sense of cultural inferiority or a pervasive transformation of culture or identity. Sherpas remain proud of their trad-itions and of their distinctiveness as Khumbu Sherpas" (Stevens 1993). Tourism has also led to a movement among Sherpa for economic self-determination. Sherpa strikes such as the one in 2014 have resulted in calls by the Sherpa for appropriate compensation for their families when accidents happen and safety measures that adequately protect Sherpas working on the mountain (Bramley 2015).

Although there might be some (including Krakauer) who remain nostalgic for the heroic age of climbing when Everest was more pristine, the fact is that a return to that age would mean a reduction of Sherpa rights and a continuation of racist and colonial stereotypes about them as a people and as workers who are essential to almost all climbing expeditions on Mount Everest. The widely held assumption of George Mallory's heroism – the belief that he "belonged" on Everest more than any other person – must be tempered by fact that Sherpa were there too, and that they belong to the mountains as much or more than the foreign climbers who are visitors. Mallory himself trained Sherpa porters to become climbers so that by 1924, Sherpa were able to supply Mallory and Irvine with oxygen canisters and other supplies at their highest camp. This labour was and is unmentioned in most accounts of Mallory's last climb. But in 1922, six Sherpas were lost in an avalanche while Mallory guided them. Although Mallory himself was devastated and fellow climber Howard Somervell was consumed with guilt, the official expedition account did not even mention the names of the Sherpas who died. After the accident, a message from the expedition was sent down the valley which said only, "all whites safe" (Jack 2013). In letters, Mallory revealed that his views of Sherpas were racist, complaining that he wanted to return home because he was tired of Tibetans, calling them a "hateful people" (Davis 2011, 344). In a letter to the secretary of the Everest committee at the end of the 1922 expedition Mallory said that he longed to no longer see "dark-skinned faces" (368). In a 1921 letter to his wife, Mallory suggested that he should bring his favourite Sherpa, a young boy called Nyima, back to England in order to be his servant because as "a coolie whose job it is to carry," he could haul their luggage to the train station and perform other menial jobs. There is no record of whether the Sherpa wished to go with Mallory, or if he knew that Mallory had called him "a clean animal" who "might inhabit part of the cellar or the outside coal shed" when he brought him home (327).

Such obviously paternalist and overtly racist attitudes are no longer part of the public face of the climbing industry in the Himalayas, but residual attitudes about Sherpas that disregard what their lives and working conditions are like still include idealizing the Sherpa of the Khumbu region and treating the setting of Mount Everest as a backdrop for mostly Western and white heroic achievement. The Sherpa themselves, as they are in the latest Everest film and in the most-read accounts of Everest climbs, remain invisible (Elmes and Frame 2008, 230). But not for lack of trying: the early efforts of Tenzing Norgay in his memoir, his son Jamling Norgay in his account of his Everest climb (Norgay 2002), the memoir by Tenzing's grandson Tashi Tenzing (Tenzing and Tenzing 2001), the recent republication in English of Ang Tarkay's 1954 memoir about his work as sirdar on Annapurna with the French team in 1950 (2016), anthropologist Sherry Ortner's study of Sherpa climbing and culture based on a decade of interviews with Sherpa people (1999), Peter Zuckerman and Amanda Padoan's book about Sherpa heroism during the 2008 K2 disaster (2013), Jennifer Peedom's documentary *Sherpa* (2015), and shorter magazine or blog articles by Sherpa writers – including Jemima Dika Sherpa (2014) and Norbu Tenzing Norgay (2015) – all try to bring context to the lives of Sherpa people and show why some of them continue to do dangerous work on Everest in the commercial era. Particularly since the 2013 brawl between Sherpas and foreign climbers (Adhikari 2013) and the accidents and avalanches of 2014 and 2015 on Everest, which led to calls for better working conditions, safety standards, pay and benefits, Sherpa climbers themselves have started to speak, within films and in articles they write themselves, about the dangers which their work conditions now pose on Everest and other high mountains (Potts 2016, Preiss 2018). It is becoming increasingly difficult to treat Sherpa climbers and porters as invisible or even as an "exotic" backdrop to the world of climbing anymore.

Accounts by and about Sherpas themselves show that the commercial era is not without its benefits for the people who go to Everest as part of their livelihood, year after year. By 2014, after the Everest Sherpa strike for better working conditions and in light of the experience many Sherpa now have as climbers and as expedition company entrepreneurs, it was obvious that the Sherpa who make Mount Everest their workplace should be understood neither as eternally cheerful servants nor as lazy and undisciplined workers who need non-Sherpa leadership. Rather, as Sherpas like past climbing legends Tenzing Norgay and Ang Tharkay have said, Sherpas do climb Everest and other high mountains because it is lucrative and the work can be exciting. But it is also dangerous work and given the problems of compensating injured workers or their families in an impoverished country, they expect to be compensated and insured appropriately (Barnes 2015). What do Sherpas think of the *Everest* IMAX film and its neo-colonial treatment of the Sherpas as almost invisible? According to Jennifer Peedom, who made the film *Sherpa* about Sherpa work conditions, they hate it (Bramley 2015).

The Myth of Decline in the Commercial Era: Women and Gender as Stunt

When businessman Richard (Dick) Bass stood on the summit of Mount Everest in 1985 with his guide David Breashears, he did not know that the plan he and his friend Frank Wells had dreamed up would help to change the world of mountain guiding. Bass was a Texas rancher and oil baron. From 1981 to 1984, he and Wells paid guides to help them do something no one had done before: to climb the highest mountain on each of the seven continents. Neither man was an expert climber, although both were fit enough to be guided up all seven mountains. Wells had to abandon the quest after he became president of the Disney Corporation in 1984. Bass kept going, and in 1985, on his third attempt, he summited Everest and thus completed the seven summits challenge (Weber 2015). He later published a book, *The Seven Summits* (1988), about the experience. Bass's accomplishment marked the beginning of the commercial era for high altitude mountain climbing. *The Seven Summits* was widely read, particularly in the United States. As he himself freely admitted, Bass was not a professional climber and considered himself to be a fit amateur. He gave full credit to his guides, saying that "we [Wells and I] were smart enough to take the best with us, guys who helped dampen and allay a lot of the fear ... Where you needed fixed ropes, they [the guides] could put them in. Frank and I would have killed ourselves if we went out there and tried to do that kind of stuff" (Weber 2015). Bass had proven that with enough money, "the best" guides could take some of the difficulty and risk out of climbing 8,000-metre peaks. He made it possible for climbers with money but without elite skills to imagine that they too could climb Everest.

According to Jon Krakauer, Bass's achievement "spurred a swarm of other weekend climbers to follow in his guided bootprints" (Krakauer 1997, 25). Other climbers with the financial means to do so began to hire professional guides to help them climb all fourteen 8,000-metre peaks, to do the seven summits, or just to climb Mount Everest. The commercial era on Everest and other 8,000-metre peaks had begun. But what had also begun was the critique of climbing Everest in this way because it seemed "unsporting" to climbers like Krakauer, who thought that Everest had become too easy (23). Climbing Everest with professional assistance appeared to go against what Krakauer himself called "the culture of ascent." Traditional climbing culture was anti-commercial to its core, and it was masculinist, competitive, and focused on community recognition: "characterized by intense competition and undiluted machismo ... getting to the top of any given mountain was considered much less important than *how* one got there: prestige was earned by tackling the most unforgiving routes with minimal equipment, in the boldest style imaginable" (23).

The commercial era appeared to directly challenge climbing authenticity. In the case of Everest, what were seen as the evils of commercial climbing implicitly connected commercialism, authenticity, and gender politics because the critique of commercialism and its excesses also contains an explicit critique of female climbers. In Laura Parker's analysis, the fact that women climb Everest at all is itself a sign of inauthenticity: "the Everest game has intensified beyond mere mountaineering adventure; it is a notch in the belt, a pursuit of Guinness Book-ish records for being the first woman, the first black man (a South African), and, more recently, the first black South African woman to summit. This spring's gaggle included Everest's first vegan, who not only eschewed meat and cheese, but also leather boots and a down-filled sleeping bag" (2015).

Parker goes on to quote Conrad Anker that "for the true climber, the story and the experience, exemplified by the way you go up the mountain, is more important than getting to the summit" (Parker 2015). This quotation follows the jibes at female and brown climbers, although Anker is talking about climbing style and ethics on commercial expeditions and not directly about gender. But the article nevertheless implicitly draws this conclusion, connecting the commercial era to what are assumed to be false climbing identities. The difference here is between "the true climber" and the false climber, who summits for the wrong reasons. The false climber has *the wrong body for Everest*. The first successful summit attempt is authentic because the climber has the right body for the job. It is always a white able-bodied man who is the first, in this version of the story. But when the first woman or the first brown person or the first blind person successfully summits, it is merely a stunt, something not serious and risky, like parachuting off the summit, a misuse of a body that has no right to be where it is. This is why false climbers, or climbers who aren't "real" enough, are taken to be a sign of mountaineering's decline into commercialism on Everest. And when they die, their deaths are "explained" as the result of personal folly, or weakness. Their bodies should never have been allowed to be on Everest in the first place.

Analyses like Laura Parker's that implicitly connect progressive politics with decline are not unusual to see in print. Walt Unsworth says much the same thing in *Everest: The Mountaineering History*, the definitive account of the climbing history of the mountain. In his description of the first ascents of Everest by women in the 1970s, Unsworth reworks A.F. Mummery's famous comment about mountaineering difficulty and gender: "According to A.F. Mummery, the celebrated pioneer Victorian Alpinist, any great mountain gradually regresses in the climber's estimation from being 'an inaccessible peak' to 'an easy day for a lady,' as the climbing of it becomes increasingly familiar. Mummery was perhaps being a little tongue-in-cheek, but there is a good deal of underlying truth in his words. There is no reason to believe that Everest will not follow this general pattern" ([1981] 2000, 462).

Unsworth makes these remarks just before he introduces the achievements of the first two women to summit Mount Everest in 1975, the Tibetan guide Phantog on the north route, and Junko Tabei of Japan on the south approach. Unsworth acknowledges that Mummery was joking – "the easy day for a lady" barb Mummery made was meant to mock male climbers who were shown up by his talented climbing partner, Lily Bristow (Parson and Rose 2003, 65–7). But Unsworth adds that Mummery nevertheless should be taken seriously. In other words, in Unsworth's estimation, the summiting of Everest by women should be understood to be akin to the category of stunt ascents as unserious achievements unworthy of serious treatment, like the first ski descent of the mountain, or the first ascent of the mountain by a quadriplegic or a child.

Not all commentators collapse these distinctions: ascents of Everest after the heroic era have been seen as simply the making of records on a continuum from identity or nationally based records to stunt ascents connected to extreme skiing or paragliding: "the most common form of record making was that based on identity: becoming the first female or the first climber of this or that nationality to reach the summit of this or that peak. Everest, as always, was the most desired destination ... and then there were records based on stunts" (Isserman and Weaver 2008, 443). In this view of records, stunt ascents are part of extreme sports records, and not identity records. It is possible in this view that Reinhold Messner's Seven Summits record for climbing the highest mountain on every continent could itself be seen as a stunt (443–4). But for Unsworth, an important historian of Mount Everest climbing, there is no continuum. Identity-based records are stunt ascents. Two things are key to Unsworth's characterization of female ascents of Everest: that climbs significant in terms of gender identity must not be authentic because the climber's body is not authentic, and that the presence of a woman is a sign of Everest becoming too "familiar," and too easy. To summit as a woman is to make a mountain climb inauthentic, even ridiculous. The climb itself is regarded as a stunt, and not a landmark achievement for climbing. Stunt discourse works to limit some climbs, and climbers – that are in fact not any less interesting or important than others – within a narrow, binary logic of worthy versus unworthy climbs. The Aymara women I mentioned in the introduction to this book, cooks and porters who climbed Aconcagua in 2019 on their own in traditional dress, because that is what they had always wanted to do, would not be credited with achieving anything in the world of climbing, within the logic of the stunt.

The power of stunt discourse can even make the climber who inhabits it conflicted. Sharon Wood, who in 1986 became the first Canadian woman to summit Everest, recounts her resistance to being on a summit team, even when her team leader and other team members (all men) tell her that it will be historic if she takes the chance offered to her. She resists at first, saying that "I have made sure to quash any special status since the beginning of the trip to avoid alienation" and stresses that it was only a strategy to get sponsors that she could make history (2019, 129). Wood's reluctance, even in the face of her team members reassuring her that she is on a summit team because of her merit, shows that she wants to earn her way and be treated as completely equal. Later, in the glare of publicity, she feels uncomfortable at the attention she receives, because she does not see herself apart from her team and hopes that her fellow climbers still see her as one of their own (198). She does not want her climb to be regarded as a stunt. She wants her identity as a climber to remain authentic, and for other climbers to respect who she is.

Mallory and Purity

Far more than other Himalayan 8,000-metre peaks, the history of Everest climbing includes a key aspect of mountaineering discourse which is connected closely to gender issues: the importance of climbing authenticity and its contrast to the idea of the stunt ascent. The stunt ascent is the antitheses of "pure" style, when a mountain is climbed by its most difficult or aesthetically pleasing line, or where climbing aids such as pitons or oxygen are not used. George Mallory, for instance, is remembered as "pure" because he did not support the use of oxygen to aid passage through the Death Zone. He thought that such mechanical aids were unsporting, a view held later by alpine climbers like Reinhold Messner, who is a vocal supporter of climbing mountains by what he calls fair means, which to him means climbing without oxygen or porters. Messner himself has called Mallory's last climb "a masterpiece in the annals of high altitude mountaineering" because of his dedication to what he calls a pure style (2001, 3) and credits Mallory's attitude to oxygen use as the inspiration for his own decision to climb Everest without oxygen (1989, 39–40). Purity discourse appears in the work of Messner as a way to connect climbing identity to climbing values. Correct climbing behaviour, narrowly defined, appears as climbing style. Pure style is presented as an obvious given here, but in fact, it is cultural, and it has a history.

Why is pure style and the memory of Mallory so important to the history of Everest? When a disaster occurs on Everest, established climbers often critique it as the result of improper climbing values. Mallory's experiences on the mountain are seen in this light as pure, because no one else was climbing the mountain in the 1920s, but also because Mallory symbolizes the selfless pursuit of climbing ideals, teamwork, climbing without mechanical aids, athleticism, and courage. Mallory, as many people have pointed out, climbed in tweed jackets and hobnailed boots. He had few of the advantages climbers have today, and yet he almost succeeded (or perhaps did). Mallory's position as the upholder of climbing authenticity becomes a standard to which contemporary climbers, particularly during disasters such as those of 1996, the 2006 abandonment of climber David Sharp high on the mountain, the 2012 disaster, and even the 2015 earthquake, inevitably come up short. In this critique, Mount Everest is sullied by the number of climbers on it, the advent of commercial climbing, and the rise in numbers and influence of amateur climbers and professional guides. The result is a climbing culture of selfishness, greed, and considerable risk. Who belongs on Everest? Not these people, surely! Sir Edmund Hillary, for example, condemned those who walked past David Sharp as callous (McKinlay 2006). Nick Heil, whose *Dark Summit* critiques contemporary mountaineering on Everest, has said in a blog post that "the growing number of climbers – most of them amateurs" contributes to deaths on the mountain (2012b), a comment which links the high numbers of commercial expeditions on Everest to what he sees as the problem of non-professional climbers on the mountain, who cannot or will not save themselves or others. Reinhold Messner has said that the preparation of fixed ropes and other services guides provided on Everest make it a tourist destination, and not an alpine challenge, saying "like in kindergarten, they go on Everest now" (Clash 2014). As we shall see, the 1996 Everest controversy was an early example of the debate about who belongs on the mountain, a linking of identity and experience with climbing style and ethics. But what is rarely pointed out is that this debate has at its heart ideas about authenticity and heroic masculinity. Amanda Padoan has observed that Mount Everest could be called "the world's highest glass ceiling" (2014) because that discourse of authenticity – and the lament for its loss – does not admit female climbers into the ranks of serious mountaineers. The lack of "values" for which many are excoriated includes an unvoiced nostalgia for a simpler time, when women and men who did not fit the classic climbing mould were not part of Everest expeditions. The critique of amateurism sometimes includes an implicit critique of women, brown men, and members of other minority groups who do not "belong" in the Death Zone with authentic climbers.

Against this picture of pure or proper climbing style and the men who can climb this way in the spirit of George Mallory, Reinhold Messner, or Sir Edmund Hillary is the history of what I will call stunt ascents of Everest. In *The Crystal Horizon: Everest, the First Solo Ascent*, Reinhold Messner names the important landmarks in the climbing history of

Everest. They include the first ascents from Tibet and Nepal, the first ridge ascents, the first ascent without oxygen (his own), and the first solo ascent (his own). He does not name any other record-breaking ascents, such as the first ascent by a woman, the oldest person to summit, the first person to ski Everest, or the first person to paraglide from the summit.[12] However, it could be argued that Messner's own ascent without oxygen could be in this stunt category, since it introduced an artificial level of difficulty that could have been alleviated by technology. Messner's feat could have been seen in the same way as the first ascent by a paraplegic or blind person, or as the first skier to push off from the summit. But it is not. Messner is almost universally regarded as the greatest living alpine style climber because of his landmark ascents of 8,000-metre peaks, particularly Everest.

Messner occupies the narrow limit between stunt and authentic climb, because he himself polices the limit. In *The Crystal Horizon,* Messner lauds the early failed solo ascent of Maurice Wilson, an eccentric Englishman who crash-landed a plane on the slopes of Everest in 1933 and attempted to climb the mountain alone as part of a mystical quest. Messner cites Wilson as an inspiration, saying "he is dearer to me than the legion of all those who anxiously build their little houses and preserve their lives for the old-age pension" (1989, 79). He also praises Earl Denman, another early solo climber of Everest whose efforts in 1947 were doomed to failure (80–3). Messner links his motivation to those of the early solo ascenders, and concludes that his desires to escape materialism, experience oneness with the world, and "go to the limits of [his] physical ability" (87) comprise his own motivation too. He probes the lives of Denman and Wilson, concluding that each of them had deep-seated psychological and spiritual reasons for doing what they did, some in common with his own. These, for Messner, lift solo ascents and ascents without oxygen out of the realm of the stunt ascent and into authentic mountaineering history. The search for a pure climbing style and a spiritual experience make the achievements serious and worth remembering.

Since no one in the mountaineering community thought that Everest could be climbed solo or without the help of oxygen until Messner did both, Messner has the authority – as Sir Edmund Hillary did – to weigh in on questions of climbing authenticity. He gets to determine what kinds of ascents are legitimate, and what kinds are not. What is inauthentic in his view are what he thinks of as stunt ascents of Everest, and the climbing of Everest by something less than what he has called "fair means" (Messner 2013). Everest's status as the highest mountain in the world, in such a view, make it a magnet for stunt ascents, which are record-setting climbs unrelated to completing new routes or making climbs more difficult. Stunt ascents include age-related or nationality-related records, such as the youngest person or the first Polish person to summit, or they are related to disability (the first blind person to ascend, or the first paraplegic), repeated ascents and extreme sports (first ski descent, first paraglide). First ascents and other achievements by women are often treated as stunt ascents in this way rather than ascents like those without oxygen. In other words, climbers who either do not have the "right" white, male, young, able-bodied identity for Everest or who are not willing to act as if they have such a body, must not have their achievements – when they are based on an aspect of their identities such as race, nationality, disability or gender – regarded as legitimate. Their records are to be remembered, in this view, as mere stunts. They cannot be authentic achievements in their own right if they do not follow prohibitively narrow criteria for what an authentic climber's achievement should look like.

Unsworth does acknowledge that A.F. Mummery was joking because Mummery was, after all, talking about the considerable talents of his climbing partner Lily Bristow on a difficult ascent of the Grépon in the Alps, and how she made the male members of the Alpine Club look amateurish by comparison. But Unsworth adds that in the case of Everest, Mummery should still be taken at his word. Leaving aside the fact that Phantog, as expedition guide and deputy leader of a Chinese and Tibetan team, led her own rope on summit day and made almost no use of oxygen beyond a few minutes (Gilman and Gilman [1993] 200, 104–5), or that Junko Tabei was part of the first all-woman team to ascend Everest and was the assistant leader and climbing leader of her expedition, Unsworth appears to go out of his way to minimize the achievements of both women, even as he mentions them in his history. The presence and achievements of women on Mount Everest therefore signals its decline as a climbing objective and the beginning of the commercial era and the prevalence of stunt ascents. Unsworth does this because the records on which his research depended portrayed these climbers as little more than curiosities. In most source material, the climber Phantog appears merely as "Mrs Phantog" (Unsworth [1981] 2000, 462) although some other accounts indicate that she was only called by her first name, not as "Mrs." Until relatively recently, there has been little information about her and her climbing history available in English, beyond some brief references, with rare exceptions (Isserman and Weaver 2008, 408; West 1998, 288).[13] Tabei, only the thirty-eighth person to ever summit Everest, the first woman to climb the seven summits on every continent, a professional climber, and one of the founders of women's climbing in Japan, is almost always introduced as a comic figure, "a bespectacled ex-schoolteacher from Tokyo" (Unsworth [1981] 2000, 462) and "a Japanese housewife" (359). First of all, Tabei was never a schoolteacher. The second, frequently repeated comment about her originated in the Associated Press news report of the climb, which was circulated in papers around the world ("Japanese Housewife" 1975; "Japanese House Wife Conquers" 1975). Tabei in English-language publications is never represented as a serious climber in her own right. Her authenticity as a climber has been denied her. By association, her ascent is pictured as less than serious, a stunt ascent by an amateur figure who is only defined by her marital relationship to her husband, not a leader or a pioneer.

In the context of Unsworth's characterization of "Mrs Phantog" and Junko Tabei as the harbinger of stunt ascents and meaningless records on Everest, Junko Tabei's response in *Honouring High Places*, a 2017 collection of her autobiographical writing recently edited and translated into English, is highly significant. Tabei's stories (and the stories of her friends) give the lie to the characterization of her as an amateur. They also provide important detail for English-language readers about the Japanese climbing scene, and the reason why Everest was so important as an objective. And finally, it is Junko Tabei who makes available in English a much fuller picture of "Phantog," who as it turns out, is actually "Pan Duo," a renowned Tibetan climber who climbed for China, and who deserves to be better known and understood. Most historians writing in English who are unfamiliar with Chinese climbing accounts have been getting her name wrong for decades.[14]

Honouring High Places was released in 2017. The English-language book began as a manuscript produced and edited in Japanese by Tabei's friend Yumiko Hiraki, who worked with Tabei, conducting interviews and selecting material, before Tabei's death that same year. After Tabei's passing, further text selection, editing, and translation from Japanese to English was done by Hiraki, Helen Rolfe, and Rieko Holtved, with assistance from Setsuko Kitamura.[15] The introduction by Tabei's friend and fellow climber Kitamura swiftly dispenses with the stereotypes of Tabei as an unserious or housewifely climber. She contextualizes the growth of the Japanese climbing scene with Japanese resurgence after the Second World War, the same reason why British teams tried to climb Everest after both world wars, and why the first ascent by a French team of Annapurna in 1950 was so important for France. She speaks of Tabei's accomplishments as a climber and as a founder of Japan's climbing club for women. She does say that Tabei did not think of herself initially as a feminist climber and accepted the "Japanese housewife" moniker, although after Kitamura admonishes her to be a better role model, Tabei starts to enter "climber" as her job in hotel registries and begins to act as a feminist, and an environmental activist as well.

In the essays themselves, Tabei is nothing like a passive or even conventionally feminine figure. The first chapter, "Avalanche," opens with a massive avalanche on Everest that buries Tabei and other climbers at a high camp, almost killing them all. Tabei is paralyzed at first, but then recovers and demands that she and the team continue, defying doctor's orders that she descend (2017, 32). In the chapter "The Meaning of Mountains," Tabei responds to stereotypical expectations of her as a female climber head-on in this passage: "During the question period [at a lecture], one of the students from the middle of the room vigorously stood up, and said, 'All women mountaineers are not good looking. Is that true?' He had based his question on a quote from a popular Japanese novelist. 'If you look at me,' I said, 'then you know that isn't the case.' That shut him up. So many questions and assumptions about body, looks, appearance – I was baffled at people's inability to dig deeper in their inquiries about mountaineering, and especially about the female mountaineer" (35).

Most surprisingly of all, Junko Tabei includes photographs of Pan Duo in *Honouring High Places*, so that it is finally clear for a contemporary, generalist, English-speaking audience who this climber was. The first photograph is of the first three women to climb Everest while they were at a climbing convention in Chamonix, France: Tabei is in the centre, on the right is Wanda Rutkiewicz of Poland, who was the third woman to climb Everest, and on the left is Pan Duo, the second woman to ascend

Figure 3.3 | The first three women to summit Mount Everest. From left, Pan Duo, Junko Tabei, Wanda Rutkiewicz. Chamonix, France, 1979.

Everest, and Junko Tabei's friend (figure 3.3). Tabei knew that Pan Duo had ascended after she had and had always been curious about her; in 1979, she finally met her at a film project about women's climbing organized by Maurice Herzog (210). There, Tabei became friends with Pan Duo, and was able to hear her story, which she recounts in her memoir. According to Tabei, Pan Duo was married to a Han Chinese tribesman and had three children, one of whom she was breastfeeding when she became part of the Chinese Everest team. She had to move to Beijing without her family and did not see her youngest child for sixteen years. She was part of a 1960 Chinese climbing team, but to her great frustration, she was ordered to climb no higher than 6,400 metres. The upper part of the mountain, she was told, is a man's world – words she received with anger. She was a Chinese communist nationalist, and so kept participating in other climbs until 1975, when – as the only remaining woman on the team – she summited Everest with eight male climbers ("Pan Duo" 2009).

After the climb, Pan Duo became a government administrator for Sport in China. She represented China at the World Conference on Women in 1995, and she carried the Olympic flag in 2008 with other athletes (Tabei 2017, 210–11). Her motivations for climbing were patriotic, she tells Tabei, while Wanda Rutkiewicz says to Tabei that she climbs for women's liberation. Both comments surprise Tabei, whose motivations for climbing were "myself and my team" (210). The conversation causes her to evaluate her own politics, and it is a key reason why Tabei with her longtime climbing partner Setsuko Kitamura organized a Mount Everest women's climbing summit in Tokyo, in 1995 (211–13). For Tabei, it was important for her "to learn more about the female perspective, especially since the number of women on Everest was increasing year by year" (211). As part of that summit, Tabei recorded the perspectives of female climbers from India, South Korea, and the United Kingdom, and she gave space too to the words of Pan Duo. She repeats the words of these climbers in *Honouring High Places* (213–14).

It is important to note that Tabei's decision to recount the life stories and motivations of other female climbers in this section of her memoir is an act of intersectional climbing feminism and it performs important political work. For example, Tabei recounts in detail New Zealand climber Lydia Bradey's story, when fellow climbers Rob Hall and Gary Ball not only denounced and even questioned the truth of her achievement, which was (in 1988) to become the first woman to climb Everest without the help of supplemental oxygen (214–15). Tabei not only hears Bradey's story at the first women's climbing summit but invites her to Japan so that her climb could be officially recorded (215). Tabei's extensive retelling of Pan Duo's story and her use of Pan Duo's own words also marks a decision to represent another Asian female climber who, because of the politics of international climbing, had been rendered almost invisible in the mainstream climbing history of Everest. Tabei's stories of her climbing career, her training for Everest, and her life as a philanthropist and environmental activist later on therefore work as a counter narrative to the story of mountaineering as the story of male achievement and heroism. The fact that Tabei speaks in her own voice about what matters to her, and that she represents other women's stories, indicates that Tabei's understanding of climbing narratives values difference and collaboration. These stories can do much to combat the ongoing narratives of sexism and racism that circulate about Everest, and to bring context for why and how people want to climb the highest mountains in the world. As Junko Tabei's friend Setsuko Kitamura says of her, "in the period when Japanese women finally gained small wings, a woman less than 153 centimetres in height flapped her wings big time and became an important figure in mountaineering history" (18). The work of *Honouring High Places* does much to dispel the image of female climbing on Everest as the work of amateurs who belong in the private sphere, or of predominately white women. It stands as an important feminist intersectional document in the history of mountaineering on Everest and elsewhere, and it contests the narrative of Everest's decline.

Conclusion: Everest and the Problem of Decline

When Everest becomes easy, the classic version of its history assumes, anyone can climb it, even married women who are not English-speaking or white. They can climb because of the advent of commercialization, not because they are good at climbing, an assumption which links the commercial "decline" of Everest with the appearance of female climbers. Since Everest itself is always discussed as "in decline" from a pure, un-sullied state as undeserving climbers try for its summit, gender politics becomes part of the myth of Everest as a mountain polluted by culture, and a climbing culture in danger of losing its values. Such assumptions bring together ideas about Western dominance, British and European imperialism, masculinity, and the "decline" of civilization (or a nostalgia for pre-capitalism). They are evoked when any of these ideals are disturbed. This picture of Everest sees women, and especially non-European women, as evidence of Everest's stunt and commercial climbing legacy, and not part of its real story of achievement. It is a powerful narrative which, as the recent film *Everest* and the success of Krakauer's version of the 1996 disaster show, still forms the dominant story of Mount Everest and its climbing history. In the next chapter, I intervene in this narrative and critique the assumptions it makes about gender, achievement, and about high-altitude climbing itself. The legacy of Mallory, the problematic relationship of Tenzing Norgay and Sir Edmund Hillary, and the impact of the 1996 disaster and the bestselling book about it, Jon Krakauer's *Into Thin Air*, have all contributed to a politics of gender and climbing that form a remarkable thread of continuity in our thinking about gender, from the Heroic Era of first ascents, the Alpine era, to the Commercial era of the present day. The dominance of *Into Thin Air* in so many debates about Everest has in fact worked to obscure Krakauer's own gender politics, and the continued problem of the representation of female climbers when their stories, most notably Lene Gammelgaard's *Climbing High*, represent a different way to understand mountaineering rhetoric about gender on Everest.

You my friends are following in the very footsteps of history, something beyond the power of words to describe. Human beings simply aren't built to function at the cruising altitude of a 747. Our bodies will be literally dying. Everest is another beast altogether.

Everest (2015)

CHAPTER 4

EVEREST: GENDER POLITICS AND THE 1996 DISASTER

In one of the North American trailers for *Everest*, a 2015 blockbuster film based on the 1996 climbing disaster on the peak, mountain guide Rob Hall, played by Jason Clark, lets his clients know what they are in for. In an inspiring speech, Hall tells his clients that they will be climbing more than a mountain. They will be entering history itself and cheating death as they do it. The experience is described as mystical, for death and history are close by. In the trailer, Hall is more than an ordinary mountain guide. He is a professional, a leader, a hero who has earned the right to speak the truth, the one who interprets the mountain and its history for the others. Hall's speech plays over breathtaking shots of climbers on a ridge while tense symphonic music plays in the background. As the trailer proceeds, we see shots of clients from Hall's company Adventure

Consultants as they come to their Base Camp and begin to work through the dangerous ice fall. Climbers struggle to summit, a deadly storm moves in, and Hall himself is stranded high on the mountain. On the phone with his wife Jan (played by Keira Knightley), Hall struggles to stay alive as Jan begs him to descend. As the words "Never Let Go" successively flash on the screen, Jan tearfully says "if anyone can make it, you can," and then a montage of images cascades: falling climbers, the Halls kissing goodbye in an airport, photographs of family members, a flashback shot of climber Beck Weathers's wife Peaches alone at home, a helicopter, Base Camp manager Helen Wilton (played by Emily Watson) praying, a bearded climber screaming "no" as the music thunders to a climax, and drops to silence and the title flashes on the screen. The trailer is well edited, with breathtaking panoramas of climbers on knife ridges in the Himalayas. It promises excitement, danger, proximity to death, and the mountain as a "beast" that can take life away in an instant, all filmed in IMAX 3D.

In the film, high altitude climbing exists firmly within male-dominated adventure discourse and the pervasive story of the heroism of mountain guides. According to the trailer, the history of Mount Everest is the history of white male heroism as men fight "the beast." Women and brown men are not pictured as agents sharing such a space. Even the mountain itself in this version of climbing is transformed from a natural geological feature to an animal that must be fought by men. My use of the male pronoun is not inclusive here. There are no female climbers in the trailer, although there were female climbers on the mountain in 1996.[1] Even in the film itself, climbers like Lene Gammelgaard, Yasuko Namba, Charlotte Fox, and Sandy Hill Pittman hardly figure at all. The women we do see in the trailer and in the film are relegated to the domestic roles of grieving wives at home or at Base Camp. In a similar vein, Sherpas, the mountain people who are most responsible for ensuring the comfort and safety of climbers on the mountain and who played important roles in the 1996 disaster, are almost invisible in the trailer: only one Sherpa appears briefly in a Base Camp tent, and he has no speaking part. In the film, Sherpas play almost no roles except as load carriers and cooks, likewise relegated to the domestic spaces of mountain camps as if they were the women who themselves only get to be servants to white male heroism, applauding its achievements and lamenting those who fall.

In 2016, twenty years after the real 1996 disaster on Everest, it seems inconceivable that this kind of racism and sexism can still be portrayed unproblematically on screen, with the help of the latest film technology. *Everest* was based on Jon Krakauer's *Into Thin Air* and purports to tell his version of the story. What does that story really involve? The 1996 disaster and Krakauer's version of what happened are central to this story of diversity as a threat and belief in the history of climbing as decline. But it is not the only story that contributes to the pervasive belief that anyone who is not a heroic man does not deserve to be a climber at all. From the story of George Mallory, to the advent of macho alpine climbing style during the 1970s, and finally to the problems of the commercial era, Everest has been at the centre of debates about authenticity and the problem of gender and racial difference. The 1996 disaster and *Into Thin Air* mark an important pivot point in the narrative of Everest and gender that built on heroic narratives of the past in order to imagine the problems of the present on the mountain. It is time to investigate how that came to be the case.

The lesson of the *Everest* trailer and of the film itself is similar to the point of much writing and thinking about Mount Everest. In many of these accounts, women are inauthentic, wrong for the mountain, or just not there. The *Everest* film focuses such bias: the trailer shows that white male mountain guides of European or North American origin are the only people with agency. They, and only they, are the rescuers, the comforters, the leaders, the team members who bond together and respect each other, the teachers who provide the ground rules for how to climb and survive. They are the ones who are "literally following in the footsteps of history" as Rob Hall says in the film, which presumably means that they follow (and are like) other climbers before them, effectively excluding women and men who are not white and English-speaking from this narrative of events, and interpreting what the mountain means in their terms alone. Since female climbers, non-European guides, and Sherpas on Everest in 1996 did play important roles as the tragedy unfolded, and since some of them did write stories of their own about what happened or have been interviewed about their version of events, it is significant that the adventure discourse of *Everest* cannot or will not admit their presence in a dramatic treatment of those events. The events of 1996, as Michael Elmes and Bob Frame have observed, have attained the status of myth, a powerful myth about the history of Everest, what they call "a leadership lesson" that simplifies what leadership is supposed to involve (2008, 215–16).

Everest is not a documentary, but it is based on Krakauer's account of what happened on Everest in 1996. Part of the ideology in the film about women, climbing, and male leadership comes from the writing that emerged from the aftermath of that disaster, when a storm on Everest claimed fourteen lives in a single day and dramatically changed the perception of Everest and mountaineering around the world. There are two reasons why the 1996 disaster has been so influential. Two rival commercial guiding operations were on Everest that year, each trying to put all of their clients on the summit. Other teams were there too, as well as the film crew for an American-made IMAX documentary. The events were tracked by satellite phone and early internet technology, making it possible for the climbs to be followed virtually, for the first time. Many of the clients on the mountain that year were American, and so American media covered the events using the new technology more closely than they had before. And so, when the disaster struck, events like Rob Hall's final phone call to his wife were widely reported and the events of 1996 were debated in media outlets around the world. The second reason has to do with the presence of journalist Jon Krakauer, an American member of Hall's Adventure Consultants team who had been there to report on the dawn of the commercial climbing era, but who ended up a survivor of the storm. Krakauer wrote an article about the disaster for the magazine *Outside* very soon after the disaster. He went on to expand that article and write the best-selling mountaineering book of all time, *Into Thin Air*, establishing for decades afterwards the importance of the 1996 disaster and its place in the climbing history of Mount Everest. *Everest* the film exists because of *Into Thin Air* and what has become the dominant narrative of the 1996 disaster and of Everest climbing itself, despite the existence of many other books and films with quite different stories to tell about what happened.

In this chapter, I want to challenge Krakauer's version of events, which has become definitive, via a critique of mountaineering authenticity. I have a wider purpose: Krakauer's picture of the tradition of mountaineering on Everest fully participates in myths about who belongs on the mountain and in the supposed decline of climbing on Everest from the more golden ages of George Mallory, Sir Edmund Hillary, and more recently, Tyrolean climber Reinhold Messner, all of whom became famous as heroes of Mount Everest. *Everest* marks what is only the latest appearance of long-held beliefs about mountaineering and authenticity centred on the highest mountain in the world, and it hews closely to the story of the mountain most familiar to non-climbers through Krakauer's version of what happened on Everest in 1996, further enshrining Everest as the scene of classic mountaineering identity as white, European or North American, and masculine. Krakauer himself has claimed that the Everest movie is not fact-based, but his own account is, calling the film "Total bull ... Anyone who goes to that movie and wants a fact-based account should read *Into Thin Air*" (Pulver 2015) and concluding that "Everest is not real climbing. It's rich people climbing. It's a trophy on the wall, and they're done" (2015). Taken together, Krakauer's comments sum up his position about climbing, his own writing, and Mount Everest: for him, there is a stark line between authentic climbing and authentic reporting of the 1996 disaster. A narrow understanding of authenticity is at the heart of the version of Mount Everest climbing history that he wishes to uphold, one that places Everest firmly within a narrative of white male heroism acting beyond market forces, inevitable decline into capitalism, and the advent of climbing diversity.

As an event in climbing history, the 1996 disaster has been overshadowed by others after it, but in itself, it represents a key moment in the climbing history of the world's highest mountain and in high-altitude climbing as a sport. It also demonstrates how the gender and race politics in at least one key account have had a negative effect on public perceptions of who belongs on Everest in the commercial era, and have pictured gender as a commercial problem for Everest. Most of the events of the 1996 disaster are not debatable, although it may be that, as survivor Lou Kasischke writes, "the truth may never be told" about what exactly happened (2015, xv). But this much is clear: in 1996 on the southern, Nepalese side of Mount Everest, a large group of climbers gathered at Base Camp in greater numbers than ever before. For the first time, there were two rival climbing companies with big groups of clients, one headed by New Zealand guide Rob Hall and one by Scott Fischer, an American. Jon Krakauer was on the Adventure Consultants team as a journalist for *Outside* magazine, which wanted him to report on the development of guided climbing on Everest. Originally *Outside* wanted Krakauer to report from Base Camp, but Krakauer dreamed of climbing Everest to realize a boyhood ambition, and he convinced the magazine to make a deal with one of the commercial outfits (Krakauer 1997, 29). Scott Fischer had tried to bid for Krakauer, but Hall outbid him (85–6). Krakauer is well aware that he is on the team as advertising (86) and he has said that this arrangement probably affected the team, admitting that "'They [Adventure Consultants] were taking chances trying to get clients to the summit because I was there'" (Pulver 2015). But Lou Kasischke adds that it was not just the guides who were affected by Krakauer's presence. Team members themselves became concerned because they thought that Rob Hall's decision-making on summit day could be affected by a journalist there to assess it. They were proved right when Hall took unnecessary risks to get some of his clients to the top (Kasischke 2015, 24–5).

What was affecting the team, ironically, was the very thing that Jon Krakauer had been sent to cover: the advent of professional guiding companies on Everest who, for a large sum of money, enabled those who could afford it to realize their climbing ambitions on the world's highest mountains. The mid-1990s mark a shift in climbing approaches to Everest and other high mountains from nationally based or independent expeditions for scientific purposes, or by world-class climbers, to the commercial era of climbing, when it became possible to climb a mountain like Everest without being a professional or keen amateur, using the expertise of Sherpas and professional guides. The commercial era had begun in the wake of American millionaire Dick Bass's successful completion of "the Seven Summits," the highest summits on every continent, with the help of his guide, David Breashears. Bass's best-selling book *The Seven Summits* of 1986 detailed his achievement and showed its readers that with a reasonable level of physical fitness and deep enough pockets, it was possible to climb Mount Everest without being an elite mountaineer. One of the results of Bass's achievement was increased traffic on all the Seven Summits, but especially on Everest in the early 1990s (Krakauer 1997, 24–6). With larger groups of clients willing to pay for the chance to climb the highest mountain in the world, the stage was set for the commercialization of Everest by the end of the 1980s.

After completing the Seven Summits himself in seven months with his climbing partner Gary Ball, New Zealand climber Rob Hall formed

Adventure Consultants with Ball in 1991 so that they could guide clients in the Himalayas just as Breashears had guided Dick Bass. Ball and Hall had realized that they would have to do even more risky climbs than the seven summits stunt to get sponsorships and be invited on important expeditions, and neither of them wanted to continue on that path. Commercial guiding on big mountains seemed less dangerous and more lucrative (41). They had seen how David Breashears had turned his guiding of Dick Bass into a lucrative climbing and film making business, and they thought that they could do something similar. But Ball died during a climb on Dhaligiri of pulmonary edema, and so Hall continued by himself to build Adventure Consultants into a major company. Between 1990 and 1995, thirty-nine of his clients summited Mount Everest. Despite the public protests of New Zealand climbing legend Sir Edmund Hillary that commercialization was disrespectful to the mountain (41), clients continued to sign up for Everest expeditions. The cost in 1996 was $65,000 USD per client: that included guiding services, oxygen, an Everest climbing permit, rope fixing, emergency services, food, and other assistance (40–1).

The other company was Fischer's Mountain Madness. In 1994 Fischer had summited Everest for the first time himself and thought – like Ball and Hall – that the time was right to become an Everest guide. Unlike Adventure Consultants, which was a highly organized and even regimented operation, Mountain Madness combined corporate sponsorship from Starbucks with a more freewheeling approach to guiding and training (82–3). Like Hall, Fischer was anxious to see his clients reach the top. He had hired Anatoli Boukreev, a Kazakhstani, as his head climber. When he lost the bid for Krakauer, he put another journalist on the team, a socialite named Sandy Hill Pittman who filed reports for magazines from a satellite phone with an internet connection at Base Camp (Boukreev and DeWalt [1998] 2002, 11). Other expeditions on the Nepalese side of Everest included a small self-service guiding operation, some national teams – including a badly organized South African team – individual climbers who planned to connect themselves to a group climbing permit, and a team led by the same David Breashears who had guided Dick Bass up Everest. He planned to film an Everest climb with an IMAX camera, filming Ed Viesturs's attempt to climb the Seven Summits without oxygen. The large commercial expeditions, Breashears's IMAX expedition, and the smaller national expeditions were all on the mountain at the same time. It would mean that there would be too many people trying to ascend during the summit window, a short time before the spring monsoon when conditions are favourable for summit attempts. As the unofficial leader of Base Camp that year, Hall tried to organize the summit bids, but the South African and Taiwanese teams refused to cooperate (Krakauer 1997, 183). By the night of 9 May 1996, all of these teams were camped in the South Col high on Everest, positioned for summit bids beginning at midnight if the winds died down and the weather was clear.

Just after midnight on 10 May 1996, the members of Fisher's and Hall's teams, along with other climbers, assembled for the summit push. But a series of difficulties began to appear. A large number of clients proceeded slowly up the fixed ropes and began to cause slowdowns. Hall's walkie-talkies were broken, leading to a miscommunication about rope fixing and another delay. Rob Hall had a set turnaround time for his team. If climbers were still proceeding to the summit by the predetermined time, they would have to turn around, since they could not make it to the summit and back to the South Col before dark. But most of Hall's team members began to experience problems. Stuart Hutchison, Lou Kasischke, and John Taske all turned around when they saw how slowly climbers were progressing. Beck Weathers became snow blind and could not go on: Hall told him to wait high on the mountain until he came down from the summit. Doug Hansen, a postal worker who had had to turn around high on the summit ridge the year before, was feeling ill and had dropped out, but Hall had convinced him to continue. Meanwhile, the Mountain Madness team was having problems of its own. Although he was normally a strong climber, Scott Fischer did not look well on summit day and was proceeding slowly. He had not set a turnaround time, preferring that climbers should climb at their own pace and make their own decisions. His head climber, Anatoli Boukreev, had decided to climb ahead quickly and so was not assisting clients.

Even with these problems, the climb on 10 May proceeded well, although slowly. One by one, climbers summited. But then a major storm caught the majority of the climbers descending from the summit with some climbers still on their way to the top, and the scene was set for a major disaster. Doug Hansen, already suffering from high-altitude sickness, was caught with Rob Hall in the storm. He never made it off the ridge. Guide Andy Harris, suffering from oxygen deprivation, tried to climb to help Hall and it appeared that he reached him, but subsequently he disappeared, and his body was never found. Hall himself eventually froze to death after his last satellite phone call with his wife, too weak to climb down to safety. Fischer died somewhere below him, despite heroic attempts by Sherpas and Boukreev to save him. Meanwhile, members of both teams tried to descend with guides, but a group of them became caught in the wind and darkness on the South Col and could not find the tents. They were forced to huddle together until those who could walk found their camp. Boukreev went into the darkness as Hutchison shone lights and banged pots, and he brought back exhausted climbers. But he had to leave Yasuko Namba and Beck Weathers, who could not move and had to be left for dead. By the morning, eight climbers had died. Beck Weathers somehow escaped being the ninth casualty by waking up and walking back to the tents after hours in the cold, walking down the mountain with frozen hands, and was then dramatically rescued by helicopter. By the end of the climbing season that month, a total of fifteen climbers had died, making 1996 the deadliest season on the mountain to that date.

These are the indisputable facts of the 1996 disaster. But the story of *Into Thin Air* in particular moves beyond the facts and creates an argument as to why the disaster occurred. That argument rests on Krakauer's portrayal of climbing authenticity as counter-cultural, masculinist, and Western, based on ideas of sacrifice connected to the figure of George Mallory or Sir Edmund Hillary, and not to anyone (but particularly women and Sherpas) who does not fit that mold. The story of Everest here is the story of decline and pollution. As I have said, Dick Bass's seven summits feat had inspired amateur climbers to realize their dreams and encouraged guides like Ball and Hall to try to create an industry to help that happen. But other climbers, including Krakauer himself, saw the dawn of the commercial era on Everest as the denigration of the mountain to "a slag heap" (Krakauer 1997, 24). The easier routes on Everest had already been climbed many times by the 1980s, and the success of Dick Bass appeared to pull Everest into the realm of an achievement for the rich and amateur, not an honour and a career-making act for the relatively poor and dedicated. In *Into Thin Air*, Krakauer understands himself as part of the latter group because of his willingness to sacrifice his life for climbing, and because of his experience on rock and ice. He writes that he is so dedicated to the act of climbing the he "lived to climb" when he was a younger man, working as a carpenter so that he could afford trips to the Bugaboos or the Alaska range (24).

Krakauer's counter-cultural values meant that in *Into Thin Air* he depicts himself as working-class, not elite, and that he sees himself as having little in common with the other members of the Adventure Consultants expedition, except for the guides – who he sees as dedicated and skilled, like himself – and Doug Hansen, a postal worker who had raised the money to climb Everest (Krakauer 1997, 46). Guide Andy Harris, for example, reminds Krakauer of a youthful version of himself: "Andy's palpable hunger for climbing ... made me wistful for the period in my own life when climbing was the most important thing imaginable" (37). But his view of his teammates, with one exception, is different. When Krakauer takes stock of his teammates as they helicopter towards the village of Lukla, he finds all of them except for Doug Hansen, who worked an additional job in construction to raise the money to climb, as Krakauer himself had done when he was a carpenter (46), to be alien to him. He calls the rest "nice, decent folks" but adds that they are "complete strangers" because for the first time, Krakauer is not just climbing with his trusted friends. He has become a client himself (46). The picture that he draws is stark: "I wasn't sure what to make of my fellow clients," he writes. "In outlook and experience they were nothing like the hard-core climbers with whom I usually went into the mountains" (46). The contrast is clear: Krakauer bonds with those who he thinks are authentic climbers, which is how he sees himself. He sees Harris's dedication and Hansen's working-class credentials as indicators of authenticity because real climbers sacrifice their lives, and their livelihoods, to climb. The others, it is implied, have not done this and so in much of *Into Thin Air*, Krakauer draws a line between them, the guides, and the working-class amateurs. The former do not, Krakauer infers, have the ambition, desire, and skills to succeed in the mountains. Their elite status makes them into tourists in his mind, not climbers, because to him, they have not sacrificed everything. In Krakauer's version of the new climbing economy, female climbers who are not on Everest to work all fall into the elite amateur category. Since the non-climbing women in Adventure Consultants are not guides (there were no female guides on Everest in 1996) they are associated with Base Camp, a domestic space, and do not play a major role in the story Krakauer tells.

Krakauer's first impressions of his teammates bear out this dividing line. He introduces Base Camp manager Helen Wilton as a "mother of four," when he does not introduce any male climbers as fathers. He remarks that expedition doctor Caroline Mackenzie is "an accomplished climber" but says little else about her achievements. In this drama, because they are not climbers, both women are meant to play supporting roles. As for the climbers, Lou Kasischke is introduced as a "gentlemanly lawyer," Yasuko Namba is "a taciturn personnel director," and Beck Weathers is "a garrulous pathologist." Stuart Hutchison is called a "cerebral, somewhat wonkish Canadian cardiologist" (45). John Taske is described as a retired anaesthesiologist who had "taken up climbing" after leaving his job, while Frank Fischbeck is "a dapper, genteel publisher from Hong Kong" (46). With the exception of brief mentions of Kasischke's successful climbing of most of the seven summits, Fischbeck's three attempts to climb Everest, and Hansen's previous attempt, Krakauer does not introduce his teammates' climbing records, and focuses on their occupations instead. Taske's climbing history is introduced as if it were a casual hobby. Hutchison's considerable climbing record goes unmentioned. Namba's record is also not mentioned and her reputation is, as we shall see, minimized later on.

One of Krakauer's surviving teammates, Beck Weathers, has endorsed Krakauer's view of events in his own memoir *Left for Dead*, calling Krakauer's account "definitive" (Weathers 2000, 12). Charlotte Fox, a member of the Mountain Madness team, has said that she sees Krakauer's account as definitive "'because he truly tried to get the facts straight'" (Sohn 2006). But not all those who were on Everest agree with Krakauer's framing of the events. Most notably, Anatoli Boukreev's *The Climb*, written with G. Weston DeWalt, is a response to Krakauer's questioning of Boukreev's actions during the disaster that provides a different view of the events. Commentators have noted frequently that *The Climb* opens up the possibility that Krakauer's account contains some fictionalized elements and subjective assessments (Garner 2010, Horrell 2011, Johnson 2012) which could be why Krakauer vigorously contested the composition of *The Climb* in the postscript to the 1999 edition of *Into Thin Air* (Krakauer 1999, 307–26). Boukreev was a professional mountaineer and guide with another team, and so responded to Krakauer on that basis, focusing on his own actions and understanding of events: he could not comment on Krakauer's picture of the Adventure Consultants team. Boukreev died in a mountaineering accident in 1999, and so *The Climb* remains his only published statement about the events of 1996.

Lou Kasischke's portrait of the team in *After the Wind*, his own memoir of the 1996 disaster not published until 2015, is another. Kasischke's memoir in particular is an important corrective to Krakauer's version of events because with the exception of Beck Weathers, whose memoir focused on his own story and recovery, Kasischke is the only surviving client with Adventure Consultants who has written about the dynamics of the team. Notably, as an Adventure Consultants client and a possible target of Krakauer's critique of commercial culture, Kasischke does not see the commercial era in the same light. Unlike Krakauer, Kasischke thinks that the commercial era had improved climbing, not caused its decline: "Professionally organized climbing significantly improved the sport. Professional alpinists led the way to developing high standards, better skills, and more responsible climbers and climbing values. This advancement, in turn, attracted a higher caliber of climber, who brought to climbing a broad array of experiences, especially in high stakes decision-making" (2015, 28).

It is key that Kasischke emphasizes the experience of team members not just as climbers, but as leaders who are capable of thinking for themselves. He calls his team members "serious, part-time climbers, proud of being amateurs" (63) and pictures the Adventure Consultants team as a team, and not just as a collection of clients who unthinkingly follow the direction of their guides. In a direct contrast to the scene in the film *Everest* where clients silently listen to Rob Hall hold forth with admiring eyes, climbers in Kasischke's account discuss decisions at length and think about the welfare of the team. There is concern about Andy Harris's lack of high-altitude experience – veteran Ed Viesturs was to have been a guide but could not because he had agreed to be part of the IMAX team, and so Harris replaced him (51). Team members become concerned later with Hall's plan to summit with the rival team and argue with Hall about it, pointing out that there was a possibility of delays that could cost them all the summit and their safety (78–81). On summit day when Hall makes a unilateral decision to climb, Kasischke points out that this is not how to run a team: "Rob never consulted with Andy [Harris] or any of us on the decision. Because the stakes were so high and the weather so questionable, for Rob to make a major strategic decision unilaterally was not a good sign. Our tent was full of experienced and well-informed climbers who had serious thoughts about what to do and why" (135). The ability of at least some of the team members to make independent decisions is probably the reason why four of them – Kasischke, Taske, Fischbeck, and Hutchison – decided on their own not to continue to the summit as conditions deteriorated because "they needed Rob the least for judgment and decision-making" (190). Weathers also decided to turn around but listened to the poor advice Hall gave him and waited high on the mountain in the cold for Hall to return, a decision that almost cost him his life (154). Doug Hansen also turned around because he said that he did not feel well, but Hall spoke with him and he resumed climbing (Krakauer 1997, 216). Kaskischke adds that Hall disregarded the advice of other climbers who saw Hansen saying that he wanted to turn back, suggesting that Hall should let him descend (Kasischke 2015, 145–6). The problem here is not the inexperience of the team members and the wisdom of their guides. It is that the team leader, intent on getting his clients to the top with a reporter present, did not consult enough with the experienced members of his own team.

The team itself is not, in Kasischke's account, starkly divided between dedicated and experienced climbers and guides, versus inexperienced clients. Throughout *After the Wind* Kasischke discusses his teammates in terms of their climbing records and experience, sometimes giving quite a different account of their abilities than Krakauer does. John Taske, for example, is described as a veteran climber who had served in an elite commando unit in Vietnam and so was used to making tough decisions (33). Rather than "wonky," Stuart Hutchison is "intelligent, and quick-witted," with fifteen years of climbing experience in the Himalayas and Alaska (46). Yasuko Namba has a "goal-oriented mindset" and is quiet rather than taciturn; Kasischke adds that she "was one of the leading female climbers in Japan and had climbed on earlier expeditions around the world with Rob. She was a national figure in Japan and all of Asia, where climbers are held in high esteem" (47). The differences between these assessments of Namba and Hutchison are particularly important. From the beginning of *Into Thin Air*, Krakauer portrayed Namba as the quintessential inexperienced client, interpreting her quiet nature as evidence of ignorance, and as we shall see, understanding her commitment not as evidence of dedication but as evidence of her lack of experience. Hutchison too, will be described as an inexperienced bumbler, so much so that years later, he complained that Krakauer's portrayal of him as a novice climber meant that he became part of the story of Everest's commercial decline, despite the evidence: "For the next five years, people would come up to me and say, 'Well you didn't deserve to be there, because you'd never climbed before,' because that's what they'd read. When I'd try to explain that, actually, I had quite a bit of experience beforehand, they would say, 'No, you didn't'" (Sohn 2006).

Finally, in what can only be assessed as an error of fact in *Into Thin Air*, Krakauer's account of turnaround times is questionable, making an assessment of his other motives for writing the book imperative. Krakauer describes Hall as adamant that his orders on summit day must be followed and that Krakauer in particular needed to be obedient: "'I will tolerate no dissension up there,' he admonished, staring pointedly at me. 'My word will be absolute law'" (Krakauer 1997, 216). Krakauer explains that he had been allowed to climb faster than the others (217) but that Hall might have to turn the group around before the summit (217), and "passivity on the part of the clients [was] encouraged on the expedition" (219). One of the orders that presumably would have to be followed was Hall's pre-set turnaround time. A turnaround time lets a climber know objectively whether she can summit by a specific time. If the climber is too far from the summit to make the time set, she should turn around to avoid being caught high on a mountain late in the day or during a storm, tired and possibly disoriented from the effort. Since summit fever can make a climber think that reaching the summit in good time is possible, a turnaround time can help climbers to make a responsible decision based on their physical condition, the weather, the condition of the snow, and other factors. According to Krakauer, "Hall had contemplated two possible turnaround times – either 1:00 pm or 2:00 pm. He never declared which of these times we were to abide by" (232). Furthermore, the day before the summit push, Krakauer says "Hall still hadn't announced what our turnaround time would actually be. Hutchison, conservative by nature, was operating on the assumption that it would be 1:00 pm" (232). And finally, Krakauer writes that Hall told Hutchison and Taske at 11:00 am that "the top was still three hours away" (233), predicting a summit time of 2:00 pm.

This is not what Lou Kasischke says occurred. He writes that "Rob set the turnaround time for 1 pm" at the final camp (Kasischke 2015, 118). He told the entire team, who had discussed it at length, and there was no doubt among them about what the turnaround time was.[2] In an interview he did for *The Climb* he says the same thing and confirms that Stuart Hutchison agreed: "we had a one o'clock turnaround time. And Stu [Hutchison] was convinced of that" (Boukreev and DeWalt [1998] 2002, 140). Why are turnaround times important, and why would Krakauer misreport the time as well as the discussions and never correct the error? Taske, Kaskischke, and Hutchison turned back before the Hillary Step between 11:30 am and 12:00 pm when they realized that with the bottleneck in front of them, they would have to wait too long to summit. Krakauer reports a bottleneck at 1:00 pm on the Hillary Step, the last challenge before the summit and the only technical climbing section of the route, because guides and Sherpas had not fixed the ropes leading to it. Nonetheless, Krakauer climbs the Hillary Step and is on the summit just afterwards at 1:12 pm, one of the first climbers to summit – just behind guide Anatoli Boukreev. He begins to make his way down but is slowed by other climbers making their way up the Hillary Step rope. Krakauer finally begins to descend after 2:00 pm. He reports the following about those after him: "the only people to reach the summit before 2:00 pm were Boukreev, Harris, Beidleman, Mountain Madness client Martin Adams, Klev Schoening, and me [Krakauer]; if Fischer and Hall had been true to their pre-arranged rules, everyone else would have turned back before the top" (1997, 261).

According to Krakauer, what happens next is that Beidleman stays on the summit, anxious about the lateness of the hour but there to help other clients. Hill Pittman summits at 2:10, followed by Charlotte Fox, the Sherpa Lopsang, client Tim Madsen, and Lene Gammelgaard, who reports later that she summited at about 2:30 pm (Boukreev and DeWalt [1998] 2002, 230). Finally, Rob Hall, Adventure Consultants guide Mike Groom, and Yasuko Namba appear. Scott Fischer does not summit until 3:40 and Doug Hansen, with Hall's help, reaches the summit after 4:00 pm (Krakauer 1997, 262–3).

Notably, Krakauer blames Fischer and Hall for not adhering to their own rules, and this assessment now forms part of the accepted wisdom about what went wrong that day.[3] In his summary, Krakauer says that "predetermined turn-around times were egregiously ignored" and then adds "extending the turn-around times may to some degree have been influenced by the rivalry between Fischer and Hall" (355). But he had already written that Hall had never settled on a time, a fact backed up by Neal Beidleman, who said on the Mountain Madness recording that Hall had recommended more than one time, but that neither was stringent (Boukreev and DeWalt [1998] 2002, 321). He adds that Hall's "cut-off time" was 10:00 am on the South Summit (321), which would mean that the turnaround time was 1:00 pm. Moreover, Krakauer had not commented on whether Fischer even had a turnaround time at all – Gammelgaard says in an interview in *The Climb* that she had never heard that Fischer even had a summit turn-around time (Boukreev and DeWalt [1998] 2002, 145). *The Climb* describes Fischer's alternate system: he would sweep climbers as last in line and turn climbers around as needed (Boukreev and DeWalt [1998] 2002, 146). It does appear that Fischer and Hall agreed to set off at the same time for the summit, an agreement they made with each other without consulting with other guides or team members (Boukreev and DeWalt [1998] 2002, 118, 312; Kaskischke 2015, 135). If it is true that for his team Hall vaguely set the turnaround time for 2:00 pm at the latest, Jon Krakauer summits exactly when he should, just after 1:00 pm, along with guides and two other clients. It would not seem that most clients were that late, summiting just after the latter turn-around time. Krakauer's criticism seems misplaced for most climbers that day, another instance of him demonstrating that less experienced clients summited too late while he, a strong climber, summited on time. But if the turnaround time to summit was 1:00 pm and was clearly a rule that Hall had set, then Krakauer himself disregarded the turnaround time and summited late, not turning back at the Hillary Step. Krakauer then would not be all that different from other clients and guides who had summit fever and could not stop themselves from continuing. Unlike those who turned back at 12:00 pm, realizing correctly that they could not get up the Hillary Step and to the summit by 1:00 pm, Krakauer made the decision to continue and as a result, was caught up in the Hillary Step bottleneck, ran out of oxygen, and could not assist Andy Harris, who was severely hypoxic (Krakauer 1997, 245). In the end, Krakauer's decision to go on to the summit meant that he was forced to climb down very quickly through the gathering storm (254–5) and so was not in a position to assist the rescue effort later that night. Indicating the summit turnaround time was 2:00 pm would keep the line clear that Krakauer had drawn between responsible, strong clients and weak clients. He is a strong client in such a scenario.

Most important of all, not reporting Hall's turnaround time means that Krakauer does not report on the most probable reason why Hall, one of the most experienced and careful mountaineering guides on Everest in 1996 who had turned his clients back from the summit push one year earlier, would disregard his own advice so flagrantly and put the members of his team in danger. Lou Kaskischke explains that at noon, Hall was at the back of the line, waiting for fixed ropes to be placed on the Hillary Step to enable climbers to safely ascend it. His junior guide Mike Groom, seeing the late hour and concerned about all the climbers who had to ascend the Hillary Step, asked Hall if turning around was a good option, and Hall said that they should continue on (Kaskischke 2015, 186). Why would Hall advocate for this? The answer is competition:

> At noon, of all the decision-making pressures Rob confronted, the force probably most influential of all was the sight of the Fischer climbers going for it ... That sight no doubt had a powerful influence, along with the sight of Jon Krakauer, Rob's expected publicity machine, also among those going for it. The only way for Rob to neutralize the leadership and business promotion publicity competition with Scott was to keep going ... If it all worked out for Scott and his team, even if by a miracle of luck, the mountaineering culture would treat Scott as a bold and courageous leader. And Rob, just the opposite if he turned back. That outcome would have a major adverse impact on Rob's expedition business. (189–90)

Most of Hall's clients had turned back already and one, Beck Weathers, was blinded and waiting in frigid conditions below for assistance. Of them all, only Krakauer, Namba, and Hansen were on the summit push, and Hansen had tried to turn back earlier. All of Fischer's clients who had started that day, without a turnaround time, were on their way to the summit. For Kaskischke, business competition explains why Rob Hall continued on to the summit hours after he should have and encouraged Doug Hansen, his weakest client that day, to continue on. It is also the initial reason, according to Kasischke, why Hall insisted on his team summiting with Fischer's on the same day, against the protests of team members in Adventure Consultants (78–81). Hall "dismissed our questions and played down our concerns with empty, aggressive rhetoric" (80) for those same business reasons, disregarding safety concerns. This is why climber Ed Viesturs, following the progress of the climbers with a telescope at Base Camp, wondered why climbers continued on after 1:00 pm (194), when it was no longer safe to summit.

Like the many small mistakes on summit day in 1996 that added up to a disastrous outcome, misreporting the turnaround time might seem to be a relatively small error to make. But that error shows that Krakauer is not reporting the facts consistently in *Into Thin Air*, and he does not do so because it is more important that he represent the gulf between guide and client, authentic climber and mere rich tourist, in an absolute way. Given that Krakauer has insisted that his account is fact-based as recently as 2015, it may seem strange that he chooses to create so sharp a divide between amateurs and guides/dedicated climbers. The reason why may lie in the residual narrative of *Into Thin Air*, originally meant to be an exposé of the guiding business. The article Krakauer had been hired to write for *Outside* was meant to cast a jaundiced eye over the Everest scene. It is no wonder, then, that Krakauer takes such pains to depict himself as a climber with counter-cultural values who, as many climbers did by the 1990s, sneered at the idea of Everest as a true climbing objective because "Everest, the purists sniffed, had been debased and profaned" (Krakauer 1997, 26). But at the same time, Krakauer writes, the possibility of climbing Mount Everest and of standing on its summit like his boyhood heroes Willi Unsoeld and Tom Hornbein proved to be irresistible (21–2). The opening of *Into Thin Air* therefore contains two narratives that sit uneasily alongside each other. The pull of Everest and the romantic possibility of summiting the highest mountain in the world sits alongside the reality of commercial guiding as a business. Krakauer's presentation of both stories about Everest, between which he is uneasily caught, help to make *Into Thin Air* compelling reading, the story of an "authentic" climber who had done difficult ice climbs with one or two friends, who is caught up in the lure of Everest, but who is also sickened by the problems of commercial guiding and what he perceives to be the lack of ability of other climbers in his expedition.

The moral, for this thread of the story, was that those who do not have the desire to sacrifice everything for the mountains do not have the right to be there. This is the argument of another bestselling book by Krakauer, *Into the Wild*, the story of idealist adventurer Chris McCandless and his tragic death from starvation in the shell of an old bus in the Alaskan wilderness. In chapter 14 of that book, Krakauer explains and defends McCandless's idealism and his risk-taking behaviour in terms of Krakauer's own foolhardy solo ascent of a dangerous mountain – the Goblin – when he was a young climber (1996, 134–9). *Into the Wild* argues that McCandless did not die from making amateur mistakes as he camped out and tried to live off the land. He died from something he could not have known about: mushroom poisoning. Krakauer wrote that the accidental nature of his death means that McCandless should be regarded as heroic, not foolish or incompetent. Like the young Krakauer, he was a dreamer; like him too, he makes mistakes, as anyone would. The basis for this position is that Krakauer sees himself and his youthful idealism in McCandless, much as he sees himself in Doug Hansen and Andy Harris. Adventurous young men like them (or like George Mallory) are to be excused from judgment and their competence defended. Much as happened with *Into Thin Air*, Krakauer's insistence that *Into the Wild* sets the record straight about McCandless because of factual reporting has received several serious challenges.[4] Guides in Krakauer's account are authentic climbers, too, who are caught up in the commercial era but, if they are "pure of heart," in Tim Cahill's memorable phrase (Coburn 2007), they are assumed to have good motives for what they do, and so are excused from judgment. Anyone who does not fit Krakauer's criteria for authenticity, however, is not excused.

That narrative of desire, authenticity, and Everest's "decline" into commercialism that was to be part of Krakauer's planned article therefore collided head-on with the events of the 1996 disaster, pushing Krakauer's original story into the best-selling mountaineering book in history, making Krakauer into an internationally famous author and sending a narrative about the problems of Everest and commercialism all over the world. The narrative frame Krakauer made about guides, clients, and authentic climbers became attached to the need to report accurately on what happened, in no small part because many of the disaster's victims had died and could no longer speak for themselves. Krakauer explains in the introduction to *Into Thin Air* that he tried to report accurately by interviewing most of the participants in the disaster several times. He writes that he made minor errors of fact and calls most of these small, with the exception of his misrecognition that caused him to wrongly report in his initial article for *Outside* how Andy Harris died (Krakauer 1997, xv–xvi). He corrected this error and apologized for it. But in a postscript to the 1999 paperback edition, Krakauer defended other judgments he made, writing that he wished to "provide the most accurate, honest account possible" (Krakauer 1999, 324). He states that his assignment for *Outside* magazine was to "assess the qualifications of the guides and clients" and saw it as his duty to "the other survivors, to the grieving families, to the historical record, and to my companions who did not come home" to provide a factual assessment of what happened (324).

Krakauer understands *Into Thin Air* to be a work of journalism with scrupulous truth claims, an ethically oriented document that must be responsible to the living and the dead. He himself makes the highest ethical claims and journalistic standards possible for what he reported. But *Into Thin Air* is also still a story of a clash between older ideas of mountaineering counterculture and the commercial era. And it is more: it is a trauma narrative that even Krakauer admits he wrote too quickly, against the advice of others (1997, xvii). Krakauer ignores advice to wait, however, because he needs to tell the story but also because the story would be more authentic: "What had happened on the mountain was gnawing my guts out. I thought that writing the book might purge Everest from my life ... I had hoped that something would be gained by spilling my soul in the calamity's immediate aftermath, in the roil and torment of the moment. I wanted my account to have a raw, ruthless sort of honesty that seemed in danger of leaching away with the passage of time" (1997, xvii).

The power of *Into Thin Air* derives from its eyewitness style that makes it seem as if the reader is there too, on Everest, as the tragedy unfolds. It does seem to be raw, confessional, and honest as it appears to diagnose the problem with Everest as the problem of authenticity in the age of commercialism. This is why *Into Thin Air* became the bestselling mountaineering account of all time. But as Krakauer's portrayal of his own teammates shows, it is not a completely dispassionate account and it is not even a completely factual account either. The narrative of Krakauer's own trauma on Everest and his original design for the piece work to create a picture of the events of 1996 that in some cases does a disservice to those who survived, and those who did not. At times, Krakauer's need to tell a compelling story and his own personal struggles as a climber overwhelms the journalistic goals of the account.

In *Into Thin Air*, many climbers on Krakauer's team and on Mountain Madness were unfairly characterized as moneyed thrill seekers without experience or ability, climbers who needed guides to help them succeed. Krakauer did this because, as he says in his postscript, his job initially was to assess the abilities of the climbers (324), and he did this job initially without asking for permission from the members of his team. His former teammate Lou Kasischke found out from Sandy Hill Pittman, who had access to the internet, that Krakauer created a "score-card" to assess his teammates during the climb and was providing that information to *Outside Online* without their knowledge (Kasischke 2015, 58–9). Kasischke says that Krakauer's scorecard, and the revelation that assessments of their performance were circulating on the internet, caused a chill effect on the team dynamics as they realized that they were being watched. Kasischke says that he "felt betrayed by Rob [Hall] for converting our private quest into something the whole world could read about, just so he could prime the publicity pump" because Hall had invited Krakauer onto the team for his own benefit (59). It is also significant that Hill, the only person with access to internet technology on Everest, had revealed what had happened.

Krakauer did not just judge members of his own team in terms of their fitness for the mountain, and it is not just his own team whose expertise and experience were discounted. For example, Klev Schoening, a member of the Mountain Madness team, is described only as being strong but having little experience in high mountains, while he describes Schoening's uncle, Pete Schoening as "a living Himalayan legend" in breathless terms (Krakauer 1997, 95). Stuart Hutchison, who Krakauer introduced earlier as "somewhat wonkish," is presented as a neophyte, someone who does not know how to make his crampons – the spikes climbers wear on their boots to give themselves secure footing on ice – fit onto his boots properly (78). Hutchison is called "high strung," a doctor "who had little time for climbing" (259) despite the fact that during the storm, Hutchison was one of the few team members in Adventure Consultants who shone lights and banged pots outside the tents in an attempt to let the stranded climbers on the South Col know where the camp was, and who went into the storm alone to find climbers when Krakauer was incapacitated (272–3). Krakauer's portrait of a team "utterly without leadership" because all guides were either dead or incapacitated (321) means that when he describes, in detail, what Hutchison does to try to organize a rescue effort with the Sherpas, Hutchison is still not described as a leader, but as an amateur with "limited climbing experience" who "did his best to rise to the occasion" (321–3).

Krakauer's most biting portrayals are directed at the female members of his own team and the women climbing with Mountain Madness. Charlotte Fox, another experienced climber, is introduced as "dynamic and statuesque" (96) although later Krakauer describes her more charitably as a "Himalayan veteran" (113) because she had summited two 8,000-metre peaks in the Himalayas. She fares better than Yasuko Namba, a climber who "seemed to know next to nothing about how to use crampons" despite the fact that there is a note on the same page that says she used them before on four very high mountains (85). She is not described by Krakauer as a respected climber in Japan, but merely as "a minor cause célèbre in Japan" because of her desire to climb Everest (184). She is someone so "overly eager" that she almost causes an accident because of what he calls her "impatience and inexperience," rather than someone who is strong or confident (184). Krakauer describes her as someone who "didn't fit the meek deferential stereotype of a middle-aged Japanese woman" (231) but proceeds to say nonetheless that she had been "a slow and uncertain climber" but now was "in a trance ... jostling her way to the front of the line" (231), making her strength seem to be rude and dangerous and underscoring the impression that she had no high altitude experience. The last scene of the book is the setting for the final assessment of Namba, a tragic scene that completely denies her any agency. Guide Neal Beidleman describes having to leave Namba to die on the South Col so that others could be saved. In his words, Yasuko is a helpless victim, someone who is "little" and who he cannot save: "'I can't help thinking about Yasuko ... she was so little. I can still feel her fingers sliding across my biceps, and then letting go. I never even turned to look back'" (301). The book ends with an inescapable conclusion: Yasuko Namba was not a good enough climber to be able to rescue herself. She was too quiet in life, overconfident on summit day, and represented as a victim in death when her guide can no longer care for her. The last image of her is not even about her: it is about Beidleman's own guilt because he cannot rescue her.

Krakauer's harshest words of all are reserved for the only other journalist on the expedition, Sandy Hill Pittman. He calls her "an indefatigable seeker of public attention" (121), questions her climbing credentials (120), and calls her "a grandstanding dilettante" (123) and symbol of "the ensuing debasement of the world's highest mountain" (124) because of her wealth and her relative lack of experience. He mocks her decision to carry an espresso maker (122) and portrays her as a frivolous member of high society (123) on the mountain and off, a woman who is proud of carrying laptops to Base Camp (today this is common practice). Krakauer ends his assessment of Hill Pittman with a devastating critique, writing that "Pittman epitomized all that was reprehensible about Dick Bass's popularization of the Seven Summits. But insulated by her money, a staff of paid attendants, and unwavering self-absorption ... she remained as oblivious as Jane Austen's Emma" (124).

After the disaster, Hill Pittman never climbed at high altitudes again, and abandoned her career in part because she was subjected to a backlash that left her in the role of "villain" of Everest (Graham 2015) and a symbol of the mountain's decline in the commercial era. Hill Pittman, now called Sandy Hill, did not respond to Krakauer's portrayal of her at the time, but did say in 2015 that "this [portrayal] came from a source who had a vested interest in crafting a dramatic story ... I guess it served a purpose for him to bury me ... in those days you could get away with destroying someone's life and flogging them with innuendo" (2015). Given that Krakauer takes care to emphasize how he has created a factual narrative, his portrayal of Hill Pittman casts her in the role of villain, in opposition to the heroic guides who have to save her. Hill Pittman conveniently symbolizes the twin evils of the commercial era: she is rich, and she is a powerful woman. In reality, Hill Pittman had been on Everest before, and was well regarded by other climbers, who call her "strong and determined" (Weathers 2000, 30), a good team member (Breashears 2008, 207), and good at providing information from the internet (Kasischke 2015, 58).

It should be clear by now that Krakauer's contention that he wrote his narrative based only on facts, as a journalist would, is not accurate – particularly in his portrayal of climbing experience, which also exhibits considerable gender bias. Women cannot be strong in *Into Thin Air*; they cannot be rescuers. They cannot, in particular, be Krakauer's rivals as chroniclers. As he writes, over time he begins to feel guilty about his judgment of his team members and possibly for assessing them online: "my sympathy for Taske, Weathers and some of my other teammates mounted ... I felt increasingly uncomfortable in my role as journalist" (Krakauer 1997, 142). But, tellingly, he also says "I had no qualms when it came to writing frankly about Hall, Fischer, or Sandy Pittman" because in his view, "they had been aggressively seeking media attention for years" (142). In his sketches of some male clients and almost all female clients, Krakauer subsumes who these figures are to the story he needs to tell of brave male guides who are rescuers, and women as victims. Another example of this occurs when Krakauer describes the huddle of climbers who tried to survive the storm on the South Col, so close to the tents. Other climbers who climbed well and were experienced, including Klev Schoening, Lene Gammelgaard, and Charlotte Fox, are only mentioned in Krakauer's account as climbers who, before the storm, summit late. Neal Beidleman is pictured as the group leader on the descent and the one with the most agency. Krakauer has already called him "one of the strongest climbers on the mountain" (260) who was nevertheless ranked low in the expedition pecking order and so did not think that he could force clients to turn around (260–1). It is Beidleman who decides that the clients on the summit have to leave at 3:10 pm, and he "gathered up Pittman, Gammelgaard, Fox and Madsen and started leading them down the summit ridge" (265), appearing to have much more agency than the other climbers and making leadership decisions. It is Beidleman who orders Gammelgaard to give up her oxygen to the failing Hill Pittman and Beidleman who slides Hill Pittman down the ridge after Fox gives her a steroid shot (267). When the climbers reach the South Col, Beidleman "led his group" and "knew" where they were when the storm hit (269–70). The guides Beidleman and Mike Groom are mentioned by name as they walk in the storm, while the Sherpas and clients are not, an implicit way of (269) identifying who the leaders of the group were, and who was following. Beidleman says, "It was total chaos ... people are wandering all over the place; I'm yelling at everyone, trying to get them to follow a single leader'" (271). It is Beidleman who senses that they are on a cliff, and has the group form a huddle (271). Most significantly, he is the person who sees the sky clear, fights with Klev Schoening about where the tents are, coaxes everyone to move and tells Boukreev how to find those who could not walk out (273). It is Beidleman, with Schoening, who tells Boukreev where to find the huddle (271). He is a leader and a hero, fulfilling his role as guide.

Boukreev, meanwhile, is portrayed as irresponsible because he descended ahead of his clients and did not use oxygen that day (274). This portrayal of the guide, who climbed to try to rescue Scott Fischer and went into the storm alone multiple times to save everyone in the huddle except for Namba and Weathers, has been controversial and Boukreev contested it in his version of events found in *The Climb*. For his part, Krakauer attacked Boukreev's editor and translator in the postscript of the 1999 edition of *Into Thin Air*. He wrote in the postscript about Boukreev with a mixture of defiance and regret because Boukreev himself died in a climbing accident in 1999 before they had reconciled (Krakauer 1999, 331–3). But Krakauer has never had to account for how heavily he relied on Neal Beidleman's account of the disaster, including his portrayal of Beidleman as key to the rescue attempt, despite the existence of competing evidence. Krakauer appears never to have made use of the most valuable document to be produced at the time of the disaster: a transcript of tapes made of a group conversation between the surviving members of the Mountain Madness team, who talked together almost immediately after the crisis had passed about what had happened. Krakauer would have known about this tape, either at the time of his first writing of the manuscript for his *Outside* magazine article or later, and so this omission is puzzling, particularly since the transcript of the tape, printed in Boukreev's *The Climb*, reveals some key problems with Krakauer's account. In the Mountain Madness transcript, it is Lene Gammelgaard with Klev Schoening, not Neal Beidleman, who both see the light from Boukreev's headlamp and begin walking towards it (Boukreev and DeWalt [1998] 2002, 348). Boukreev gets directions to find the weak climbers from Gammelgaard and Schoening, not from Beidleman, who was not from his team (348). Schoening is mentioned in Krakauer's account briefly, but not Gammelgaard, who was there and was key to the rescue attempt. One reason why she may not appear could be connected to a telling moment in the transcript when Beidleman tries to say what Gammelgaard was doing on the South Col, claiming that everyone was panicking. Gammelgaard corrects his version of events, reminding him that she was calm, and that he was the one who was panicking (365). When Beidleman tries to say again what Gammelgaard was doing, she says "don't speak for me ... I can speak for myself" (355). She does not speak on the tape as much as some of the other climbers and has to remind Beidleman more than once that she is there (364) and can speak for herself when she wishes to do so. Klev Schoening backs up her version of events (357).

It is easy to see how Gammelgaard, and her role in the events, was overlooked, and why her account of the disaster is almost never mentioned. Although she resists the image of herself as a passive client, a woman whose point of view can be overlooked, the record shows that Gammelgaard herself was a strong climber with her own clear ideas of what to do in an emergency. The Mountain Madness approach, which did not prescribe climbing times, did result in almost all the members of that team surviving the ordeal. The way that she was ignored during the discussion is similar to how her memoir about the events, *Climbing High: A Woman's Account of Surviving the Everest Tragedy* has also been overlooked or even erased. *Climbing High* was the first book to be published about the 1996 disaster, but it was not read at the time by English speakers, because it appeared in Danish first. An English version did not appear until 2000. Once Krakauer's version of events appeared, it became the foundational narrative to which all others responded. Gammelgaard's version of events, and her philosophy of climbing Everest, would not be available to English speakers for another four years. She almost does not appear in Krakauer's story at all, perhaps because Krakauer never interviewed her. But with the Mountain Madness transcript, *Climbing High* deserves to be considered as an alternative story of what happened on Everest, and an eloquent counter-narrative to Krakauer's story of heroic guides, incompetent women, and helpless clients.

Climbing High was not written to be a definitive account of the disaster, but it was written to be accurate in its details and in Gammelgaard's feelings on the climb. Its diary-like style, called by the *New York Times* review "intimate and impressionistic" (Sanders 1999), moves the account away from journalism, creating a sense of Gammelgaard's entire experience on Everest, and not just an account about the disaster itself. Gammelgaard, a therapist ([1996] 1999, 10), wrote therapeutically for two weeks after the tragedy had occurred while she was on her way back to Denmark from the Himalayas, but could only write at first, "*Scott is dead*" (ix, italics in original). Her publisher tried to get her to write her book immediately, and she told him that she was not ready, asking him to trust her own process. At a writing retreat, she completed it in 1996 (x). The style of *Climbing High* may have been inspired by the negative example of Gammelgaard's own mountaineering reading: "reading about mountaineering is getting dull because it's becoming obvious how uniformly we think, express ourselves and are driven by recognizable inner forces" (40). Gammelgaard makes use of a journal she kept about the climb: "I wrote before I left Denmark, I wrote at Base Camp, I wrote on the mountain and I wrote after the tragedy had unfolded in all its enormity" (ix). The use of journals and journal-like writing done very soon after the disaster give the account immediacy and provide accurate details of conversations and observations. Some of the style in *Climbing High* preserves that journal work: there are dates at the heading of "entries" and the book is written in the present tense. Other parts of *Climbing High* act as a scrapbook, reproducing documents. In a section called "Preparations," Gammelgaard transcribes letters from Mountain Madness organizers and copies in the program distributed to expedition members (13–16). She transcribes the original climbing plan (85) and a letter from Scott Fischer (12). She transcribes in his own words the story Mountain Madness Sherpa and climbing logistics leader Lopsang told her "again and again" about finding Scott Fischer high on Everest, too frozen to respond to Lopsang's attempt to save him (197–8) and she transcribes a Danish press agency brief about the disaster (198–9). Like Krakauer, Gammelgaard wanted to present events accurately, writing "I have tried to act as a camera lens, recording what I experienced, presenting my teammates as I saw them" (x). She says that she relied on her journals to provide the immediacy of the moment and accuracy where possible, but that she cannot be completely objective because of oxygen deprivation (x).

Unlike Krakauer's picture of climbers like herself, Gammelgaard represents herself as a strong and ambitious climber who wants to succeed on Everest, but only if Chomolungma allows it (Gammelgaard [1996]

1999, 19). She is respectful of the mountain environment and the Sherpa people, whom she loves (46, 49, 60, 72). They also have great respect for her and tell her so when they climb up to rescue her on her way down (190). She writes extensively about the Sherpas on the expedition by name and in detail (49, 62, 81–2, 89, 118), and with Boukreev, tries to eat their style of food whenever possible, forgoing fancier European items (118–19). She is not a wealthy climber and has to raise money through corporate sponsorship in order to be part of the team (33–5, 53).

Climbing High shows that the culture of the Mountain Madness team differed from that of Adventure Consultants: Mountain Madness climbers were encouraged to climb at their own pace, and Gammelgaard saw that it made her team cohesive (69). Partly as a result of this culture, Gammelgaard understands guides like Boukreev as teachers, but not as substitutes for her own efforts. When Anatoli Boukreev meets her and expresses surprise that a woman wants to climb Everest, she decides to try to understand why he acts as he does, rather than react negatively to his assumptions about women: "Another code obviously operates in Anatoli's world, but I'm accustomed to that code and that type of response, and have nearly forgotten my past battles on that account. I need not answer, need not fight to prove anything. All I want is to get to the top of Everest. And talking won't get me there. Only the actual climb will reveal whether I've got it or not. So I keep my mouth shut" (41).

In the end, she befriends Boukreev by listening closely to him and trying to understand him (73–4). She and Boukreev come to respect each other's differences and trust each other (120). In the end, this is probably why Boukreev relies on her information to rescue the climbers from the South Col huddle. As he takes off her crampons for her when she gets to the tents, she says, "'Anatoli, the others are out there. They're dying,'" and points the way before she enters her tent. Anatoli hears this, then returns and receives more precise directions from Gammelgaard: "'You have to head straight across the rock, not upward across the ice. Straight across the rock. No longer than half an hour'" (184). It is impossible to mistake the precision of these directions, which Gammelgaard gives twice.

Climbing High, unlike most Everest books by women, does have feminist overtones – due to Gammelgaard's awareness of the history of women climbers, and of female friendship, as well as her quiet determination to move past sexism when she encounters it. Gammelgaard discusses other female climbers whom she admires, including British climber Alison Hargreaves (30–1, 155), whose autobiography she reads (51), and *On Top of the World* by British climber Rebecca Stephens. She uses a fundraising idea by Stacey Allison, the first American woman to summit Everest (34). She recounts her sorrow at seeing the body of climber Hannelore Schmatz on her way up the mountain because Schmatz is a woman and reminds her of "the destiny of my female kin" (25). She writes about her feelings of inadequacy when she meets Klev and Pete Schoening and so she looks forward to meeting Charlotte Fox and Sandy Hill Pittman, writing "we might team up, to kind of equalize things" (54). She describes Pete Schoening as "skeptical about having women on the expedition" because he is from an earlier climbing era – but adds that she senses no disapproval from him when they do spend time together (57). She, Fox, and Hill Pittman laugh about their body image ideas, and decide to pose in bikinis as a joke (58). Later, Hill Pittman confesses to her that "she hadn't expected another woman to be supportive" of her when Gammelgaard waits for her as they climb through the dangerous Ice Fall section (101). In one interesting moment, she meets Yasuko Namba when she visits the camp of Adventure Consultants, finding her "modest and pleasant" (118). The meeting provides a moment of solidarity: "When we [Namba and Gammelgaard] were introduced, we held hands just a slight touch longer than the men and I did. There aren't many women on Everest, and I sense a solidarity among us. Everest has plenty of space for us all" (118).

But there are moments of sexism as well. She finds Neal Beidleman "patronizing" when he treats her as a beginning climber: Fischer reprimands him (70). She writes of her frustration when Fischer will not let her climb without oxygen: Gammelgaard knows that if she climbs with it, she will not be able to build her climbing resume easily because it will not be as much of an achievement to summit Everest with oxygen (131–2). She therefore feels that Fischer is blocking her career, a particularly galling thing since she acclimatizes faster than all other climbers and is stronger than most of them (62, 132). She even temporarily loses her motivation to succeed in her anger (136).

Gammelgaard's description of events as the storm gathered and broke diverge in important ways from Krakauer's version. The differences point to Krakauer's desire to show that Beidleman, and not the female clients, male clients, or Sherpas, is in charge because he is a guide. Gammelgaard mentions that "Charlotte, Neal, Sandy and Tim" are leaving the summit and she realizes that she needs to go with them (173), a contrast to Krakauer's picture of Beidleman "gathering" up the climbers. On the descent, Gammelgaard recalls that no one except Hill Pittman is struggling, that Tim Madsen is "calm and deliberate" (174). Beidleman, in Krakauer's account, orders Gammelgaard to give up her oxygen to Sandy Hill Pittman: in *Climbing High*, Gammelgaard says that she and Beidleman "confer and discover that Sandy's oxygen bottle is approaching empty. As I am the strongest among us, she and I exchange oxygen containers" (174). She leads the descent with Klev Schoening, passing Yasuko Namba (she does not mention the guide Mike Groom with her), and she and Klev discuss how to head for the camp (176–7). But the lights they think are those of the camp are those of the other climbers, including two Sherpas who tried to lead them, but become lost (178).

Gammelgaard writes: "Klev and I are in agreement. We hardly need words" to know what should be done about making an action plan now that the group is lost. But Beidleman, Gammelgaard says, is panicked (178). Gammelgaard decides to let Schoening convince Beidleman to be methodical and so she leaves "it to Klev to talk to Neal" (178). The Sherpas disappear and as they form the huddle to keep warm, Gammelgaard again praises Tim Madsen for his calm as he keeps shouting to his girlfriend, Charlotte Fox, to stay awake, and of Beidleman says "Neal tries to guide, but I sense fear underneath his words" (180). She represents Klev Schoening and herself as calm on the South Col, huddling with the others before they look around, then realizing at the same time as Beidleman that they must get up and find the tents before they freeze to death. Beidleman moves the group forward (182). In the end, Schoening says "'I know where we are, and I know where the camp is,'" and Gammelgaard believes him. She is the climber who says "'Klev, light!'" and sees where the tents are, saving the group (183). As I mentioned, Gammelgaard also directs Boukreev to where the huddle is located on the South Col a second time. Beidleman said in an interview with IMAX filmmaker David Breashears that he turned and pointed when Boukreev asked him where the huddle was before he went into his own tent (183).

Even when the effects of oxygen deprivation, exhaustion, and panic are taken into account, it is clear that Krakauer's version of events relies heavily on an interpretation of Beidleman's role as leader during the disaster, *because he is a guide.* Krakauer's own ideology about passive clients and guides as leaders means that he discounts the roles played by others in the disaster, most notably Klev Schoening, Tim Madsen, and Lene Gammelgaard. Beidleman clearly did provide some leadership and personally assisted Sandy Hill Pittman, as he describes in the Mountain Madness group recording (Boukreev and DeWalt [1998] 2002, 354). The recording shows too that he did not order Gammelgaard to give up her oxygen, but discussed it with her, and that Schoening and Gammelgaard led the way down to the South Col (356–8). And finally, the recording shows that even when Beidleman forgets that Gammelgaard was there, she was not panicking, and played a role in the rescue, she reminds him, and he acknowledges this as well as his own feelings:

Neal: Well, sorry to indicate that I thought everybody ran with fear and adrenaline. [Klev laughs.] I did. I didn't realize that Lene was totally under control.
Lene: I was totally under control within myself, Neal.
Neal: I'm glad.
Lene: I am too. (365–6)

The process of getting to the South Col, forming a huddle, eventually walking to find the tents, and helping Boukreev to find the other survivors was a group decision-making process because as Beidleman said on the Mountain Madness recording, "it wasn't really clear that there was a leader versus a non-leader or followers at that point" (360). In an interview published in *The Climb*, Gammelgaard underscores this as she gives credit to Beidleman's effort when the group descended to the South Col: "At that point, Gammelgaard said that the group was doing a good job, 'Neal is doing the right things, the best things you can do. He is doing what I do, what Klev would do, what Tim would do.'" They were working as a team, not being led, according to Gammelgaard, but cooperating in their individual efforts to survive (Boukreev and DeWalt [1998] 2002, 162).

It is clear that Gammelgaard is making a specific effort in her comments to credit Beidleman as a climber who is on par with what the other climbers are capable of doing, and to dispel any notion of guide and client hierarchy. In this version of events, women and men, however they could, tried to make the decisions that would save their lives and tried to help each other. They were not, as Krakauer claimed, "a team in name only [because] we would ascend as individuals, linked to one another by neither rope nor any sense of loyalty. Each client was in it for himself, pretty much" (Krakauer 1997, 213). The gathering storm and subsequent events made the climbers from each team into a group that did try to save each other, and whether or not they were clients or guides became irrelevant.

Why is Krakauer so bent on proving that group teamwork was not possible, and why does he insist on the idea that in the commercial era, there could be only individual clients on a guided expedition? One possible explanation is his need to maintain his narrative of guide/client hierarchy and what he maintains that has done to traditional climbing culture. But connected to this is the possibility that Krakauer himself felt cut-off from his own team because he was an embedded reporter whose "score card" of other climbers in Adventure Consultants did not engender their trust in him. Another possible reason is that Krakauer himself is not a team player but does not admit this openly. He climbed to the summit alone, partly because he was a strong and fast climber who often received permission to climb out ahead of the group (217). He chafes on summit day when he is asked to climb with the others, a situation that he calls as foregoing of "self-reliance" in favour of "passivity," another betrayal of traditional mountaineering culture (219). At the famous Hillary Step, he dreams of leading the climb to fix the rope, "as any serious climber would" (237) before realizing that this was a guide's job. He summits before any of his team members and descends alone, receiving some help from Martin Adams – he misidentifies him as guide Andy Harris because he is oxygen-deprived (253). He offers help to Beck Weathers but does not press the matter. And, most important of all, Krakauer blames "guide-client protocol" for why he did not help Andy Harris when he did see him struggling at the South Summit, below the Hillary Step. He calls it "inconceivable" that he did not help Harris, who he regards as an equal in ability, but says Harris "had been cast in the role of invincible guide, there to look after me and other clients; we had been specifically indoctrinated not to question our guides' judgement" (245). One of the most powerful aspects of *Into Thin Air* is Krakauer's honesty with himself at this moment, when he blames himself for inadvertently causing the death of Harris and for not helping Namba, saying, "the stain left on my psyche is not the sort of thing that washes off after a few months of grief and guilt-ridden self-reproach" (352). But the power of such statements lies in their incomplete affect: Krakauer has not healed from the experience, as he says in the preface to the book, and he wrote the memoir partly to try to dispel his own demons. The effort fills the book with emotion, but it is also the source of judgment. I believe that Krakauer was suffering from the effects of trauma when he wrote this account, and so *Into Thin Air* must be considered as a trauma narrative more than a work of journalism. Therefore, Krakauer's candid admission of guilt, although it is real and deserves respect, is accompanied by his indictment of guide culture, which he says had "indoctrinated" him. That explanation may serve, but it is evident that Krakauer's own position as a journalist and his decision not to work with others in a team setting were facts as well. It is also evident that Krakauer does not turn to his own position and his own style as an explanation for his actions, but rather insists that guide culture, and his acceptance of it, is the most plausible explanation for what went wrong in his case, and what is wrong with Everest, in all cases.

If *Into Thin Air* were truly a dispassionate record, it could have represented other points of view about the disaster with more accuracy, particularly since Krakauer claims that his account can be trusted because he interviewed all participants and wrote his account to the highest journalistic standards. But it is clear from competing evidence that Krakauer either did not interview everyone, or he did not listen to what some survivors were saying. It is inarguable that he did not pay much attention to any of the female climbers who survived and what they might have to say. His representation of Namba, a woman of colour whose first language was not English, is disturbing. But we are not left without alternate views of what happened, and the story of women on Everest can be discerned. Lene Gammelgaard's account, the Mountain Madness recording, interviews for *The Climb*, and David Breashears's later interviews for his film and book *Storm Over Everest*, taken with Lou Kasischke's own understanding of events found in *After the Wind*, provide a more complete picture of what women and men, Sherpas, clients, and guides faced on Everest in 1996. These alternate stories of what happened show that there should be limits placed on the claims Krakauer makes for his own account. Krakauer may indeed have tried hard to report the facts. But the story arc of his account aims to preserve the hierarchy of guide and client relations, supporting Krakauer's larger argument about incompetent climbers and professional guides, and the history of Everest as the theatre for a narrow understanding of what comprises leadership, heroism, and commitment. Everest, in Krakauer's version of climbing history, is a tragic theatre for neo-colonial white male masculinity, a story of mountaineering's abandonment of its own ideals. But it is not the story that everyone else on the mountain had to tell, and it is that story that we should take into account when we think about what can be learned from the 1996 disaster.

The Story of Decline and the Counter-Narratives of 1996

One outcome from decentring Krakauer's version of the 1996 disaster is that it becomes possible, through counter-narratives, to understand climbing on Everest in the commercial era as more than merely a pollution of the mountain, or as a decline from the heroic era symbolized by Sir Edmund Hillary and George Mallory, a decline that tacitly sees the presence of women on Everest and the professionalization of Sherpas as part of the problem, not a new development. Counter-narratives about what Everest can mean, and what mountaineering can be do exist: Tenzing Norgay's denunciation of British expedition culture and his alternate vision of what Everest represents is central to his account of the 1953 first ascent of the mountain. Arlene Blum has discussed sexist behaviour – the leader assumed that women could not lead or set ropes – when she was part of an American Everest expedition in her memoir *Breaking Trail* (Blum 2005, 240–2, 251–2) and has also detailed other instances of anti-semitism and sexism related to the American Alpine Club and its approval process for climbing permits for Everest and other Himalayan peaks (366–7). French climber Anne Bernard applied to join the 1922 Everest expedition, and was told that applications from women would not be considered because "the difficulties would be too great" (Rose and Douglas 1999, 58). Lydia Bradey, the first woman to climb Everest without oxygen, had her achievement publicly doubted by her teammates Gary Ball and Rob Hall, until she was eventually exonerated (Rose and Douglas 1999, 199, Feanley 2015). In the case of the 1996 disaster, Lene Gammelgaard's account is often disregarded in favour of Krakauer's. It is time to place that memoir in perspective and to unseat it as the definitive account, not only of what actually happened, but also of what mountain climbing can mean.

What can be learned from the counter-narratives of Everest? Everest is not a theatre for heroism, or a pure mountain tragically defiled by human beings. And Everest is not a "storybook paradise where only the pure of heart and well intentioned were admitted" (Coburn 2007) because its climbing history, from the beginning, includes a history of racial, class, and gender biases that were set into motion when Everest was mapped by the British empire, named for an English bureaucrat, declared to be the highest place on earth and made the focus of national and personal obsessions. The myth of Everest has often been used to obscure this history, and to discount other ways of thinking about the mountain, climbing it, and of being a climber, particularly during the commercial era. A critical look at Everest necessitates undoing the myth of climbing authenticity that underpins the fantasy of Everest's ascent and decline in public consciousness as well as its attendant myths of amateurism, professionalism, and purity of heart. Everest is not just "there." Everest has long been a symbol of human achievement. As Chomolungma, it is part of how Sherpa people have come to understand the world. In the same way, the story of climbing authenticity on Everest is just that, one possible story of what it means to be in the mountains. Gender issues form an important part of that story, not as a sign of decline, but of change.

CONCLUSION

OTHER ANNAPURNAS

I leaned on my ice axe, and looked up at the steep slope above, carefully putting my feet in the huge holes in the snow, following the climber in front of me, the heavy rope dragging along the ground and connecting me to him. That slope was just a drift somewhere on Parker Ridge in the Rocky Mountains of Canada, but to my mind, it was the Lhotse Face of Mount Everest, and I was climbing it. After years of reading about climbing and decades of hiking and camping, here I was actually learning how to use an ice axe, crampons, and ropes, practising crevasse rescue, blinking up at the sun beating down on the ice and snow that made everything around me look like diamonds. The ridge gleamed in the sun like a piece of metal. If I looked down for too long, I realized, I would get vertigo, so I looked up again. I reached up to see if I had my sunglasses on. I did. It was so bright I couldn't even tell. Somewhere below me, another student in the climbing school yelled out "woo hoo! Happy birthday to me!" It was her fortieth birthday. What a way to spend it, I thought. I was never going to be what I thought of as a "real" climber: I was already in my thirties, and I had not spent my teenage years rock climbing. But at least I was out there, learning how to be on the higher mountains of the Canadian Rockies. I could do this, I thought again. I really could.

But on that same day, the summit experience and euphoria that I felt was tempered, just as a false summit can deflate the hopes of a climber trying to reach the top of a mountain. I saw the female instructor suggest strategies for teaching our group, and heard her ideas get shot down by the other two male instructors. From the way she replied I could tell that this was a regular occurrence. As I watched her try to negotiate with men whom she could easily outclimb and who clearly saw themselves as superior to her, I began to think about all the climbing stories I had read, and particularly about *Into Thin Air*. Despite its message of disaster, something about that book had inspired me to go into the mountains and learn how to climb higher than I ever had before. It was the reason why I was on that mountain slope, fumbling with ropes, trying to understand how to climb in a harness, getting used to wearing crampons on my boots.

At that moment, I realized that *Into Thin Air* was not actually for people like me. It was a warning about me, and how I could not belong, unless strong men guided me. I was not a climber. I did not belong. The story of climbing, told over and over again in thrilling adventure stories, was never about me or even for me.

How could it be that the most popular book about climbing ever written could say the things it did about women and openly lament a vanished era of masculine dominance and heroism, with the help of Sherpa "servants"? Why is sexism so integral to everyday climbing life, and what role do its thousands of stories play in perpetuating that fact?

That is when and why I decided to write about mountaineering nonfiction and gender one day. More than two decades after the publication of *Into Thin Air*, after I had learned about crevasse rescue, ice climbing, and how to use crampons, and made my way across glaciers and up some of the crumbly rock walls of the Canadian Rockies, some things have changed for the better in mountaineering representation. *Alpinist* magazine has become a place where women in climbing are starting to write about their lives and the kind of climbing they do without simply borrowing terms from heroic discourse.[1] The film *Sherpa* (2015), a feature documentary about the work conditions of Sherpa guides and climbers on Mount Everest in 2014, the year of a deadly avalanche that killed sixteen Sherpas, has won major awards and has excellent international distribution. *Buried in Sky* (2013) by Peter Zuckerman and Amanda Padoan, the product of years of research in Pakistan and Nepal, not only tells the story of Sherpa and Bhote climbers who saved climbers on K2 in 2008, it also recounts their motivations for climbing and their own views about the world, in their own words. Jemima Dika Sherpa's 2015 essay for *Alpinist*, "Three Springs," describes gender politics in Sherpa communities, the complex relationship of Sherpa communities with the climbing industry, and pervasive "positive" attitudes about Sherpa people in light of the 2014 fight between Sherpas and foreign climbers on Everest. The 2019 Banff Mountain Film Festival featured a panel called Cultural Barriers in Climbing, with the aim of opening up the conversation about sexism, colonialism, racism, ableism, and the need for diversity for climbers, and for what represents achievement in climbing. There are online communities dedicated to helping bring more diversity to climbing, such as Melanin Base Camp and competitions aimed at female and BIPOC participants.[2] The experience of climbers on mountains like Everest has become a training ground for female Nepalese climbers. Commercialism has therefore brought opportunities in addition to well-publicized problems (Gugglberger 2015, 609). Pasang Llamu Sherpa Akita has become the first fully certified female Sherpa mountain guide, and in 2016, she won the National Geographic People's Choice Adventurer of the Year award for her efforts in helping Nepal recover from the effects of the 2016 earthquake (Potts 2016). Junko Tabei's memoir *Honouring High Places: The Mountain Life of Junko Tabei* won the 2018 Mountain History award at the Banff Mount Book awards competition. There is even the remote possibility that Nepal will regulate climbing on its routes up Everest, providing standards for guiding outfits and reducing the number of permits for Everest (Arnette 2019).

Some things still need to change. The climbing community remains overwhelmingly male-dominated and focused on extreme adventure as the definition of cutting-edge climbing. The image of women in climbing remains ableist and white, in part because the discourse of adventure that keeps heroism central to mountaineering nonfiction has proven difficult to shift, and so women still have to try to be heroic in the same way that men are expected to be. The narrative of mourning for the heroic era of climbing found within the pages of *Into Thin Air* is challenged very rarely, as is the common belief that Krakauer's account is definitive, and the last word on Himalayan climbing in the commercial era. Neither a non-European/North American cis-gendered man, nor a trans or gender-queer climber has yet won a Piolet d'Or lifetime achievement award. The narrative of commercialism and decline on Mount Everest is still pervasive, and it still keeps those mountaineering writers and filmmakers, the ones who tell the story of mountaineering as a story of masculinity and extreme achievement, firmly in the spotlight as the focus of the normative narrative of climbing history. The definition of climbing stardom and what is seen as success in the mountains is still narrow, and reliant on neo-colonial ideas about adventure that ignore the environmental, cultural, and economic impact of mountaineering tourism on some of the most vulnerable, and precious, places on earth.

But once it becomes possible to see how gender in the stories of mountaineering has done its work and continues to influence what stories of climbing we think are possible to create, other stories of what it means to live and move in the mountains can emerge. The "other" Annapurnas of our lives that Maurice Herzog wrote of more than fifty years ago can take shape in the stories told about climbing mountains, in ways that do justice to the diversity of climbers, and to the mountains themselves.

The cholita climbers of Bolivia, who opened this book, stood on the summit of Aconcagua in January 2019. Now, they are training for a new goal: Everest. As before, they will climb to the summit as themselves, in skirts, to honour their culture and the lives their mothers and grandmothers led. But they see a future too. Why Aconcagua? Why Everest? Because, one of them says, they need to: "We did it [climbed Aconcagua] for all the women who are discriminated against, they told us we were not going to be able to do it, it was very hard for us to get there, a lot, but we want to continue, we need so many mountains!" (Ski-Guru 2019).

NOTES

INTRODUCTION

1 In *False Summit*, the terms "mountaineering," "climbing," and "climber" are related to general mountaineering, as opposed to more specific kinds of climbing such as rock climbing, bouldering, sport climbing, extreme mountain activities such as BASE jumping, or ice climbing, although some articles about climbing do combine all activities and call them "climbing," particularly when ideas of community or group identity are invoked. General mountaineering refers to climbing mountains with ropes and other equipment, including techniques and equipment for moving on ice and snow. There are different styles of general mountaineering, including siege-style climbing with large teams on high mountains, alpine-style climbing with smaller teams and minimal equipment, or solo climbing. When I refer to high-altitude climbing (particularly in the Himalayas or the Karakoram), I refer to climbs that have parts of the route above 1,500 metres, which is where the air is thinner, and there is a possibility of illness from the lack of oxygen. See Anne Wislowski (2017).

2 *Alpinist* magazine, an important climbing opinion source, regularly features stories about female climbers and climbers of colour (https://shop.hol publications.com/products/alpinist-magazine-issue-66?variant=205874357535 60), including Anaheed Saatchi's article "Your Climbing Is Political Whether You Like It or Not," which features interviews with diverse climbers (2020). The 2019 Banff Mountaineering Film and Book Festival, one of the most important festivals of its kind in the world, featured a panel called "Climbing through Barriers," with mentors and guides from Brown Girls Climb, Indigenous Womxn Climb, and Brothers of Climbing among others, discussing this topic: "what if you found yourself in love with the outdoors but there was no one who looked like you or who you could relate to?" See https://www.banffcentre.ca/banff-mountain-film-book-festival for the catalogue copy. The online community Melanin Base Camp, started by Danielle Williams in 2018, is dedicated "to increase ethnic minority and LGBTQ+ participation in the outdoors" (2020). The Flash Foxy group provides an online community, climbing festival, and education for female climbers (2020) and the No Man's Land film festival began as a feminist climbing festival, but now supports the work of Black, Indigenous, and People of Colour (BIPOC), and the LGBTQ+ community as well (2020). Also see Gugglberger (2015) for a detailed study about the history of Sherpani and Nepalese women's climbing.

3 Nanga Parbat, the ninth-highest mountain in the world, is another possible site for a similar investigation, but most critical materials about the climbs of Nanga Parbat are in German, due to the obsession with the mountain as the "mountain of destiny" for many German climbers, and issues related to gender on the peak were not unique to it. For an overview of the importance of Nanga Parbat to Germany, and to Nazi Germany as well, see Harald Höbusch, *Mountain of Destiny* (2016).

4 See Amrita Dhar's "Travel and Mountains" for an example of an overview of mountain travel using an intersectional critique, particularly in its detailed treatment of Sherpa climber Ang Tarkay's memoir *Sherpa* (2016, 358–9).

5 High-altitude mountaineering refers to the practice of climbing mountains when oxygen apparatus is used, or when the decision not to use oxygen is seen as the assumption of an additional risk. This is usually at altitudes above 7,000 metres or 22,960 feet above sea level. Above that height, medical conditions such as HACE and HAPE could become a factor for climbers. See UIAA Medical Advice papers for details: https://www.theuiaa.org/mountain-medicine/ medical-advice/.

6 Simon Bainbridge's point that most of the English Romantic poets also considered themselves to be mountaineers and did write about climbing in their poetry is well taken, although he does not discuss how or whether the poets

under discussion were widely read as mountain writers and understood by their readership to be climbers, as the Victorian mountaineers Edmund Whymper, Albert Mummery, or Leslie Stephen would have been. See Bainbridge (2012).

7 Climbing has a significant readership, which in turn creates more climbers, and more writers. For example, Reinhold Messner was inspired as a child by the stories of the British expeditions to Everest ([1982] 1989, 30) and later was inspired by the minimal equipment of those early expeditions to climb Everest "by fair means" (40). In *A Youth Wasted Climbing*, Canadian rock climber and editor of the magazine *Gripped* David Chaundy-Smart finds an escape from his boring suburban life and an inspiration to try climbing when he reads about Chris Bonington and his team's 1970 attempt on Annapurna in his local library (2015, 29–30). Jon Krakauer's childhood heroes were Tom Hornbein and Willi Unsoeld, whose daring climb of Everest, detailed in *Everest: The West Ridge*, fuelled his own dream of climbing the mountain (1997, 21–3). David Roberts was inspired by Maurice Herzog's *Annapurna* to become a climber himself (2002, xiii).

8 Life writing studies has a significant amount of work about confession and its relationship to testimony. Leigh Gilmore's early work on confession in the chapter "Policing Truth" from *Autobiographics* connected it to questions of power and the vulnerability of the confessing subject ([1994] 2003). See Gillian Whitlock, *Soft Weapons* (2007), for a discussion of the politics and circulation of testimony, Margaretta Jolly's introduction to Meg Jensen and Jolly's collection *We Shall Bear Witness* (2014) for a discussion of the role of testimony within the discourse of human rights reporting, Molly Andrews on the complex relationship between trauma and testimony in Jensen and Jolly, and Kay Schaffer and Sidonie Smith's study of personal storytelling and online human rights campaigns in Jensen and Jolly.

9 See Heggie (2019, 12–13). Chapter 3 of Heggie's *Higher and Colder* also has a detailed treatment of racism, class politics, and sexism in extreme research environments, including mountain locations.

10 See Reuben Ellis's *Vertical Margins* (2001) and Bayers (2003) for a discussion of mountaineering, masculinity, and British-American imperialism. For discussions of mountaineering and masculinity, see Dummit (2004), Erickson (2003), Frohlick (1999), Morin et al. (2001), Ortner (1999), Hansen (2013), and Reidy (2016). Overtly postcolonial critiques of masculinity are found in Slemon (2008, 1998, 2012), Frohlick (2004), and Purtschert (2016).

11 For examples, see Engel (1971), Reichwein and Fox (2004), Routledge (2004), Skidmore (2006), Waldroup (2014), Gugglberger (2015). Gugglberger, however, does connect the development of Nepali women's climbing to national discourse in Nepal and ideas about women's empowerment. Roch (2013) discusses the advent of women's climbing in the Victorian Era with reference to the ideology

of "the new women," which does connect gender theory about that period with climbing.

12 A notable exception which proves the rule can be found in Peter Zuckerman and Amanda Padoan's account of Sherpa heroism on K2 in 2008, *Buried in the Sky*. The climbing Sherpa Chhiring and the Korean team's cook Ngawang Bhote say of the Korean team that they felt the presence of the Koreans was a bad omen because the Korean ceremony to placate the goddess of K2 failed, and because the leader of the Korean team, Mr Kim, had caused problems with Sherpas on Mount Everest the year before about a rock the leader thought was a good omen for their climb, which at one point went missing (2013, 104–5). Chhiring and Ngawang's assessment of the Korean team is based on omens, ceremonies, and their experience with the team's style, rather than on assumptions about what their climbing style should or should not involve.

13 A more recent article by Phillips about sexual harassment in climbing is less positive and does identify problems for women in the climbing world, reflecting the impact of the #MeToo online campaign to raise awareness. Phillips writes that 47 per cent of women surveyed by #SafeOutside reported that they were sexually harassed while they were climbing. She uses her own experience and those of others to underscore that even behaviour not seen as overt harassment still affects "women's access to climbing free of fear, anxiety or discomfort" (Philips 2017b).

14 For example, Swann, Crust, and Allen-Collinson's study of Mental Toughness (MT) uses data from fourteen mountaineers (2016); Allen-Collinson, Crust, and Swann's sociological-phenomenological study of weather and the climbing body derives data from interviews with nineteen climbers (2018); Brymer and Schweitzer's phenomenological study within psychology (again based on inter-views) is of extreme mountaineering and the idea of the ineffable (2017). Dianne Chisholm's feminist theoretical explication of Simone de Beauvoir's phenom-enological writing on Merleau-Ponty is different in that it uses rock climbing (and specifically, the example of American climber Lynn Hill, because she is most widely known as a free climber) as a test case for evaluating how women experience movement within the lived body. The study concludes that gender forms a "background" to Hill's account of lived experience in her memoir. Hill's memoir is read as evidence of the lived body, not a construction of experience or a representation (2008).

CHAPTER ONE

1 Bonington's description of the role of Sherpas on his team may not be accur-ate. Junko Tabei observed to a friend and fellow climber that the Sherpas on

Bonington's team appeared to be not allowed to eat meals until after the British climbers were finished, and that the relationship between Sherpas and British climbers on that team did not appear to be equitable. Tabei was known to share equipment and work equitably with Sherpas, particularly on Everest in 1975. Personal correspondence, Yumiko Hiraki, 11 May 2020.

2 Quotations from *Annapurna: A Woman's Place* are from the first edition, unless otherwise indicated.

3 For a discussion of the misnaming of Pan Duo as "Phantog" in English-language climbing histories, memoirs, and in the press, see chapter 3.

4 For a sustained discussion of the problem of sisterhood in light of other conditions of inequality, see Lorde (1984, 144–212).

5 See Arlene Blum's website for a full account of her workshops at http://www.arleneblum.com/.

CHAPTER TWO

1 Although Houston never used this phrase directly, during the tape-recorded conversation he had with his team in Base Camp he says that "we entered the mountains as strangers, but we left as brothers." This phrase is repeated and given a longer explanation which connects the phrase to rope in the official account of the 1953 expedition by George Bell ([1954] 2009, 137). When the team meets twenty-five years later to talk about events, Bates refers to "the Brotherhood of the Rope established on K2" (McDonald 2007, 139–40). Houston made a film about the American expeditions to K2 called *The Brotherhood of the Rope*, and the phrase is also the title of Bernadette McDonald's biography of him. According to Stephen Slemon, the idea that mountain climbers form a brotherhood appears as early as 1926 in a eulogy for George Mallory (2001, 237) but I believe that the phrase in its entirety can be reasonably attributed to Charlie Houston and other members of the 1953 expedition.

2 See the introduction for a discussion of *Tents in the Clouds*, Monica Jackson and Elizabeth Stark's account of the 1955 Himalayan's women expedition. In her foreword to the 2000 edition, Arlene Blum mentions that American women did not know about this expedition or about the efforts of other British women climbers during the 1960s. There was not another all-female climbing team (with male Sherpa support) in the Himalayas until the Tokyo Women's Mountaineering expeditions, led by Junko Tabei, in 1970 and 1975.

3 According to Salman Rashid, a Pakistani travel writer who has walked the original trade routes with Balti guides and described his travels in the 2011 book *The Apricot Road to Yarkland*, Balti families in the area told him that the original name of K2 was Chhogho Ri (Great Mountain) in Urdu. Rashid glossed his book

in an article about place names, where he writes that the mountain is called Cho-ghiri or Chogor by the Balti people, and Chongoli by the Chinese in the border area (Pracha 2013, Rashid 2011). See his blog post excerpt from his 2011 book for a discussion of the name Chogor and a theory of the naming of Chhogho Ri by the traders (Rashid 2014). However, a 2015 debate among Wikipedia editors (including Balti speakers) established only that Choghiri is in use by some Balti people, but not widely (Talk: K2/Archive 3, 2015). There is no print evidence why Montgomerie, who named K2, did not learn what local traders called the mountain. Presumably if he had found out, he would have renamed it, as he renamed K1 Masherbrum when he learned this name.

CHAPTER THREE

1 Cho Oyo, the sixth highest mountain in the world and widely regarded as the easiest to climb was second at 3,136 summits in 2013. Most 8,000-metre peaks had fewer than 500 successful summits in 2013. See "Stairway to Heaven" (2013) for the statistics.

2 For an overview of mapping of Mount Everest and British imperialism before the Great War, see Isserman and Weaver (2008, 1–34, 72–82), Unsworth ([1981] 2000, 11–19), and Davis (2011, 43–79).

3 For a discussion of the continuities between counter-cultural approaches and Golden Age approaches to climbing and masculinity, see Sherry B. Ortner (1999, 36–41). For the beliefs about the connection between George Mallory and contemporary climbing, see David Hahn's comments in Hemmleb et al. (1999, 123), and Messner ([1982] 1989, 39–40).

4 The decline narrative about Everest in the mainstream press is ubiquitous. Book-length explorations of Everest's "decline" in the face of commercialization include Kodas (2008), Heil (2009), and Krakauer (1997).

5 Mallory's relationship with his wife Ruth was very close and affectionate. Mallory wrote often to Ruth while he was on Everest expeditions, telling her of the details of his travels and his thoughts and feelings about climbing. Many of his letters to Ruth survive. See Davis (2011, 162–5) for examples. Ruth did not want Mallory to go to Everest in 1921 because she did not want him to leave his family for months (Davis 2011, 204). The second Everest expedition also meant that Mallory would be away for months (380). As he considered whether to return to Everest again in 1924, Mallory "was deeply conflicted, torn between his family and his fellow climbers" (479).

6 For a detailed examination of how Mallory was perceived before he went to Mount Everest with an annotated bibliography of sources, see Davis (2011, 168–85, 601–4).

7　There are many biographies and historical analyses of George Mallory and his last climb with Andrew Irvine. The most detailed historical account of Mallory and the 1924 expedition can be found in Holzel and Salkeld (1996, 2000). Wade Davis's biography of Mallory, *Into the Silence* (2012), focuses on Mallory's life and character more generally, with an analysis of the impact of the First World War on Mallory's generation. Unsworth summarizes the theories about what happened to Mallory and Irvine before Mallory's body was found in 1999 ([1981] 2000, 126–41). For analyses of what might have happened to Mallory after his body was found in 1999, see Firstbrook (2003), Hemmleb et al. (1999), Anker and Roberts (1999), Breashears and Salkeld (1999), Messner (2007), and a *National Geographic* film directed by Anthony Geffen about Conrad Anker's finding of Mallory and re-enactment of the conditions of the 1924 climb, *The Wildest Dream* (2010).

8　It is not clear in *The Wildest Dream* how the finding of Mallory was actually filmed. Anker says in *The Lost Explorer* that he discovered the body, realized that he had not brought his camera, and then sat and waited for the other climbers (Anker and Roberts 1999, 19). When the other climbers arrived, they took photos, shot video, and discussed how to investigate the body. Some of the video shows Anker as if he is approaching the body for the first time; other shots show events – such as the discovery of the clothing labels – presumably as they unfolded in real time.

9　See Dhar (2019, 345). Ullman is credited as the solo author of *Man of Everest* on the book's cover, but the book is based on Tenzing's story. To indicate the nature of this collaboration and to signal how naming conventions work in Nepal (Tenzing is Tenzing Norgay's surname), I have cited the book as Ullman and Tenzing.

10　Sherpa naming conventions are complex, and in the case of Tenzing Norgay, who lived in Nepal and India, and whose family had migrated to Nepal from Tibet, they are even more so. In *Man of Everest*, Tenzing says his first name (Tenzing) and his second name (Norgay, which means fortunate) have undergone many changes. His clan name was Ghang La. He sometimes used Sherpa as a last name, to honour his people. He clarifies that he uses Tenzing as his name and that he is not concerned about last names. For details, see Ullman and Tenzing ([1955] 2010, 24). His grandson, Tashi Tenzing, writes that Tenzing's full name was Tenzing Norgay Bhutia because he had migrated from Tibet, but he used Sherpa as his last name. According to him, "Tenzing was, and is still, known in Nepal and India as Tenzing Norgay Sherpa. Tenzing and Norgay were his first and middle names" (Tenzing and Tenzing 2001, xxi). Following common convention and Tenzing's own usage, in this book Tenzing Norgay is referred to by his first and middle names, and by his first name.

11 For examples, see the photographs of Sherpas (all are smiling) in Hornbein (1965), Ortner's discussion of Sherpas and the "childlike" trope (1999, 41–5), and Morris's portrayal of Sherpas as childlike ([1974] 1997, 32, 36).

12 These statistics were compiled by Elizabeth Hawley, a widely accepted authority on Himalayan summit attempts, for Coburn (2007, 248–9).

13 A notable exception is a more complete history of Phantog (as she is called there) in Peter and Leni Gillman's (1993) 2000 collection. Phantog's early life, climbing career and her thoughts about her Everest climb and her life afterwards are included, probably based on Zhao Zonglu's one-page interview with her – done in 1986 – in the English-language magazine *Beijing Daily Review*. Also see Gillman and Gillman ([1993] 2000, 104–5).

14 The confusion about Phantog's name and the scant details available in most accounts about her appears to have arisen in part from the complexities of translating Chinese names and climbing accounts into English, but not entirely. See the previous note for Gillman and Gillman's article: even though Pan Duo is called Phantog there, this account of Pan Duo's life at least seems to be based on one of the few sources available in English about her, Zonglu (1986) where she is called "Phanthog." A 2009 English-language account (also based on the *Beijing Daily Review* article) about the sixtieth anniversary of Pan Duo's achievement does not mention her name as "Phantog" or "Phanthog." It was republished as part of the Wayback Machine project ("Pan Duo" 2016). Given how difficult it has been to ascertain who Pan Duo was or what she accomplished, Junko Tabei's inclusion of Pan Duo's biography with additional details about her is significant.

15 Special thanks to Yumiko Hiraki for telling me about the complex production history for *Honouring High Places*. Personal correspondence with the author, 11 May 2020.

CHAPTER FOUR

1 In the "international" version of the *Everest* trailer, Japanese climber Yasuko Namba appears as a hiker, but she is not identified and has no speaking part. In that same trailer, a line of Sherpa climbers is shown, but they are not identified and do not speak. The North American versions of the trailer do not even include these scenes.

2 Personal correspondence with Lou Kasischke, 2016. In *The Climb*, it is reported that "Hall had hedged around setting a specific turnaround time" and different climbers understood the time differently (Boukreev [1998] 2002, 146), which gives support to Krakauer's story. No source is given for this information, however, and no other climbers have gone on record that the time was not 1:00 pm.

3 For an example, see Dwight Garner: "A generally accepted rule is that climbers who aren't within shouting distance of Everest's summit by 1 or 2 pm must be turned around in order to descend before nightfall" (1998).

4 Krakauer initially argued that poisoned seeds McCandless ate caused his death, and that he could not have known they would hurt him. This theory has been contested. Krakauer then argued for other causes, and these have also been disputed. See Saverin (2013) for a summary of the debate. A journalist has claimed that Krakauer invented material in order to create McCandless's motivations and cause of death, misreading McCandless's journal entries and reporting deliberately that all books in the abandoned bus belonged to McCandless and were annotated by him. In fact, Krakauer had been told by the actual owner of the books that McCandless was not the owner, the books had been left there the previous January before McCandless came to the bus, and there is no proof that McCandless was the annotator. Krakauer refused that explanation (Medred 2016). This allegation is significant, because much of Krakauer's analysis of McCandless's time at the bus depends on assuming that the annotations are McCandless's.

CONCLUSION

1 For an example, see Ives (2019).
2 For examples of attempts to make climbing more diverse, see note 2, introduction.

REFERENCES

"2018 Honoured Ascents." 2018. *Piolets d'Or*. 22 September. https://www.piolets dor.net/index.php/en/archives/home-3/2018-honoured-ascents.

Abel, Georgie. 2017. "A Feminist Review of Climbing How-To Guides." *Alpinist*, 27 November. http://www.alpinist.com/doc/web17f/wfeature-feminist-review-of-climbing-how-to-guides.

Adhikari, Deepak. 2013. "The Everest Brawl: A Sherpa's Tale." *Outside*, 13 August. https://www.outsideonline.com/1929351/everest-brawl-sherpas-tale.

Allen-Collinson, Jacquelyn, Lee Crust, and Christian Swann. 2018. "Embodiment in High-Altitude Mountaineering: Sensing and Working with the Weather." *Body and Society* 25, no. 1 (28 November): 90–115. https://doi.org/10.1177/1357034X18812947.

Anker, Conrad, and David Roberts. 1999. *The Lost Explorer: Finding Mallory on Mount Everest*. New York: Simon & Schuster.

Arnette, Alan. 2010. "Search for THE Camera: Everest Historian Tom Holzel." *Outside*, 3 February. https://www.outsideonline.com/1815566/search-camera-everest-historian-tom-holzel.

 – 2019. "Will New Rules Reduce Crowds on Mount Everest?" *Outside*, 15 August. https://www.outsideonline.com/2400987/mount-everest-crowds-new-rules-nepal.

Aron, Nina Renata. 2017. "Lesbians Battled for Their Place in 1960s Feminism." *Timeline*, 19 January. https://timeline.com/lesbians-battled-for-their-place-in-1960s-feminism-25082853be90.

Austin, Charlotte. 2017. "The Psychology of Climbing with Women." *Verticulture*, 7 March. https://www.outdoorresearch.com/blog/article/the-psychology-of-womens-climbing.

Bainbridge, Simon. 2012. "Romantic Writers and Mountaineering." *Romanticism* 18, no. 1: 1–15.

Barcott, Bruce. 1996. "Cliffhangers: The Fatal Descent of the Mountain-Climbing Memoir." *Harper's*, August: 64–9.

Barnes, Henry. 2015. "On Strike at 8,848 Metres: *Sherpa* and the Story of an Everest Revolution." *Guardian*, 19 December. https://www.theguardian.com/film/2015/dec/19/on-strike-8848-metres-sherpa-film-everest-revolution.

Bass, Dick, and Frank Wells, with Rick Ridgeway. 1988. *The Seven Summits*. New York: Grand Central Publishing.

Bayers, Peter L. 2003. *Imperial Ascent: Mountaineering, Masculinity, and Empire*. Boulder: University Press of Colorado.

Beaumont, Peter, and Ed Douglas. 2011. "Everest Expedition to Find Irvine's Remains Slammed as 'Distasteful.'" *Guardian*, 7 August. https://www.theguardian.com/world/2011/aug/07/everest-expedition-irvine-remains-distasteful.

Bederman, Gail. 1995. *Manliness and Civilization: A Cultural History of Gender and Race in the United States, 1880–1917*. Chicago and London: University of Chicago Press.

Bernstein, Jeremy. 1965. *Ascent: The Invention of Mountain Climbing and Its Practice*. New York: Simon & Shuster.

Blum, Arlene. 1980. *Annapurna: A Woman's Place*. San Francisco: Sierra Club Books.

 – 1998. *Annapurna: A Woman's Place (20th Anniversary Edition)*. San Francisco: Sierra Club Books.

 – 2005. *Breaking Trail: A Climbing Life*. Orlando: Harcourt.

Boardman, Peter. 1978. *The Shining Mountain: Two Men on Changabang's West Wall*. London: Hodder & Stoughton.

Bonatti, Walter. (1998) 2010. *The Mountains of My Life*. Translated and edited by Robert Marshall. London: Penguin Classics.

Bonington, Sir Chris. 2001. *Annapurna South Face: The Classic Account of Survival*. New York: Adrenaline Classics.

Booth, Alison. 2004. *How to Make It as a Woman: Collective Biographical History from Victoria to the Present*. Chicago: University of Chicago Press.

Boukreev, Anatoli, and G. Weston DeWalt. (1998) 2002. *The Climb: Tragic Ambitions on Everest*. New York: St Martin's Press.

Bowley, Graham. 2010. *No Way Down: Life and Death on K2*. London: Viking Penguin.

Bramley, Ellie Violet. 2015. "A Mountain of Trouble: The Roots of the Sherpas' Grievances." *Guardian*, 29 December. https://www.theguardian.com/film/2015/dec/19/on-strike-8848-metres-sherpa-film-everest-revolution.

Breashears, David. 2000. "Breashears on Mallory and Irvine." Interview by Andrew North. *Lost on Everest*. Nova Online. PBS (November). https://www.pbs.org/wgbh/nova/everest/lost/mystery/breashears.html.

– 2008. "The Hour by Hour Unfolding Disaster." *Storm over Everest: Front Line*, 13 May. http://www.pbs.org/wgbh/pages/frontline/everest/stories/unfolding.html.

Breashears, David, and Audrey Salkeld. 1999. *Last Climb*. Washington: National Geographic Society.

Brown, Bill. 2008. "Thing Theory." *Critical Inquiry* 28 (Autumn): 1–22.

Brown, Chip. 2014. "Sherpas: The Invisible Men of Everest." *National Geographic Sites*, 26 April. http://news.nationalgeographic.com/news/special-features/2014/04/140426-sherpa-culture-everest-disaster/.

Brown, Rebecca. 2002. *Women on High: Pioneers of Mountaineering*. Appalachian Mountain Club Books.

Brymer, Eric, and Robert D. Schweitzer. 2017. "Evoking the Ineffable: The Phenomenology of Extreme Sports." *Psychology of Consciousness: Theory, Research, and Practice* 4, no. 1 (March): 63–74. DOI: 10.1037/cns0000111.

Buhl, Hermann. 1956. *Nanga Parbat: Pilgrimage*. London: Hodder & Stoughton.

Burke, Edmund. (1757) 1971. *A Philosophical Enquiry into the Origin of Our Ideas of the Sublime and Beautiful*. New York: Garland Publications.

Butler, Judith. 2006. *Gender Trouble: Feminism and the Subversion of Identity*. New York: Routledge.

Carpenter, Hayden. 2015. "New Route and Deaths on Annapurna – World's Deadliest Mountain." *Rock and Ice*, 28 July. http://rockandice.com/climbing-news/new-route-and-deaths-on-annapurna-worlds-deadliest-mountain/.

Chaundy-Smart, David. 2015. *A Youth Wasted Climbing*. Banff: Rocky Mountain Books.

Child, Greg, and Jon Krakauer. 1987. "The Dangerous Summer." *Outside*, March. http://web.archive.org/web/20030824070929/http://web.outsideonline.com/news/specialreport/alison/K20mag.html.

Chisholm, Dianne. 2008. "Climbing Like a Girl: An Exemplary Adventure in Feminist Phenomenology." *Hypatia: A Journal of Feminist Philosophy* 23, no. 1 (Winter): 9–40.

Clark, Liesl, and Audrey Salkeld. 2015. "The Mystery of Mallory and Irvine '24." *Lost on Everest: PBS ONLINE*, 5 August. http://www.pbs.org/wgbh/nova/everest/lost/mystery/.

Clarke, Owen. 2019. "Indigenous Bolivian Women Summit Aconcagua." *Rock and Ice*, 29 January. https://rockandice.com/climbing-news/indigenous-bolivian-women-summit-aconcagua/

Clash, Jim. 2014. "Climbing Legend Reinhold Messner." *Forbes*, 19 September. http://www.forbes.com/sites/jimclash/2014/09/19/climbing-legend-reinhold-messner-like-kindergarten-they-go-on-everest-now/.

Clements, Philip W. 2018. *Science in an Extreme Environment: The 1963 American Mount Everest Expedition*. Pittsburgh: University of Pittsburgh Press.

Coburn, Broughton. 2007. *Everest: Mountain without Mercy*. MacGillivray Freeman Films.

Cosgrove, Ben. 2014. "High Society: LIFE with Hillary and Tenzing after the First Ascent of Everest." *TIME/Life*, 18 April. http://time.com/3879614/mount-everest-photos-of-edmund-hillary-and-tenzing-norgay-1953/.

Curran, Jim. (1994) 1995. *K2: The Story of the Savage Mountain*. Seattle: The Mountaineers. Reprint, London: Hodder & Stoughton. Citations refer to the Hodder & Stoughton edition.

– 1987. *K2: Triumph and Tragedy*. Boston: Houghton Mifflin Co.

Da Silva, Rachel, ed. 1992. *Leading Out: Women Climbers Reaching for the Top*. Seattle: Seal Press.

Davis, Wade. 2011. *Into the Silence: The Great War, Mallory and the Conquest of Everest*. London: Bodley Head.

Dhar, Amrita. 2019. "Travel and Mountains." In *Cambridge History of Travel Writing*, edited by Nandini Das and Tim Youngs, 345–60. Cambridge: Cambridge University Press.

Diemberger, Kurt. (1989) 1991. *The Endless Knot: K2, Mountain of Dreams and Destiny*. Munich: F. Bruickmann KG. Translated by Audrey Salkeld. Seattle: The Mountaineers.

Douglas, Ed. 2009. "Mallory: The Everest Enigma." *Independent*, 2 March. http://www.independent.co.uk/arts-entertainment/films/features/mallory-the-everest-enigma-1634977.html.

– 1999. "Roped into Mallory's Legend." *Observer*, 3 October. https://www.theguardian.com/theobserver/1999/oct/03/focus.news1.

Dummit, Christopher. 2004. "Risk on the Rocks: Modernity, Manhood and Mountaineering in Postwar British Columbia." *BC Studies* 141 (Spring): 3–29.

Egan, Susanna. 2011. *Burdens of Proof: Faith, Doubt and Identity in Autobiography*. Waterloo: Wilfrid Laurier University Press.

Eisenstein, Zillah R. 1981. *The Radical Future of Liberal Feminism*. New York and London: Longman.

Ellis, Reuben. 2001. *Vertical Margins: Mountaineering and the Landscapes of Neoimperialism*. Madison: University of Wisconsin Press.

Elmes, Michael, and Bob Frame. 2008. "Into Hot Air: A Critical Perspective on Everest." *Human Relations* 61, no. 2 (February): 213–41.

Engel, Claire. 1971. *Mountaineering in the Alps: An Historical Survey*. London, UK: Allen and Unwin.

Erickson, Bruce. 2003. "The Colonial Climbs of Mount Trudeau: Thinking Masculinity through the Homosocial." *topia: a Canadian journal of cultural studies* 9 (Spring): 67–82.

Everest. 2015. (Film.) Directed by Baltasar Kormákur. Universal Pictures.

Feanley, Laurence. 2015. *Lydia Bradley: Going Up Is Easy*. London: Penguin.

Firstbrook, Peter. 2000. *Lost on Everest: The Search for Mallory and Irvine*. Contemporary Books: Chicago.

"Five Women Who Deserve the Piolet d'Or Lifetime Achievement Award." *Gripped*, 8 March 2018. https://gripped.com/news/five-women-who-deserve-the-piolet-dor-lifetime-achievement-award/.

Flash Foxy. 2020. https://flashfoxy.com/.

Free Solo 360. (Film.) Directed by E. Chai Vasarhelyi and Jimmy Chin. National Geographic Documentaries, 2018. https://www.framestore.com/work/free-solo-360.

Frohlick, Susan. 1999–2000. "The 'Hypermasculine' Landscape of High-Altitude Mountaineering." *Michigan Feminist Studies* 14: 83–106.

– 2003. "Negotiating the 'Global' within the Global Playscapes of Mount Everest." *Canadian Review of Sociology and Anthropology* 40, no. 5 (December): 525–43.

– 2004. "'Who Is Lhakpa Sherpa?': Circulating Subjectivities within the Global/Local Terrain of Himalayan Mountaineering." *Social and Cultural Geography* 5, no. 2 (June): 195–213.

– 2005. "'That Playfulness of White Masculinity': Mediating Masculinities and Adventure at Mountain Film Festivals." *Tourist Studies* 5, no. 2 (August 1): 175–93.

– 2006. "'Wanting the Children and Wanting K2': The Incommensurability of Motherhood and Mountaineering in Britain and North America in the Late Twentieth Century." *Gender, Place & Culture: A Journal of Feminist Geography* 13, no. 5 (October): 477–90.

Gammelgaard, Lena. (1996) 1999. *Climbing High: A Woman's Account of Surviving the Everest Tragedy.* New York: HarperCollins Perennial. Seal Press.

Gardien, Claude. 2020. "Catherine Destiville." The 2020 Piolets D'Or. 27 July. https://pioletsdor.net/index.php/en/21-po-carriere/liste-po-carriere/109-2020-catherine-destivelle.

Garner, Dwight. (1998) 2010. "Coming Down." *Salon*, 26 October. https://web.archive.org/web/20110111112541/http://www.salon.com:80/wlust/feature/1998/08/cov_03feature3.html.

Gau, Ming-Ho (Makalu). 2007. "Everest 2007: Makalu Ming-Ho Gau Looking Back in Anger." Interview. *Explorersweb*, 13 March. https://www.explorersweb.com/everest_k2/news.php?id=15761.

Gillman, Peter, and Leni Gillman. (1993) 2000. "Women on Top." In *Everest: Eighty Years of Triumph and Tragedy*, edited by Peter Gilman, 104–5. Seattle: The Mountaineers.

Gilmore, Leigh. 1994. *Autobiographics: A Theory of Women's Self-Representation.* Ithaca: Cornell University Press.

− 2003. "Jurisdictions: *I, Rigoberta Menchú, The Kiss*, and Scandalous Self-Representation in the Age of Memoir and Trauma." *Signs* 28, no. 2: 695–718.

Graham, Regina. 2015. "Socialite Mountaineer Portrayed by *Into Thin Air* Author John Krakauer as a 'Privileged Villain' Breaks Silence ahead of Everest Blockbuster Based on 1996 Mountain Tragedy and Says 'I Was an Easy Target.'" *Daily Mail*, 18 September. http://www.dailymail.co.uk/news/article-3239442/I-easy-target-Socialite-mountaineer-villainized-John-Krakauer-breaks-silence-ahead-Everest-blockbuster-based-1996-mountain-tragedy.html.

Gugglberger, Martina. 2015. "Climbing beyond the Summits: Social and Global Aspects of Women's Expeditions in the Himalayas." *International Journal of the History of Sport* 32, no. 4 (February): 597–613.

Haladyn, Julian Jason. 2016. "Friedrich's 'Wanderer': Paradox of the Modern Subject." *RACAR: Revue d'art canadienne/Canadian Art Review* 41, no. 1: 47–61. http://www.jstor.org.login.ezproxy.library.ualberta.ca/stable/43855855.

Hall, Lincoln. 2008. *Dead Lucky: Life after Death on Mount Everest.* New York: TarcherPerigee.

Hansen, Peter H. 1995. "Albert Smith, the Alpine Club and the Invention of Mountaineering in Mid-Victorian Britain." *Journal of British Studies* 34 (July): 300–24.

− 2013. *The Summits of Modern Man: Mountaineering after the Enlightenment.* Boston: Harvard University Press.

"Hazards of the Alps." 1923. *New York Times*, 22 August. https://www.nytimes.com/1923/08/29/archives/hazards-of-the-alps.html.

Heggie, Vanessa. 2019. *Higher and Colder: A History of Extreme Physiology and Exploration*. Chicago: University of Chicago Press.

Heil, Nick. 2009. *Dark Summit: The Extraordinary True Story of Everest's Most Controversial Season*. New York: Henry Holt.

— 2012a. "Tragedy at 29,000 Feet: The 10 Worst Disasters on Everest." *Outside*, 26 April. http://www.outsideonline.com/1930356/tragedy-29000-feet-10-worst-disasters-everest.

— 2012b. "Mount Everest Suffers from Too Many Climbers and Deteriorating Conditions." *Daily Beast*, 23 May. https://www.thedailybeast.com/mt-everest-suffers-from-too-many-climbers-and-deteriorating-conditions.

Hemmleb, Jochen, Larry A. Johnson, and Eric R. Simonson. 1999. *Ghosts of Everest: The Search for Mallory and Irvine*. Seattle: The Mountaineers.

Herrar, Heinrich. 1959. *The White Spider*. London: R. Hart-Davis.

Herzog, Maurice. (1952) 1997. *Annapurna: The First Conquest of an 8,000-metre Peak*. Translated by Nea Morin and Janet Adam Smith. London: Pimlico.

— 1980. Foreword. In *Annapurna: A Woman's Place*, by Arlene Blum, ix–x. San Francisco: Sierra Club Books.

Hewes, Ben. 2003. "Priest's Crucifix Buried on Everest." *Newsquest Media Group*, May. http://www.thecross-photo.com/Priests_crucifix_buried_on_Everest_by_Ben_Hewes.htm.

Hillary, Sir Edmund. (1955) 2003. *High Adventure: The True Story of the First Ascent of Everest*. New York: Oxford University Press.

Höbusch, Harald. 2016. *"Mountain of Destiny": Nanga Parbat and the German Imagination*. Rochester: Camden House.

Holehouse, Matthew. 2013. "Margaret Thatcher: A Pioneering Woman with No Time for Feminists." *Telegraph*, 8 April. http://www.telegraph.co.uk/news/politics/margaret-thatcher/9979922/Margaret-Thatcher-a-pioneering-woman-with-no-time-for-feminists.html.

Holmes, Richard. 1993. "Biography: Inventing the Truth." In *The Art of Literary Biography*, edited by John Batchelor, 15–26. Oxford: Clarendon Press.

Horn, Robert. 1996. "No Mountain Too High for Her." *Sports Illustrated Vault*, 29 April. *Sports Illustrated* 84, no. 17: 9–10. http://sportsillustrated.cnn.com/vault/article/magazine/MAG1008036/1/index.htm.

Hornbein, Thomas F. 1965. *Everest the West Ridge*. Seattle: The Mountaineers, 1980. San Francisco: Sierra Club.

Horrell, Mark. 2010. "8 Reasons Why False Summit Claims Are Made." *Footsteps on the Mountain* (blog), 10 December. https://www.markhorrell.com/blog/2010/false-summit-claims/.

— 2011. "The Krakauer Syndrome." *Footsteps on the Mountain* (blog), 8 June. https://www.markhorrell.com/blog/2011/the-krakauer-syndrome/.

Houston, Charles S., and Robert H. Bates. (1939) 2000. *Five Miles High: The Thrilling True Story of the First American Expedition to K2*. New York: Dodd, Mead and Co. Reprint, New York: The Lyons Press. Citations refer to the Lyons Press edition.

– (1954) 2009. *K2: The Savage Mountain*. New York: McGraw Hill Co. Inc. Reprint, Guildford, CT: The Globe Pequot Press. Citations refer to the Globe Pequot edition.

Howkins, Heidi. 2001. *K2: One Woman's Quest for the Summit*. Washington, DC: National Geographic Adventure Press.

Hozel, Tom, and Audrey Salkeld. (1996) 2000. *The Mystery of Mallory and Irvine*. Seattle: The Mountaineers.

Hunt, John. (1953) 2003. *The Ascent of Everest: Mount Everest Expedition, 1953*. Garden City, NJ: International Collectors Library, 1953. Seattle: The Mountaineers, 1993, 1998. London: Hodder & Stoughton, 2001. London: Hachette, 2003. Citations refer to the Hachette edition.

Ireton, Sean, and Caroline Schaumann, eds. 2012. *Heights of Reflection: Mountains in the German Imagination from the Middle Ages to the Twenty-First Century*. Woodbridge, UK: Boydell & Brewer.

Isserman, Maurice, and Stewart Weaver. 2008. *Fallen Giants: A History of Himalayan Mountaineering from the Age of Empire to the Age of Extremes*. New Haven and London: Yale University Press.

Ives, Katie. 2017. "An Oral History of the First U.S. Ascent of Annapurna (Oh Yeah, and It Happened to Be the First Female Ascent Too)." *Outside*, 11 April. https://www.outsideonline.com/2170021/annapurna-women.

– 2019. "The Ice Mirror." *Alpinist*, 8 March. http://www.alpinist.com/doc/web19w/wfeature-a65-sharp-end-the-ice-mirror.

– 2020. "The Measure of a Mountain." *Alpinist*, 6 March. http://www.alpinist.com/doc/web20w/wfeature-a69-sharp-end-measure-of-a-mountain.

Jack, Ian. 2013. "Sherpas and Climbers on Everest Never Used to Fight – So What Changed?" *Guardian*, 3 May. https://www.theguardian.com/commentisfree/2013/may/03/sherpas-climbers-everest-fight.

"Japanese Housewife First Woman to Climb Everest." 1975. *Prescott Courier*, 18 May. https://news.google.com/newspapers?nid=886&dat=19750518&id=nqdMAAAAIBAJ&sjid=XlADAAAAIBAJ&pg=2353,1804690&hl=en.

"Japanese Housewife Conquers Everest." 1975. *Evening News*, 17 May. https://news.google.com/newspapers?nid=1982&dat=19750517&id=r_ZGAAAAIBAJ&sjid=_jMNAAAAIBAJ&pg=5231,2968751&hl=en.

Jemima Dika Sherpa. 2014. "Three Springs." *Alpinist*, 25 April. http://www.alpinist.com/doc/web14s/wfeature-three-springs-everest.

Jillani, Shahzeb. 2014. "Amir Mehdi: Left Out to Freeze on K2 and Forgotten." *BBC News*, 7 August. https://www.bbc.com/news/magazine-28696985.

Jolly, Margaretta, and Meg Jensen, eds. 2014. *We Shall Bear Witness: Life Narratives and Human Rights*. Madison: University of Wisconsin Press.

Johnson, Chloe. 2012. "*Into Thin Air* v. *The Climb*: A Book Review, and Why We've Clearly Learned Nothing since 1996." *Fresh Air Fort Collins*, 7 June. http://freshairfortcollins.com/into-thin-air-v-climb-book-review-why-weve-clearly-learned-nothing-since/.

Johnston, Barbara. 1994. "The Commodification of Mountaineering." *Annals of Tourism Research* 21, no. 3: 459–78.

Jordan, Jennifer. 2005. *Savage Summit: The Life and Death of the First Women of K2*. New York: HarperCollins.

– 2010. *The Last Man on the Mountain: The Death of an American Adventurer on K2*. New York: W.W. Norton and Company.

Jurgalski, Eberhard. 2019. "True Summits or Tolerance Zones?" *8,000ers.com*. 31 July. http://www.8,000ers.com/cms/.

Kasischke, Lou. 2015. *After the Wind: Tragedy on Everest One Survivor's Story*. Harbor Springs, MI: Good Hart Publishing.

Kennedy, Maeve. 2015. "Camp Correspondence: Letters Reveal George Mallory's Flirtatious Side." *Guardian*, 27 May. https://www.theguardian.com/uk-news/2015/may/27/camp-correspondence-letters-reveal-george-mallorys-flirtatious-side.

Kiester, Shey. 2013. "Ueli Steck's Annapurna South Face Solo." *Alpinist*, 11 October. http://www.alpinist.com/doc/web13f/newswire-ueli-steck-south-face-annapurna.

Kodas, Michael. 2008. *High Crimes: The Fate of Everest in an Age of Greed*. New York: HarperCollins.

Koerner, Joseph Leo. 2009. *Caspar David Friedrich and the Subject of Landscape*, 2nd edition. London: Reaktion Books.

Krakauer, Jon. 1996. *Into the Wild*. New York: Villard.

– 1997. *Into Thin Air: A Personal Account of the Mt Everest Disaster*. New York: Anchor Books.

– 1999. "Postscript." In *Into Thin Air*, 303–37. New York: Anchor Books.

Lejeune, Philippe. 1989a. "The Autobiographical Pact." In *On Autobiography*, 1–30. Edited by Paul John Eakin. Translated by Katherine Leary. Minneapolis: University of Minnesota Press.

– 1989b. "The Autobiographical Pact (bis)." In Lejeune, *On Autobiography*, 119–37.

Lorde, Audre. 1984. "Age, Race, Class, and Sex: Women Redefining Difference." In *Sister Outsider: Essays and Speeches*, 114–23. Freedom, CA: The Crossing Press.

McDonald, Bernadette. 2007. *Brotherhood of the Rope: The Biography of Charles Houston*. Seattle, WA: The Mountaineers Books.

– 2011. *Freedom Climbers*. Toronto: Rocky Mountain Books.

Macfarlane, Robert. 2003. *Mountains of the Mind: A History of a Fascination*. London: Granta Books.

McGlen, Nancy E., Karen O'Connor, Laura van Assendelft, Wendy Gunther-Canada. 2005. *Women, Politics and American Society*. New York: Pearson Longman.

McKinlay, Tom. 2006. "Wrong to Let Climber Die, Says Sir Edmund." *New Zealand Harald*. 24 May. https://www.nzherald.co.nz/nz/news/article.cfm?c_id=1&objectid=10383276.

McQuillan, Gene. 1998. "'No Anthems Playing in My Head': Epiphany and Irony in Contemporary Mountaineering Writing." *Aethlon: The Journal of Sport Literature* 16, no. 1: 49–65.

Manzolini, Elizabeth. 2016. *The Everest Effect: Nature, Culture, Ideology*. Tuscaloosa, AL: Alabama University Press.

Marshall, Robert. 2009. *K2: Lies and Treachery*. Carreg Press.

Mathews, Donald G., and Jane Sherron de Hart. 1990. *Sex, Gender and the Politics of ERA*. New York and Oxford: Oxford University Press.

Mazel, David, Ed. 1994. *Mountaineering Women: Stories by Early Climbers*. College Station: Texas A&M University Press.

Medred, Craig. 2016. "The Fiction That Is Jon Krakauer's 'Into the Wild.'" *Anchorage Daily News*, 28 September. https://www.adn.com/books/article/fiction-jon-krakauers-wild/2015/01/10/.

Melanin Base Camp. 2020. https://www.melaninbasecamp.com/.

Messner, Reinhold. (1982) 1989. *The Crystal Horizon*. Ramsbury: The Crowood Press. *Der Glaserne Horizont*. 1982. Munchen: BLV Verlagsgesellschaft.

– 1982. *K2: Mountain of Mountains*. New York: Oxford University Press.

– 2000. *Annapurna: 50 Years of Expeditions in the Death Zone*. Translated by Tim Carruthers. Seattle: The Mountaineers.

– 2001. *The Second Death of George Mallory: The Enigma and Spirt of Mount Everest*. Translated by Tim Carruthers. New York: St Martin's Press. *Mallory Zweiter*.

– 2002. *Die Nackte Berg – Bruder, Tod, und Eimsandkeit*. Munich: Piper Verlag.

– 2003. *The Naked Mountain*. Translated by Tim Carruthers. Seattle: The Mountaineers.

– 2013. "What I've Learned." *Rock and Ice*. http://www.rockandice.com/latesnews/reinhold-messner-what-i-ve-learned.

Mitchell, Richard G., Jr. 1983. *Mountain Experience: The Psychology and Sociology of Adventure*. Chicago and London: University of Chicago Press.

Morin, Karen M., Robyn Longhurst, and Lynda Johnson. 2001. "(Troubling) Spaces of Mountains and Men: New Zealand's Mount Cook and Hermitage Lodge." *Social and Cultural Geography* 2, no. 2: 117–39.

Morin, Nea. 1968. *A Woman's Reach: Mountaineering Memoirs.* New York: Dodd Mead.

Morris, Jan. (1974) 1997. *Conundrum.* London: Penguin Books.

– (1958) 2000. *Coronation Everest: Eyewitness Dispatches from the Historic Hillary Climb.* Shorthills, NJ: Burford Books.

Mortenson, Greg, and David Oliver Relin. 2006. *Three Cups of Tea.* New York: Penguin Books.

Noble, Chris. 2013. *Women Who Dare: North America's Most Inspiring Women Climbers.* Falcon Guides.

No Man's Land Film Festival. July 2020. http://nomanslandfilmfestival.org/.

Norgay, Jamling Tenzing. 2002. *Touching My Father's Soul: A Sherpa's Journey to the Top of Everest.* New York: HarperCollins.

Norgay, Tenzing Norbu. 2015. "Business as Usual on Mount Everest Must Change." *Outside,* 20 April. https://www.outsideonline.com/1968671/business-usual-everest-must-change.

Ortner, Sherry B. 1999. *Life and Death on Mount Everest: Sherpas and Himalayan Mountaineering.* Princeton: Princeton University Press.

Palmer, Catherine. 2002. "'Shit Happens': The Selling of Risk in Extreme Sport." *Australian Journal of Anthropology* 13, no. 3 (December): 323–37.

"Pan Duo: China's First Woman on Top of World." (2009) 2016. *CCTV.com,* 27 September 2009. Republished in *The Wayback Machine Internet Archive,* 11 July. https://web.archive.org/web/20160711093503/http://www.cctv.com/english/special/tibet/20090927/104002.shtml

Padoan, Amanda. 2014. "Breaking Mount Everest's Glass Ceiling." *Daily Beast,* 30 March. http://www.thedailybeast.com/articles/2014/03/30/breaking-mount-everest-s-glass-ceiling.html.

Parker, Laura. 2015. "Will Everest's Climbing Circus Slow Down after Disasters?" *National Geographic Online,* 13 May. http://news.nationalgeographic.com/2015/05/150513-everest-climbing-nepal-earthquake-avalanche-sherpas/.

Parnel, Ian. 2006. "Victors of the Unwinnable." *Alpinist* 16. http://www.alpinist.com/doc/ALP16/unwinnable-parnell.

Parsons, Mike, and Mary B. Rose. 2003. *Invisible on Everest: Innovation and the Gear Makers.* Philadelphia: Northern Liberties Press.

Philips, Noël. 2017a. "No Man's Land: The Rise of Women in Climbing." *Climbing,* 24 October. https://www.climbing.com/people/no-mans-land-the-rise-of-women-in-climbing/.

– 2017b. "Safe Outside: The Facts about Sexual Harassment and Assault in the Climbing Community." *Climbing*, 27 August, revised 30 August. https://www.climbing.com/news/safe-outside-the-facts-about-sexual-harassment-and-assault-in-the-climbing-community/.

"Piolet d'Or 2009, The Winners." 2009. *Planetmountain.com*, 2 May. https://www.planetmountain.com/en/news/events/piolet-dor-2009-the-winners.html.

"Piolets d'Or 2016: Four Ascents Honoured." 2016. *Planetmountain.com*, 7 April. https://www.planetmountain.com/en/news/alpinism/piolets-dor-2016-four-honoured-ascents.html.

Potts, Mary Anne. 2016. "This Sherpa Woman Is Our Adventurer of the Year." *National Geographic*, 4 February. https://www.nationalgeographic.com/adventure/adventure-blog/2016/02/04/pasang-lhamu-sherpa-akita-adventurer-of-the-year/.

Pracha, Maheen. 2013. Review of *The Apricot Road to Yarkland*. *Salman Rashid* (blog), 2 February. http://odysseuslahori.blogspot.com/2013/02/the-apricot-road-to-yarkand.html.

Preiss, Danielle. 2018. "One-Third of Everest Deaths Are Sherpa Climbers." *NPR Parallels*, 14 April. https://www.npr.org/sections/parallels/2018/04/14/599417489/one-third-of-everest-deaths-are-sherpa-climbers.

Pulver, Andrew. 2015. "'Total Bull': *Into Thin Air* Author's Opinion of Everest Movie." *Guardian*, 28 September. https://www.theguardian.com/film/2015/sep/28/jon-krakauer-into-thin-air-opinion-everest-movie.

Purtschert, Patricia. 2016. "Aviation Skills, Manly Adventures and Imperial Tears: The Dhaulagiri Expedition and Switzerland's Techno-Colonialism." *National Identities* 18, no. 1: 53–69.

Rashid, Salman. 2014. "The Long Wait in Xinjiang." *Salman Rashid* (blog), 3 February. http://odysseuslahori.blogspot.com/2014/02/Kashgar-Yarkand.html.

– 2011. "Place Names – II." *Express Tribune*, 2 September. https://tribune.com.pk/story/243567/place-names--ii/.

Rébuffat, Gaston. (1956) 1957. *Starlight and Storm: The Ascent of Six Great North Faces of the Alps with a Section on the Technique of Mountain Climbing*. Translated by Roland Le Grand. New York: E.P. Dutton & Comp. Inc. Originally published as *Étoiles et tempêtes*. Paris: Arthaud. Citations refer to the 1957 edition.

Reichwein, PearlAnn, and Karen Fox. 2001. "Margaret Fleming and the Alpine Club of Canada: A Woman's Place in Mountain Leisure and Literature, 1932–1952." *Journal of Canadian Studies* 36, no. 3 (Fall): 35–60.

– eds. 2004. *Mountain Diaries: The Alpine Adventures of Margaret Fleming, 1929–1980*. Edmonton: Alberta Historical Society.

Reidy, Michael. 2016. "Mountaineering, Masculinity, and the Male Body in Mid-Victorian Britain." *Osiris* 30, no. 1: 158–81.

"Reinhold Messner and Peter Habeler, 40 Years Ago Everest without Supplementary Oxygen." 2018. *Planetmountain.com*, 5 May. https://www.planet mountain.com/en/news/alpinism/reinhold-messner-and-peter-habeler-40-years-ago-everest-without-supplementary-oxygen.html.

"Respecting Annapurna and Its History." 2017. *Inside Himalayas*, 13 August. https://www.insidehimalayas.com/respecting-annapurna-history/.

Richards, Dan. 2016. "In the Footholds of Dorothy Pilley: How My Great-Great Aunt Became a Climbing Inspiration." *Guardian*, 15 September. https://www.theguardian.com/travel/2016/sep/15/dorothy-pilley-climbing-dan-richards-adventure-travel.

Ridgeway, Rick. (1980) 1999. *The Last Steps: The American Ascent of K2*. Seattle: The Mountaineers.

Ritchie, Gayle. 2019. "Interview with Simon Yates – 'The Man Who Cut the Rope' in Award-Winning Film *Touching the Void*." *Courier*, 23 February. https://www.thecourier.co.uk/fp/lifestyle/entertainment/834260/interview-with-simon-yates-the-man-who-cut-the-rope-in-award-winning-film-touching-the-void/.

Roberts, David. 1968. *The Mountain of My Fear*. New York: Vanguard.

– 1981. "Hazardous Routes." *Outside*, 29–33, 85–7.

– 2002. *True Summit: What Really Happened on the Legendary Ascent of Annapurna*. New York: Simon & Shuster.

Roche, Clare. 2013. "Women Climbers 1850–1900: A Challenge to Male Hegemony?" *Sport in History* 33, no. 3, (September): 236–59.

Rose, David, and Ed Douglas. 1999. *Regions of the Heart: The Triumph and Tragedy of Alison Hargreaves*. London: Penguin Books.

Routledge, Karen. 2004. "'Being a Girl without Being a Girl': Gender and Mountaineering on Mount Waddington." *BC Studies* 141 (March 1): 31–58.

Ryan, Mick. 2005. "Climb Like a Girl – Part I." *UKC: UK Climbing.com*, 5 April. https://www.ukclimbing.com/articles/features/climb_like_a_girl_-_part_1-107.

Samuel, Henry. 2015. "French Mountaineers Take On 'World's Most Perilous Climb' up Annapurna." *Telegraph*, 5 September. https://www.telegraph.co.uk/news/worldnews/europe/france/11846754/French-mountaineers-take-on-worlds-most-perilous-climb-up-Annapurna.html.

Sanders, Erica. 1999. "Mountain Madness." *New York Times*, 18 July. http://www.nytimes.com/books/99/07/18/reviews/990718.18sandert.html.

Saatchi, Anaheed. 2020. "Your Climbing Is Political Whether You Like It or Not." *Alpinist* 69 (Spring). https://shop.holpublications.com/products/alpinist-magazine-issue-69?variant=32406910861400.

Saverin, Diana. 2013. "The Chris McCandless Obsession Problem." *Outside*, 18 December. https://www.outsideonline.com/1920626/chris-mccandless-obsession-problem.

Sawer, Patrick. 2015. "The Secret Relationship between Climbing Legend George Mallory and a Young Teacher." *Telegraph*, 28 October. http://www.telegraph.co.uk/history/11960859/The-secret-relationship-between-climbing-legend-George-Mallory-and-a-young-teacher.html.

Scully, Lizzy. 2003. "In the Footsteps of Fanny: Climbing in the Karakoram." *Climbing Magazine* no. 222 (June). http://climbing.com/current/wmnkarakrm/.

Sedgwick, Eve Kosofsky. 1990. *Epistemology of the Closet*. Berkeley and Los Angeles: University of California Press.

Shah, Saeed, and Joe Pilkington. 2011. "Greg Mortenson's Dizzying Fall from Grace." *Guardian*, 22 April. https://www.theguardian.com/books/2011/apr/22/greg-mortenson-three-cups-tea.

Shelley, Percy Bysshe. 1816. "Mont Blanc: Lines Written in the Vale of Chamouni." *Poetry Foundation*. https://www.poetryfoundation.org/poems/45130/mont-blanc-lines-written-in-the-vale-of-chamouni.

Ski-Guru. 2019. "The 'Cholitas Escaladoras' (Climbing 'Cholitas') Are Going for Everest." *Ski-Guru*, 13 May. https://www.the-ski-guru.com/2019/05/14/cholitas-escaladoras-climbing-cholitas-everest/.

Skidmore, Colleen. 2006. *This Wild Spirit: Women in the Rocky Mountains of Canada*. Edmonton: University of Alberta Press.

Simonson, Eric, Joachim Hemmleb, Larry Johnson. 1999. "Ghosts of Everest." *Outside*, 1 October. https://www.outsideonline.com/1909046/ghosts-everest.

Simpson, Joe. 1997. Introduction. In *Annapurna: The First Conquest of an 8,000-metre Peak* by Maurice Herzog, xiii–xvi. Translated by Nea Morin and Janet Adam Smith. London: Pimlico.

– 2003. *The Beckoning Silence*. New York: Vintage.

– (1989) 2004. *Touching the Void: The True Story of One Man's Miraculous Survival*. New York: Harper Perennial.

Slemon, Stephen. 2008. "The Brotherhood of the Rope: Commodification and Contradiction in 'The Mountaineering Community.'" In *Renegotiating Community: Interdisciplinary Perspectives, Global Contexts*, edited by Diana Brydon and William D. Coleman, 234–5. Vancouver: University of British Columbia Press.

– 1998. "Climbing Mount Everest: Postcolonialism in the Culture of Ascent." *Canadian Literature* 158 (Autumn): 15–35.

– 2012. "Tenzing Norgay's Four Flags." *Kunapipi* 34, no. 2: 32–41.

Smith, Sidonie, and Julia Watson. 2010. *Reading Autobiography: A Guide for Interpreting Life Narratives*, 2nd edition. Minneapolis: University of Minnesota Press.

Sohn, Tim. 2006. "Impossible to Forget." *Outside*, 15 August. https://www.outsideonline.com/1909151/impossible-forget.

Steele, Peter. 1972. *Doctor on Everest*. Vancouver: Raincoast Books.

"Stéphane Benoist: The South Face of Annapurna and the Importance of a Climbing Partnership." 2013. *PlanetMountain.com*, 12 November. https://www.planetmountain.com/en/news/alpinism/stephane-benoist-the-south-face-of-annapurna-and-the-importance-of-a-climbing-partnership.html.

Stevens, Stanley F. 1993. "Tourism, Change, and Continuity in the Mount Everest Region, Nepal." *Geographical Review* 83, no. 4 (October): 410. DOI: 10.2307/215823.

"Stairway to Heaven." 2013. *Economist*, 29 May. http://www.economist.com/blogs/graphicdetail/2013/05/daily-chart-18.

Stout, David. 2014. "Everest Climbing Season in Doubt as Sherpas Issue Ultimatum to the Authorities." *Time*, 20 April. http://time.com/69829/everest-climbing-season-in-doubt-as-sherpas-issue-ultimatum-to-authorites/.

Styles, Showell. 1950. *The Mountaineer's Week-End Book*. London: Seeley, Service & Co.

Swann, Christian, Lee Crust, and Jacquelyn Allen-Collinson. 2016. "Surviving the 2015 Mount Everest Disaster: A Phenomenological Exploration into Lived Experience and the Role of Mental Toughness." *Psychology of Sport & Exercise* 27 (August): 157–67.

Tabei, Junko. 2017. *Honouring High Places: The Mountain Life of Junko Tabei*. Edited by Junko Tabei and Helen Rolfe. Translated by Yumiko Hiraki and Rieko Holtved. Calgary: Rocky Mountain Books.

"Talk: K2/Archive 3." 2015. *Wikiwand.com*, 1 May. https://www.wikiwand.com/en/Talk:K2/Archive_3.

Tenzing, Judy, and Tashi Tenzing. 2001. *Tenzing and the Sherpas of Everest*. New Delhi: HarperCollins.

Terray, Lionel. (1961) 2001. *Conquistadors of the Useless: From the Alps to Annapurna*. Translated by Geoffrey Sutton. London: Bâton Wicks; Seattle: The Mountaineers. *Les Conquérants de l'inutile*. Paris: Guérin, 1999. Citations are to The Mountaineers edition.

Tharkay, Ang. [1954] 2016. *Sherpa: The Memoir of Ang Tharkay*. Seattle: The Mountaineers.

Ullman, James Ramsey, and Tenzing Norgay. (1955) 2010. *Man of Everest – The Autobiography of Tenzing*. London: Gibson Square Books.

Underhill, Miriam O'Brien. (1971) 1992. "Manless Climbs." In *Give Me the Hills*. New York: Dodd Mead. Reprint, in *Leading Out: Women Climbers Reaching for the Top*, edited by Rachel da Silva, 3–12. Seattle: Seal Press.

Unruh, Nathan. 2020. "False Summits." *Sidecar*, 1 July. https://www.sidecaredge.com/false-summits/.

Unsworth, Walt. (1981) 2000. *Everest: The Mountaineering History*, 3rd edition. Seattle: The Mountaineers; London: Baton Wicks.

Vause, Mikel, ed. (1990) 1999. *Rock and Roses: Mountaineering Essays by Some of the World's Best Women Climbers of the 20th Century*. La Crescenta, CA: Mount'n Air Books.

Viesturs, Ed, with David Roberts. 2009. *K2: Life and Death on the World's Most Dangerous Mountain*. New York: Broadway Books.

Waldroup, Heather. 2014. "Hard to Reach: Anne Brigman, Mountaineering, and Modernity in California." *Modernism/Modernity* 21, no. 2: 44–66.

Weathers, Beck. 2000. *Left for Dead: My Journey Home from Everest*. New York: Dell.

Weber, Bruce. 2015. "Richard D. Bass, Ski Resort Developer Who Climbed Tallest Peaks, Dies at 85." *New York Times*, 30 July. http://www.nytimes.com/2015/07/31/sports/international/richard-d-bass-ski-resort-developer-and-climber-of-tallest-peaks-dies-at-85.html.

Webster, Paul. 2000. "Phantom Haunts Hero of Summit." *Guardian*, 28 May. https://www.theguardian.com/world/2000/may/28/paulwebster.theobserver.

Whelehan, Imelda. 1995. *Modern Feminist Thought: From the Second Wave to 'Post-Feminism.'* New York: New York University Press.

West, John B. 1998. *High Life: A History of High-Altitude Physiology and Medicine*. New York: Oxford University Press.

The Wildest Dream. 2010. (Film.) Directed by Anthony Geffen. BBC, National Geographic, Altitude Films.

Williams, Cicely. 1973. *Women on the Rope: The Feminine Share of Mountain Adventure*. London: George Allen & Unwin.

Willis, Clint. 2006. *The Boys of Everest: Chris Bonington and the Tragedy of Climbing's Greatest Generation*. Cambridge: Da Capo.

— 2001. "Introduction." In *Annapurna South Face: The Classic Account of Survival*, by Sir Chris Bonington, xi–xviii. New York: Adrenaline Classics.

Whitlock, Gillian. 2007. *Soft Weapons: Autobiography in Transit*. Chicago: University of Chicago Press.

Wislowski, Anne. 2017. "Learn This: Understanding Altitude Illness." *Climbing*, 6 October. https://www.climbing.com/skills/learn-this-understanding-altitude-illness/.

Women of K2. 2003. (Film.) Directed and co-produced by Jennifer Jordan and Jeff Rhoads. National Geographic, Fox Television Studios, Skyline Ventures Production.

Wood, Sharon. 2019. *Rising: Becoming the First Canadian Woman to Summit Everest*. Toronto: Douglas & McIntyre.

Wren, Christopher. 1987. "Climb and Tell, or It's a Long Way from Annapurna." *New York Times*, 15 February: 2007. https://www.nytimes.com/1987/02/15/books/climb-and-tell-or-it-s-a-long-way-from-annapurna.html.

Zonglu, Zhao. 1986. "Mountaineering Heroine: 10 Years Later." *Beijing Daily Review*, 11 August, 27. http://www.massline.org/PekingReview/PR1986/PR1986-32.pdf.

Zuckerman, Peter, and Amanda Padoan. 2013. *Buried in the Sky: The Extraordinary Story of the Sherpa Climbers on K2's Deadliest Day*. New York: W.W. Norton and Co.

INDEX

Chogolisa, 130

Chogor, 236. *See also* Chhogho Ri; Choghiri

cholita, 3–4, 230

Chomolungma, 8, 143, 145, 165–8, 217, 225.
  See also Everest

Clark, Jason, 191

Climb, The (Boukreev), 201–2, 205–6, 215,
  221

climbing, 144–50, 153–65, 169–93, 195–209,
  211–25, 227–39; aesthetic qualities of,
  19, 63, 77, 145, 152, 181; alpine style, 56;
  amateurism and, 182, 184, 225; athleticism
  and, 26, 151, 181, 188; authenticity of, 6, 16,
  40, 142–5, 147, 149–51, 153, 178, 181, 185,
  195; Aymara women and, 3–5; body, 26,
  32–4, 40, 69, 82–3, 136; celebrity and, 19,
  28, 131, 150; civilization and, 36, 58–9, 98,
  108, 146–7, 189; Commercial Era, 172, 177;
  commercialization and, 83, 98, 174, 178–9,
  196–7, 236; counterculture, 116, 210; discrimination and, 4, 66, 72, 230; diversity
  and, 5, 141, 193, 195, 229–30; early, 20;
  embodiment and, 35–6, 95, 153; equality,
  need for, 31, 38, 66–7, 71–2, 81, 116; ethics
  and, 17, 19, 94, 141, 145, 154, 159–62, 178,
  182, 210; Golden Age of, 41, 43, 116, 148,
  236; hazards of, 29, 42, 72, 95, 97; Heroic
  Era, 46, 57, 190; high-altitude, 9, 11, 14, 47,
  56, 83, 85; inauthenticity and, 40, 178, 180,
  183, 193; inequality and, 3–6, 24, 31, 66–7,
  69–70, 235; inexperience and, 136, 203,
  212; publicity, 19, 55, 58, 180, 207, 211;
  racism, 22, 66, 171, 173, 175, 189, 193, 229,
  233; selfhood, 147; siege style, 9, 44–7,
  49–51, 57–9, 62–3, 74–7, 102, 105–7, 140,
  159, 231; solo climbing, 34, 43, 80, 113,
  123–4, 138, 183, 209, 231, 237; women,
  20–2. *See also* mountaineering

Climbing High (Gammelgaard), 190, 216–18,
  220

closeted, 68, 83, 116

Clouds from Both Sides (Tullis), 132

Clough, Ian, 85

Cobden, Stella, 151

Coburn, Broughton, 142, 209, 225, 238

Compagnoni, Achille, 113

Conundrum, 32–3

Coronation Everest (Morris), 32, 172

corpse, 84–5, 155–9, 161

Couzy, Jean, 50

Craig, Robert, 107, 113

crampons, 23, 91, 211–12, 218, 227–8

Cranmer, Piro, 102–3

crevasse, 48, 87, 102, 118, 227–8

Crowley, Aleister, 98

Crystal Horizon, The (Messner), 12, 182–3

Curran, Jim, 97–8, 102–6, 126–9, 135–6

Curzon, Lord, 143

Czerwińska, Anna, 123

da Silva, Rachel, 20

Darjeeling, 8, 173

Dark Summit (Heil), 182

Davis, Wade, 162, 236–7

Dead Lucky (Hall), 16

Denman, Earl, 183

Desio, Ardito, 114

Destiville, Catherine, 25

DeWalt, G. Weston, 197, 201, 205–6, 215, 221

Dhar, Amrita, 14, 232, 237

Dhauligiri, 8, 47, 116, 130, 197, 233

Diemberger, Kurt, 121–2, 124–37

Dika, Jemima, 31, 170, 176, 229

disability, 93, 184

documentary film: culture of mountaineering and, 13, 18–19; festivals and, 10;
  Everest and, 154; IMAX, 5, 149, 177, 192,
  194, 197, 202, 220; *Sherpa*, 176; *Wildest
  Dream*, 156, 159, 237

Douglas, Ed, 17, 138

Drinkwater, Barbara, 68

Durrance, Jack, 103–4

Egan, Susanna, 15

Eiger, 13, 90, 93

Eisenstein, Zillah, 66, 68

El Capitan, 80, 114

Elizabeth II (queen), 21, 168, 172

Elmes, Michael, 176, 193

England, 59, 130, 146, 153, 175, 183

Erickson, Bruce, 233

Estrada, Huayllas, 3–4

Everest, 8, 229–30, 233, 235–9; 8000-metre
  peaks and, 9, 56; British 1920s expeditions, 47, 144; British 1953 expedition,
  78, 163–72; climbs without oxygen and,

masculinity, 22, 33, 52–4, 34–5, 44, 106–7; alpine style and, 58–9, 146, 236; climbing and, 20, 28, 32, 85, 90, 147; colonial, 8, 167, 189, 233; dominance of, 25–6, 33, 178; heroism and, 5, 45, 55, 58, 62, 105–7, 112, 147, 182; machismo as, 4, 28, 31–2, 58–9, 65, 73, 119; George Mallory and, 151, 153–4; manliness, 51, 53–4, 84; narrow idea of, 5, 33, 224; sovereignty and, 34–5; Romantic, 14, 34, 56, 144; siege style and, 51, 61, 105; whiteness and, 20, 24, 33, 44, 154, 169

Masherbrum, 97, 236

Maudit, Chantal, 137–9

Mazeaud, Pierre, 131

Mazel, David, 20, 64, 83, 89

McCandless, Chris, 209, 239

McDonald, Bernadette, 17, 94, 100, 121–3, 125, 235

Mehdi, Amir, 113, 169

memoir, 22, 55; adventure discourse and, 13, 18; affect and, 128–9, 132; cultures of climbing and, 11, 19; as documentation, 12, 16, 156, 201, 216; gender and, 7, 22, 27–30, 32–3, 86, 115, 234; identity construction and, 12–13, 27; inspiration of, 55, 233; nationalism and, 53, 165; popularity of, 9, 229; Sherpa writers of, 163–5, 176, 232; settling scores in, 13, 126, 161, 163, 201–2, 224; truth claims of, 13–16, 223; women writers of, 14–15, 21, 78, 187–8, 216–22. *See also* autobiography

Merkl, Willy, 13

Messner, Reinhold: assessment of Annapurna climbs, 42, 55–6; George Mallory and, 55, 153–4, 181, 236–7; reputation of, 12–13, 148, 180, 183, 195; sexism and, 66, 85; support for alpine style, 83–4, 115, 121, 148, 182

Miller, Irene, 80

Millett, Kate, 66

Mingma, 72–3

Miodowicz-Wolf, Dobroslawa, 124

Mitchell, Richard, 10

Mitra, Rabindranath, 163

Miyolangsangma, Jomo, 166

modernity, 30, 51, 146

Montgomerie, 97, 236

Morris, Jan, 32–3, 162, 168, 172

Mortenson, Greg, 15–16

mountain film festivals, 10–11, 25, 27, 34, 229, 232

Mountain Madness, 197–8, 201, 205–6, 211–12, 215–18, 221, 223

Mountain of My Fear, The (Roberts), 13, 55, 79

mountaineering, 6–7, 26, 63, 82–3, 108–9; authenticity and, 40, 150, 181–3; bodies and, 82–3; brotherhood and, 88–93, 100–1, 114 (*see also* brotherhood: of the rope); commercialization of, 83–4, 98, 148; corporeal sovereignty and, 34, 37; culture of, 5–6, 10, 30, 58–9, 61, 82, 95, 115; decline and, 40, 179; film and book festivals about, 10, 25–6, 80; equipment, 23, 87, 88, 90–2 (*see also* rope); feminism and, 66–7, 85–6; gender and, 19–20, 33, 65, 82, 179; Golden Age of, 41, 114; ideals of, 94, 102, 105, 110, 140, 161; masculinity and, 20, 33–4, 85, 139, 147; modernity and, 22, 144; nonfiction and, 7–10, 15–19, 21, 27, 45, 86; Romanticism and, 13–14, 36, 144–5; sexism in, 79, 80–1, 94, 115; Sherpas and, 69, 135, 173; skills, 102, 106; whiteness and, 24, 141; women and, 14–15, 20–1, 25, 63–7, 69–70, 186; writing and, 11, 86. *See also* climbing

Mountaineering Women (Mazel), 20

Mountaineer's Week-End Book, The (Styles), 87

Mountains of My Life, The (Bonatti), 16, 113, 169

Mrówka, 124–7

Mummery, Albert, 179, 184, 233

Muztagh Tower, 98

Naked Mountain, The (Messner), 13

Namba, Yasuko, 203, 219; characterization in Everest, 192, 238; death, 199, 212; Everest climb, 205, 220; racist assumptions about, 23–4, 201, 212, 223

Nanga Parbat, 8–9, 12–13, 56, 122, 126, 130, 232

National Geographic, 79, 82, 146, 148, 155, 229, 237

nationalism, 36, 55, 84, 105, 107, 162, 165, 187

Nelson, Bill, 8